OHIO

Books by Dick Perry

Raymond and Me That Summer
The Roundhouse, Paradise, and Mr. Pickering
Vas You Ever in Zinzinnati?
Ohio, A Personal Portrait of the 17th State

Plays by Dick Perry

Go From Me
The Briefcase Bohemian of the 7:54
Forever the Wild Sweet Voice of Lovers
There'll Never Be Another Bongo
Who'll Teach My Baby Razor-Blades?

OHIO

A Personal Portrait of the 17th State

by Dick Perry

Photography by Bruce Goldflies

Foreword by Hugh Downs

Doubleday & Company, Inc.

Garden City, New York,

1969

Contents

Foreword

One of my friends who has lived in New York City so long that he is considered a Manhattan native actually comes from a southeastern Ohio village. Whenever he spies a car with Ohio tags, he looks to see if, by chance, he knows its occupants. I know exactly how he feels because I'm from Ohio, too. I was born in Akron and brought up in Lima. In Ohio I began my broadcast career. To Ohio I return on occasion to play summer stock. And as a small boy—full of wonder and peanut butter—I used to gaze at Indian Lake and pretend it was the sea.

But the riddle of Ohio is this. The Ohio of my friend is not *my* Ohio. My roots are in the prairie of the western half of the state, his in a mountain hollow. Still other Ohios exist—the industrial crescent of cities surrounding Warren and Youngstown, the craggy Ohio River Valley, the little islands offshore Sandusky, and the hundred and one duplicates of Louis Bromfield's *Pleasant Valley*. Although many books have been written about my native state, each writer—like Bromfield, for instance, or Sherwood Anderson—has written with passion about only his particular corner of it. Or, if about the entire state, the books are usually school texts from which all passion, poetry, and humor have been drained, making them excellent classroom fare but heavy going for the armchair dreamer. In other words, for many years Ohio has been in need of a bard to tell all its story in a non-academic book written for the man-on-the-street.

Now the search for its bard has ended. Here is the story of Ohio told by not one but two bards: Dick Perry with words and Bruce Goldflies with pictures. Dick Perry is an award-winning playwright, novelist, humorist, and—by his own admission—"a casual historian and martini buff." Bruce Goldflies is schoolteacher, piano tuner, septic tank repairman, and photographer. These two Ohio natives visited the state's eighty-eight counties—a feat which before only the governor had accomplished—to create what they call a "personal portrait of the 17th state."

Perry—a free spirit bewildered only by the Chamber of Commerce bulletins that inundated him—is not above melancholy in his Ohio story. Some of Ohio strikes him as sad, and he says so. On the other hand, some of Ohio struck him as hilarious. He notes that, too, making this probably the only story told of Ohio that contains one-liners. Of one university, he writes, "They say it is the mother of fraternities, but no one ever says who the father is." Geography did not bother him. He applied logic. The result is, the true southeastern corner of the state—geographically—has been located in West Virginia. Perry's research uncovered the fact that Ohio is where most police whistles come from. *And* most canned Chinese food. Every city, town, or village with 1500 or more people was visited. Smaller hamlets were visited, too; Perry noting that one such hamlet when visited had no one home. I have the feeling that if *all* histories were as casual and as humorous—and at times as passionate and as melancholy—the reading of history could easily replace the national pastime of baseball.

The secret of Perry's writing, I believe, is that he is a humorist who know when *not* to be funny. Passages in the boog reflect this. His study of the Amish farmers is moody and solemn. His seeking the roads that Sherwood Anderson wrote of in *Winesburg, Ohio* is an adventure in sentiment but not sentimentality. Deserted farmhouses—"with broken windows for eyes," he wrote—left him depressed. So did some cities. Through his writing we can sense the power and the dynamics of Ohio but we can also sense some of its loneliness. The photographs of Bruce Goldflies capture, in total, this over-all majesty and over-all human quality of the state. Both Perry and Goldflies are quick to point out that this is their version of the state and that each Ohioan has his own Ohio. Happily, Perry and Goldflies are as I am, fond of this state we call home.

All too often we are inclined to cast aside writing that reads too easily or is too casual. Such writing seems to us to have been created without effort. And thereby, because no effort seems to have gone into it, the writing has little value. Having written books myself I can only say that the hardest writing in the world is the writing which appears the easiest to the reader. To read this book has been to watch an artist at work. Perry makes it appear almost too simple. But it isn't. Here is proof of that old adage:

The true art is the concealment of art.

I wonder what Dick Perry could do with the whole United States? Or, for that matter, the whole world? I can just see it now: a casual study of the Roman Empire—with one-liners yet!

Hugh Downs

OHIO

1

Before Governor James A. Rhodes came, Ohio was covered with water.

Then the prehistoric sea went, dinosaurs appeared, so did glaciers, and before you knew what was happening, eons trickled by and election posters were tacked on telephone poles throughout the state, Dayton having more telephones per hundred people than Columbus, Columbus having more than Cleveland, Cleveland having more than Cincinnati, and Cincinnati having more than Gratis which, other than having fewer telephones than Cincinnati, keeps its Christmas lighting on its streets from one season to the next.

The point is, although many interesting things in the state did, Ohio itself did not happen overnight.

Ohio—Mother of eight Presidents (though Virginia disputes this; both states claim William Henry Harrison); stomping ground of Johnny Appleseed; birthplace of Clarence Darrow, Thomas Edison, James Thurber, and Clark Gable; seventeenth state; inventor of chewing gum; scene of the first minstrel show; and creator of the fly-swatter—is geographically a 41,122-square-mile contradiction.

But first things first. Technically Ohio enters the lists as a state in the east north-central portion of the United States. For borders it has Michigan, Pennsylvania, West Virginia, Kentucky, Indiana and Canada. The Ohio River, though, belongs to Kentucky. On the other hand, part of Lake Erie—of all the Great Lakes, it is the smallest and most shallow—does belong to Ohio. Any old friendly Iroquois can tell you that Ohio probably got its name from Oh-he-yo, a train caller's version of "great river." To the trivia collectors may we suggest that Ohio's bird is the cardinal, its capital Columbus, its flower a scarlet carnation, its nickname the Buckeye State, its intentions honorable, and its dialect German, Slavic, rube, hillbilly, Chinese, and teen-age hip?

To an Ohio resident—wherever he lives—some other part of his state seems unreal. If he lives in the flattened-out and now-drained Black Swamp area in the northwest, the idea that southeast Ohio contains lonely and misty mountains strikes him as far-fetched. If he shivers on the shores of Lake Erie, buffeted by arctic winds that turn his lake to ice, that the Ohio River flowing so sweetly borders his tax duplicate seems ridiculous. The reverse is true. Dwellers in mountain hollows on the edge of Ohio's national forest—which comes as a surprise to most Ohioans who didn't know they had one—flatlands do not belong here but in Kansas with Aunt Em. To those along the Ohio River the thought that Ohio plays host to ocean-going freighters is a pipe dream better left unpiped.

In other words Ohio is a patchwork quilt of diversity. For us—photographer Bruce Goldflies and myself—to compress this state into one compact ball so that all will be pleased with its bounce is asking much. I wrote once of Cincinnati that there are as many Cincinnatis as there are Cincinnatians because each sees the city from his own point of view. The same is true of Ohio. There's an awful lot of it out there. And there's an awful lot of you. This book will represent only our point of view and our point of view is, we happen to be fond of this state. This book will not be written to delight scholars who in measuring the heat from the sun miss the sunset's beauty. Nor will this book warm the cockles of a statistician's heart. He'll not learn from us how many short tons of whetstone Ohio annually coughs up. Numbers are for the birds, and on that note, we'll note statistically that in Ohio for every man, woman, and child there are fifty birds.

So much for statistics.

Rather, we shall look—in a reasonably amiable fashion—at Ohio's great cities, its vast countryside, and its diverse people—the Italians of Cleveland, the Amish of Sugarcreek, the Appalachian poor in the city slums, the remnants of German families who once made up Cincinnati, and upon occasion whatever farmers' daughters are attractive enough. We'll visit little towns like Siam, Tarlton, Williamsport, Weavers Corners, and Irwin, some of which are hardly more than crossroads heading full speed into the twilight of yesterday. We'll visit towns along Lake Erie: Ashtabula, Bellevue, Beulah Beach, Conneaut (which they pronounce funny), Huron, Lorain, Sandusky, Toledo, and—of course—Cleveland. We'll visit river towns: Dover, Cincinnati, Elyria (it *is* a river town), Martins Ferry, Steubenville, Ripley, Portsmouth, and the rest. We'll rubberneck at the sights, a few not listed in your tour books. There's the Make-Believe Motel in Colfax east of Lancaster. One wonders if it is for real? And where else but Delaware on a hot September afternoon are snow-mobiles for sale? And is that Elyria church steeps *really* painted pink? And Greenfield's High School, it was *really* given to the city for the inventor of the horse collar? In New Vienna, did we see correctly? Fire engines sleeping in an ex-movie house? Consider Zanesville's Y Bridge; sometimes after crossing you end on the same side of the river that you started from. And, yes, book-lovers, there *is* a *Winesburg, Ohio*—in fact as well as fiction. You'll find it in Amish country near Sugarcreek, but it's not the Winesburg, Ohio, Sherwood Anderson wrote about. *That* Winesburg, Ohio is really *Clyde*, Ohio; and to confuse you more, Anderson wasn't born there; he was born in Camden, Ohio.

If you have a thermometer fetish, note that the mean annual temperature for Ohio is 51 degrees. The southern part of the state averages 53.2 degrees and the northern part averages 49.5 degrees. Ohio has from 150 to 178 frost-free growing

2

Ohio has wet borders.

A frozen pond in Oxford

days and necking nights, but in the southwest and sometimes along the lake shore farmers may get lucky and end up with 198 frost-free days. If factory tours get you so excited you can't sleep, note that steel is produced in Cleveland, Youngstown, Canton, plus other smaller cities (Middletown, for example, has wonderful smog from its mills); in Akron you'll find rubber products; in Toledo motor vehicles and parts; in Cincinnati soap, machine tools, and appliances; Dayton is known for cash registers, refrigerators, and Ted Ryan; and Yellow Springs, thanks to Antioch College, produces a new breed of thinkers, some with beards, some with brains, and some with both.

Where did the Ohio settlers come from? Well, oversimplified, the New Englanders headed for the Western Reserve in the northeast part of the state. Folks from Virginia and Kentucky settled in the southern part. Also, many of the eastern and southern Ohio settlers were Scotch-Irish or Pennsylvania German. Ohio in the nineteenth century was inundated with immigrants from Germany and Ireland, the Irish settling mostly in cities, but the Germans in villages and rural areas as well. Toward the end of the nineteenth-century Cleveland and the other industrial cities in northeastern Ohio were swamped with Italians, Jews, Slovenians, Hungarians, and Poles. But by the middle of the nineteenth century, Ohio was pretty well settled save for the Black Swamp area in the northwestern part of the state. That section can be called Ohio's last frontier. It's settled now, though. So there Ohio was—and is—with eighty-eight counties and statehood. The smallest county? Lake with 232 square miles. The largest? Ashtabula with 706 square miles. Both are side by side in the northeast corner.

Did you know that in addition to Ohio producing enough salt to supply the nation with salt for 150 years, the state produced the youngest major league baseball player: Joe Nuxhall who at fifteen pitched for the Cincinnati Reds?

And did you know—but enough of this. Rather than dump Ohio's oddments and charms helter skelter into your lap, let us try for order. Let us remain calm and make sense of this. Ohio can be divided and presented to you several ways. For instance, we could sort the state out geographically. The true geographer will quickly point out that, via geography, Ohio has three distinct sections. First there are the hills and mountains—the Allegheny Plateau—that makes the eastern and southern part of Ohio anything but a grand place to roller-skate. These are the hills that spill over into Ohio from the Smokies in Pennsylvania and West Virginia. They vary—some gentle, some angry—and toward the west they tend to become more plateaus than hills. The second geographic division is that area which stretches along Lake Erie between Cleveland, say, and the state corner over to Michigan and Indiana. These flatlands are called the Lake Plains, but where creeks and rivers are, you get some pretty good-sized hills and gullies. And, to wrap

Ohio is many octagonal barns

matters up, the geographers suggest that the rest of Ohio—the part not in the Allegheny Plateau or Lake Plains—lies in the Central Plains Area.

Ohio can also be divided by its drainage basins. Ohio has two. That part of the state that trickles into Lake Erie is one. The part that trickles into the Ohio River is the other. So much for hydrography.

Ohio can also be divided by its drinking habits. Cleveland drinks more Cointreau than Cincinnati. Cincinnati drinks more Triple Sec than Cleveland.

And, if pressed, Ohio can be divided into eighty-eight counties, which it has been anyway.

Agriculturally Ohio can be divided three ways: level areas where the tall corn grows, areas of gentle and not-so-gentle hills where general farming and dairying are the order of the day, and areas strictly hilly woodlands where there might be general farming but certainly no lowing herd. Or, agriculturally, Ohio can be divided into two distinct sections: where tobacco is grown and where tobacco isn't grown. Or, two other divisions: where the hogs are and where the hogs aren't. But ask yourself, are these divisions, for our purpose, kosher?

For the purposes of this particular book and for your peace of mind we shall divide Ohio into four equal parts, letting cities and pig farms fall where they may, and that will be that. To divide Ohio into four equal parts is simple. Our method —or *methodology*, if you feel long words lend enchantment—is to draw one line through the middle of the state from north to south. We draw another line through the middle of the state from east to west. If governments can create artificial boundaries, redistricting by whim or whammy, so can we. Our division, for example, puts Cleveland in the northeast quadrant and Cincinnati in the southwest quadrant. Columbus—smack dab in the middle of the state, if you are not too technical, that is; the exact center of Ohio is, some say, Delaware—posed a problem which we casually solved one rainy afternoon while standing on the corner of Broad and High Streets watching the girls go by. We decided to put everything that was in Columbus northwest of Broad and High into Ohio's northwest quadrant, everything southeast of that corner into the southeast quadrant, and so on, thus letting *all* Ohioans feel they were a part of the state capital. This did create additional artificial divisions. The northeast part of Ohio which already had Akron, Cleveland, and Youngstown got Marzetti's Restaurant and the Kappa Kappa Gamma sorority. The northwest part of Ohio which could already boast of Toledo and Sandusky could now boast of the Ohio State University and the Jai Lai Restaurant. The capital building, southeast of the intersection, joined that part of the state which already possessed Marietta and Athens. The southwest quadrant found Cincinnati, Dayton, and Springfield the proud possessors of the Neal House. You can see what kind of book this is going to be: the problems we could not solve we have swept under the rug.

Almost every town has old-fashioned neighborhoods.

There are better books than this if Ohio history is your hobby. For a quick look backward, however, all you have to do is stumble across the nearest Indian mound, which Ohio has lots of. The Great Serpent Mound is in Adams County, and there's Fort Ancient in Warren County. Which Indians were here? At the most, Ohio never had more than 15,000, the first being the Erie Tribe along the shores of Lake Erie. They lasted till about 1650. Then the Iroquois exterminated them. In the early eighteenth century Ohio contained Indians from the Miami, Shawnee, Huron, and Delaware tribes. Hunting was easier then than now. You could have got beavers, wolves, bears, wild turkeys, deer, and a bunch of other things. Ohio still has opossums, raccoons, fox, polecats, squirrels, and ground hogs. And rabbits because they breed like rabbits. When Ohio started it was covered mostly with trees, only 5 per cent was without forest. Subdivision developers have rearranged that percentage with bulldozers. Here you'll find the red and white oak, hard maple, beech, elm, white ash, tulip, poplar, and red maple tree.

As for the real history of the state, the Indians came first, then the French, then the English, then the Revolutionary War, and then Standard Oil stations and Holiday Inns. There! That should delight the speed-reader's heart. But we have glossed over so much. For instance, what of the rebellion at Fort Fizzle near Glenmont in Holmes County? Says one report, "The uprising 'fizzled out' as soon as a force of soldiers arrived to settle the disturbance."

Anyway, around 1818 Ohio began to get interested in canals. Work started the Fourth of July, 1825, near Newark, on a canal that would run serenely from Cleveland to Portsmouth, from the top of the state to the bottom on the east side. By 1845, a second canal linking Cincinnati and Toledo was in operation. The first was the Ohio and Erie Canal; the second the Miami and Erie Canal. Because of canals, towns blossomed—or never happened. Akron happened because of the Ohio and Erie water route. Cleveland—and not Lorain—is the big city of the lake because the canal ended there. However charming the canals, along came puffer-bellies to shove them into the past. In 1850, after the canals had been operating a decade or so, the state had 299 miles of railroad track. Eight years later the state had 2788 miles of tracks, slow-motion canal boats fell into decline, and by 1877 the canals entered their last days. They lingered as wet and lonely derelicts for years, sections were leased or sold, parts of them became railroad or highway rights-of-way, and today only a few canals linger as short stretches of memory here and there in state parks.

Ohio and the Civil War? Ohio ranked third in the number of troops committed: sending 340,000 off to battle. Some say 310,000 went. The actual number, like the end of the Civil War, is still in dispute. Of that number, however, only 9000 were drafted. Death claimed 11,000 Ohioans—the violence of war itself,

Two canals opened Ohio's interior.

Great ovens for brick-making. Sugarcreek.

that is—while sickness and disease accounted for the death of 13,000 more. How many deserted? Eighteen thousand. Any major battles fought here? Nope. A few scares, the Great Battle of Fort Fizzle, and that was about it. Cincinnati was threatened by the Confederates in both 1862 and 1864. The battles never happened.

In 1931 an Ohio tax was put on cigarettes.

Whither goes Ohio storkwise? In 1940 the population was (approximately) seven million, by 1950 nearly eight million, by 1960 nearly ten million, and projections call for highs in 1970 of eleven million, 1975 twelve million, and by 1985 well over thirteen million. Academically—or wisewise—the Ohio Board of Regents projects the enrollment of Ohio colleges and universities. In 1964 the state had more than a half million college-age residents of which fewer that 45 per cent put on freshman beanies. In 1969, say the regents, we have over 700,000 such youngsters and half of them will go on to college. By 1980 we shall have, estimated, more than 900,000 people in the college-age population and nearly 70 per cent will go to college. In other words, Ohio should have as many urchins *in* college by 1975 as it had altogether in 1964. Says the state, "While the future rate of population increase is expected to be slower than the state has experienced in the past, in actual numbers, Ohio's population is forecasted in increase by more than 2.5 million people by 1980. This is the equivalent of adding another Columbus, Cincinnati, Toledo, Akron, Dayton, Youngstown, and Canton to Ohio's population."

Although the first Ohio State Fair never got off the ground because of an outbreak of cholera in the mid-nineteenth century, the fair itself has been going strong ever since. At various times the state fair was held in Cleveland, Cincinnati, Toledo, Springfield, Newark, Sandusky, and Zanesville. Now it is held on a 37 splash of land in Columbus because there it is within easy reach of most Ohioans. Here, each year unless sidetracked by the midway ring-toss or the leggy majorettes from the one hundred high school bands, you'll find the world's largest state-fair horse show as well as the world's largest exhibition of livestock. Ohio leads the nation in the number of fairs held annually. Drive around Ohio during the summer and early fall and you'll find that fairs are as impossible to avoid as smashed bugs on your windshield. Food festivals, those organized gatherings bent on touting this or that area's food crop, are held from early spring when "the maple sap runs at Chardon" to "when the 'Great Pumpkin' casts his spell over Circleville in October." (Who says government handouts don't get poetic?) There's the Apple Festival in Jackson, because within a thirty-five-mile radius of Jackson from 350,000 to 500,000 bushels of apples are produced each year. Or, consider the Apple Butter Festival in Burton during which the chamber of commerce

Sulky Racing—County Fair musts.

Ohio is football—and Football is Paul Brown.

peddles maple cream and the Burton Volunteer Fire Department has an ox roast. Also in Burton is the Butter Churn Festival; chief attraction is the churning of 400 pounds of butter. In Geneva, the Grape Jamboree, featuring the Concord grape, and held in Geneva because this lakeside community lies in the center of an area where each year 20,000 tons of grapes are picked. The sweetest town on earth? Medina says that's Medina—during the Honey Festival. Medina is the home of the A. I. Root Company, pioneer supply house for beekeepers. As noted, the Maple Festival is held in Chardon when the saps starts running and the model sugar house opens to the public; has a log-chopping contest, too. Milan has the Melon Festival, a Labor Day weekend event, because more than 200 acres of muskmelons are grown around there; watermelons, too. Sugarcreek has the Ohio Swiss Festival, a cheesy and crowded event in Amishland; within ten miles of Sugarcreek are twenty-one factories that crank out tons of Swiss cheese each year. Columbus says it has an Oktoberfest held in a month that will come as no surprise to you, the offerings being sauerkraut, sauerbraten, wiener schnitzel, hasenpfeffer, and hot dogs. German singing societies fill the air with music. Versailles offers Poultry Days because Versailles is the leading poultry and egg producer in the Midwest. Egg smorgasbord is there. So, they say, is the world's largest barbecue pit. One omelet is made in a skillet eight feet in diameter, requiring 1440 eggs to produce, and a snow shovel to turn the creation. Pumpkin waffles and pumpkin burgers and pumpkin milk shakes are the thing in Circleville during the Pumpkin Show in the fall. Also, after you've downed the 1440-egg omelet, you can go to Circleville for dessert: they've baked a 274-pound pumpkin pie that requires twelve gallons of pumpkin and thirty-six pounds of sugar. The pie pan is five feet in diameter. Corn-on-the-cob is the highlight of Millersport's Sweet Corn Festival—big tender ears of fresh corn fresh from the field served piping hot and dripping with butter—ten cents each. No Ohio town holds a bicarbonate of soda festival, but one should. We note these festivals for another purpose: most city dwellers think of Ohio as nothing but towns and cities. We've a lot a country charm hereabouts—even when the frost isn't on the pumpkin over Circleville.

In addition to having more fairs than any other state, Ohio has the dubious honor of holding the record for the world's longest prison escape: forty-four years. A man, sentenced to death for his part in a robbery where a murder was committed, took off from prison here in 1920 and was not recaptured until 1964. Also, the world's record for the most consecutive rides on a roller-coaster—305 rides to be exact—has been held by an Ohioan, Bob Cole, while in the employ of a Cleveland radio station; the record was made at Cedar Point. The previous record had been held by an Iowan who rode 303 times. The first airship to land on the roof of a building did so in Cleveland in 1919. Akron had the first auto paddy wagon in 1899. The world's first electric trolley clanged through the streets of Cleveland in 1884 and, to make a long story short, all the Liederkranz cheese in the world is made in Borden's plant in Van Wert. Aren't you glad you sat down to read instead of watching an old movie on the tube?

It seems that chambers of commerce—large, small, and minuscule—have kindly flooded us with such diverse material, touting the charms of this community and that one. Awe-inspiring. If what we read is correct, every other Ohio community, regardless of size or sootfall, is "a fine place to work, live, and play." Also, most seem to be "fine places to raise children." No quarrel, though. Ohio is a state full of hundreds and hundreds of home towns each preoccupied with the sweet thought that of all communities, it is the best; and therefore the assorted chambers broadcast this fact far and wide via printed brochures. But if this book is to have any value it should not try to be all things to all Ohioans. This book will not list every community as the garden spot of America. Some communities are more charming than others, some downright beautiful, but some should never have happened. In *our* opinion, that is. We each have in our hearts the perfect community, but beauty is in the eye of the beholder—that goes for what you think of fat women and that goes for what you think of communities. Thus, this book might make you angry. But look at the subject this way: what you think of Steubenville is your business. And Geneva-on-the-Lake? Well, to like that sort of thing one must like that sort of thing. To us, however, Geneva-on-the-Lake seems a sad and lonely little swinger of a town, filled with good intentions and too many vacation cabins, in season hardly more than a noisy midway where one can, if he cares to, sleep in. But on the other hand, wasn't nearby Geneva the home of P. R. Spencer who created the Spencerian Method of Penmanship? And isn't Geneva-on-the-Lake now—when everyone else goes home—a quiet and serene setting by an inland sea, a place of fresh air, fog, and beauty? One man's meat, we suggest kindly, is another man's Geneva-on-the-Lake.

Question is, who are we to presume to write and photograph Ohio? We're both Ohio natives, but so are a lot of other people. Because we hail from the southwestern corner of the state, we are not overly familiar with the rest of the state. This is true of the rest of you, though, because we each know our own back yards better than we know the back yards of another city. Being strangers therefore to most of our native land we can view it with the mixed feelings of strangers and natives. Much of Ohio we had to *un*learn. Akron had always struck us as distasteful conglomeration of buildings from which automobile tires spewed; we could not imagine it as a beautiful city (Akron natives feel this way a little, as if shy about what Akron really is), but Akron surprised us by being one of

17

A Friends Church. Barnesville.

the most charming cities in Ohio. Some towns which we thought would charm us left us cold. Some Bruce Goldflies liked. Some I did. Some communities found us at cross-purposes, one of us liked it, the other didn't. No fist fights, though. We resolved the matter as gentlemen should—with glares. But we do not pretend to be academic souls operating with some great moneyed grant so that we might look dispassionately at our Ohio. We have not been subsidised by chambers, the state, or industry. Simply put, he is a photographer, I am a writer, both of us have gone through life teetering on the brink of solvency, and this is the way *we* see Ohio. We did not, as I suggest, look upon Ohio dispassionately. If anything, we looked upon it with awe and pleasure. Because Ohio *is* a great state. And we, via this book, have just discovered most of it. We'd like to pass our discoveries along to you, Bruce with pictures, I with words.

Having divided the state into four sections, Bruce and I looked carefully into each. True, freeways make short shrift—whatever that means—of getting from one place to another, but for the most part, Bruce and I avoided these magnificent roads. They are swift, but they miss much that is truly Ohio. Example: take the freeway east from Columbus and before you know it, there you are on the Pennsylvania Turnpike. In between the hills have been softened, the curves gentled, and the towns bypassed. You have to deliberately turn off the freeway to reach Barnesville, a pleasant community in the eastern hills of Ohio and upon one of which sits one of the largest Friends Meeting House in the world. You have to get off the freeway, when traveling between Cleveland and Cincinnati, to see Ashland, another pleasant community and also the balloon capital of the nation —or has the pill cut inroads into that industry? Travel the freeways between Toledo and Cleveland and you miss a lot of junky little resort towns but you also miss Huron, one of the prettiest towns we have on Lake Erie. Travel between Cleveland and Zanesville via freeways, your journey will be swift, but as you hurl yourself along the great valleys near New Philadelphia, you'll not see—a few hills to the west—back roads where the Amish buggies are. No, freeways are for the swift, not the sightseer. The only sightseeing done on freeways is when you are parked with impatience on the burm, out of gas, and have time to frown with distaste at the scenery. So much for freeways. We ignored them, but they are there, and they are handy.

How closely did we examine the innards of Ohio? Well, we think we know what makes it tick. Sometimes Bruce and I traveled together. Sometimes we traveled separately. Traveling separately sometimes we met by design—and by accident—the strangest places: on a Shaker Heights trolley, on the Y bridge in Zanesville, in the hog barn at the state fair, on the docks in Sandusky, and once when he was leaning sadly against a restaurant in one of our northern cities; he

19

had just taken a picture of the place when some thug, bent on evil, pointed a gun at him and advised Bruce that a daylight robbery was then in progress; the thug took money, cameras, and Bruce's good will toward men—and the police, an efficient lot in most Ohio cities, recovered the first two items. Also, Bruce and I met in Holiday Inns which Ohio has many of; but for real adventure, we started out together to stand—exactly—on the northwest corner of the state, that well-defined line on the map where Ohio touches both Indiana and Michigan. We had thought, earlier, of taking a picture of the exact four corners of Ohio. We got to the point, approximately, by dirt road, map, and compass. But when we looked around: nothing. Cornfield on one side of the road. Stand of trees on the other. Not a house or Stuckey Stand in sight. We drove a few miles to the nearest farm house which turned out to be in Michigan, asked the farmer where Ohio stopped and Michigan started, but he wasn't sure. A farmer in Indiana wasn't sure, either. And to think that once Ohio and Michigan almost had a shooting war between its militia over that boundary. No marker there. So Bruce and I gave up the project of picturing the four corners of Ohio. Also, Ohio doesn't *have* four corners to begin with. Look at a map and tell us where the southeast corner would be. The southernmost point in Ohio is not east. The easternmost point is not south. Careful projection and poor logic puts the southeast corner of Ohio in West Virginia which doesn't seem right at all.

In our travels we saw many creeks which were labeled rivers and many rivers which were labeled creeks. The Wabash River, for example, runs through Ohio and trickles into Indiana, but you can't tell by looking at it.

In one fashion or another Bruce and I visited nearly every Ohio community that has—or claims to have—2500 people or more. We visited many smaller communities in between. Some were so small they weren't home the day we popped in. But cursory appraisals and lickety-split snap judgments based on a quick once-over? Not really. For weeks at a time we were on the road, backtracking, taking second and third and fourth and fifth looks at each town. We had to. This may come as no surprise to you but weather makes a difference. Arrived once in Lorain on a gloomy, rain-swept day, drove by the Rube Goldberg gadgetry of the steel mills and noticed, with melancholy, that even the YMCA by the mill was covered with mill grime. Spent the afternoon and evening in that Gloomy Gus of a city, talking to people, and all the while getting colder and sadder and lonelier. That was one impression of Lorain. The next visit, however, the sun was shining, the sky was so blue you could taste it, and our impression of Lorain shot up high as the sky. Even when we talked with people on that visit, the people seemed friendlier. But, you see, the town and the people had not changed. What had changed had been the weather and our attitude. So we visited—and revisited—cities. Some that we didn't like at first we came to be fond of. Others which had brought out our fondness became, on subsequent visits, communities you could give back to the Indians.

On the other hand, a word of caution to you who seek the seamy side of reality and pretend that nice people and nice towns are things of the past. While Ohio is not perfect and only an idiot would pretend that it is, Ohio is nevertheless a state that contains more pleasant than angry people, all of whom—the pleasant and the angry—are well-intentioned. Ohio, being a big state bubbling with life, sometimes has big troubles. Entire streets have been gutted by the match of the rioteer. Angers and dreams are surfacing in the breasts of many Ohioans. Here we have the Ku Klux Klan and here we have the more militant of the Black Power groups. But here, too, we have all the rest of us—white and black—sitting around in between, trying to do what is right, not knowing what right is, and thus we live from sunup to sundown, filled with the hopes and never knowing that fill the souls of men everywhere. This book does not suggest "the wonderful world of Ohio" is all that wonderful. But this book does suggest that Ohio is no better or no worse than any other state in any of these matters. We did not put this book together to sugar-coat the state nor to tear it asunder.

We put it together and present it, herewith, because we got a kick out of discovering Ohio. If you must traffic in ferment, ferment elsewhere.

On that note we'll start our visit to Ohio.

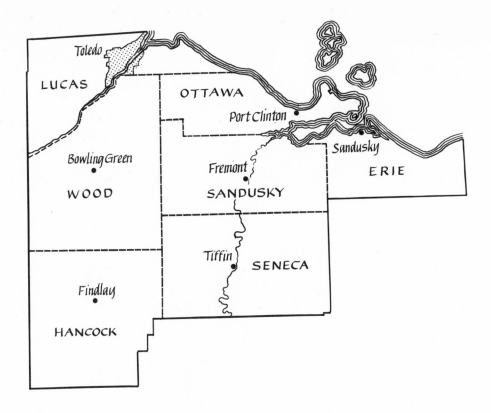

2

Shall we start with the northwestern quarter of Ohio—that part which includes Toledo, Sandusky, and the Jai Lai in Columbus? Very well. Lake Erie runs 230 miles across the top of Ohio, the better and more natural harbors being the Maumee and Sandusky bays. At the western tip of Lake Erie where the Maumee River empties into the lake is Toledo. Toledo was not always there. Long before the advent of the Toledo *Blade*, moveable type, Faith Baldwin, and—for that matter—Lake Erie itself, where Toledo is glaciers were. These glaciers were huge, noisy, and rowdy. They stood hundreds of feet high. Groaning and protesting these glaciers moved slothlike to the south, pulverizing rocks and leaving much litter. When the ice melted the result was the formation of a big lake at the bottom of which was Toledo. This lake drained south for a while to form the Wabash, Ohio, and Mississippi rivers. Then the lake drained the other way via the St. Lawrence River into the Atlantic Ocean. One of the original Lake Erie shores ran through Napoleon a far piece southwest of Toledo. The lake drained more and there was Toledo. When the lake left, it left behind muck—rich and   23

After the sea left, mud!

Lake Erie

alluvial—perfect for night crawlers and plant life. Slow motion into the eerie silence of the teenage Black Swamp came trees from the south: ash, maple, and elm. On the other hand, oak, hickory, and walnut trees sought the more sandy and higher lands. Then came the gobble of wild turkeys and the swift shadows of prehistoric wolves who paused now and then to bay prehistoric laments to the moon.

After them came people.

After them came Standard Oil stations.

Historically this is Perryland, not the writer's but Oliver Hazard's, because he figured in a lot that transpired in that section, the time being the early nineteenth century, the state capital being Zanesville, and Oliver Hazard Perry being a naval officer who would rather fight than switch. We speak here of the War of 1812. Although most Ohioans favored the war, when General Hull surrendered in Detroit, Ohio suddenly found itself wide open for the Red Coats to enter and do creative destructive mischief. In 1813 General William Henry Harrison defended Fort Meigs—now Perryville—repulsing soundly two separate British attacks. Farther south, near Fremont—which now has 21,000 residents and 1800 members in its YMCA—Major George Croghan beat off—soundly again, nothing was done unsoundly in those days—a large British and Indian force, sending them packing with his one cannon and his 150 angry men. The real battle, though, took place *on* Lake Erie itself near Put-in-Bay. There Perry clobbered the British Navy and allowed Harrison to get to Canada in time for the Battle of the Thames which, as far as Ohioans were concerned, ended the War of 1812. They went around after that naming everything they could lay their hands on after Oliver Hazard Perry.

At Put-in-Bay is a 352-foot monument: The International Peace Monument beneath which are the remains of three American and three British officers. The monument, by the way, is the second highest national monument in the country, taller even than the Statue of Liberty. And over it flies that tin-goose trolley, the island-hopping Ford Tri-Motor plane that links Ohio's off-shore islands with the nearest Kroger Store.

And down there, off to the east, is Sandusky.

To most people, Sandusky with its 120 industrial establishments and its preoccupation with miniature lighthouses in front of buildings is not a city at all. To most people Sandusky is something pleasant that must be got through if one is to reach Cedar Point out in the bay. Cedar Point is within the city limits of Sandusky but with its roller-coaster and cotton candy it seems a noisy and festive entity of its own. Cedar Point is one of the oldest resorts our country has and one of the nicest, the resort being established on part of the land that made up

Lake Erie lighthouse.

Cedar Point love bug.

the king-sized land grant by which the Connecticut refugees—burned out by the British—could rebuild inland. These land grants acquired the name "Firelands"—and that is how Sandusky, Cedar Point, and the sauerkraut factory began. Cedar Point did not always have its roller-coaster. In the 1820s, said one historian, Cedar Point "was a bit of wild land seven miles long, sheltering in its long arms Sandusky Bay. It was covered with timber and a sandy beach edged the shore. There was at that time no large amount of navigation on the lake and no lighthouse reared its head on the point . . ." Now the place has the thousand-room Breakers Hotel which early visitors got to by riding from the docks a little Toonerville Trolley. Also, magnificent yachts, some of foreign registry, used to tie up at the docks, too, in order that the passengers from the sea might partake of the hospitality. Now, though, Pepsi-Cola moderns hurl themselves swiftly across a sleek causeway but the result, once there, is the same: enjoyment. In the fifties Cedar Point almost went the way of all flesh. Trustees for the G. A. Boeckling estate—he being the gentleman who made Cedar Point a sparkling reality—wanted to peddle the whole shooting match to private developers who wanted to turn the Point into a fancy subdivision. Yelps of pain and protest were heard from the governor's office to Cleveland's Euclid Avenue bars. When the state itself wanted to step in and make Cedar Point a state park, Sandusky residents and the man collecting tickets on the giant ferris wheel said no thanks. To make a long story short, the Boeckling heirs themselves stepped in to save the day—and there Cedar Point stands. Thousands upon thousands swarm there during the summer season, and the thousand-room Breakers Hotel—painted glistening white and filled with wonder, honeymooners, and memory—stands, old and proud and elegant. And on the hot sands of the cool beach, in season, sprawl out-of-season bikinied girls so tempting as they bake themselves under the sun that for us to think of other things—like the natural resources of the Sandusky area being sand and stone and perhaps, fish—takes all the will power we can muster. A blonde strolls by—or is *undulates* more apt?—and the fact that Erie County where Sandusky is has over 100,000 acres of farmland is a fact that seems to us nonessential. And though Sandusky is one of the nation's major coal-loading ports, our minds are elsewhere. The season at Cedar Point runs from May to Labor Day and so do we. Each year the Miss Ohio Pageant is held there. We are content to sit on the beach and gape at the ones who got away.

If you insist that every item in Ohio must have deep meaning, stay clear of Cedar Point because Cedar Point with its rides and hotel and hot-dog stands is exactly what you think it is: family amusement park and pleasant Ohio tradition. On the other hand, there sits Sandusky year round, chilly in the winter when the lake turns to ice, and crowded in the summer when carloads of families

Relaxing. Cedar Point.

Indian performer. Cedar Point.

descend upon the place. Even if there were no Cedar Point—a sad thought, really —Sandusky, being more than cotton candy, would have meaning and importance. Here where sea gulls cry for the taste of ocean salt sits a well-tended city and county seat that contains 34,000 souls. On the silent streets along the waterfront when Cedar Point hibernates you can see great stone wineries sleeping in the winter sun, drowsy with wet memories of the grape and of the past. Here in 1849 was the same terrible cholera epidemic that made many cities in Ohio cry. See Sandusky's Cholera Cemetery at Harrison and Madison Streets. Here, too, through these same waterfront streets and in the shadow of some of these same buildings, the buildings then being young, passed huddled and frightened blacks on their way to Canada and to freedom. Much history here and much beauty. That's Sandusky.

The streets of this city stretch out from the downtown district like lopsided spokes of a whopperjawed wagon-wheel, extending east and south and west. To the east: beyond the homes is industrial; shopping centers are there and the Cedar Point Causeway, Sunday traffic jams waiting to happen. Avoid the main thoroughfares and Sandusky is a typical midwestern town: this street has gentle one-family homes surrounded by tall trees, that one is lined with old frame houses that have slipped, with little grace, into old age. Always, of course, suburbia and the outcroppings of it. But East Water Street downtown—with buildings both old and new—is a page torn from the past, tinkered with a little, perhaps too much, perhaps not enough. This conglomerate of architecture has character and charm. It is no mass-produced shopping center, antiseptic and mundane.

On the town square—more of a grand boulevard—a little red popcorn wagon stands, its high wheels motionless, its horse long since gone.

To the west, along the convoluted shore of Sandusky Bay, huge and complicated machinery litters the sky, machinery that lifts entire railroad coal cars high into the air, upends them, and with dark spewing pours coal one hundred tons at a time into the black and dark belly of a waiting lake vessel, a vessel that holds 3000 tons of coal. This great car dumper has been in Sandusky since 1939. Should its Tinker-Toy size intrigue you, by all means visit the Lower Lake Dock Company and see the loading of vessels yourself. Tours can be arranged, but give them a few days notice, please.

Another Sandusky plant is the General Parts Division of the Ford Motor Company which in Sandusky makes, among other items, bumper jacks and door locks General Motors makes ball-bearings in Sandusky, the Inland Boat Company makes steel cabin cruisers that are sometimes nearly fifty feet long, and down the street a ways the Lyman Boat Works creates inboard and outboards by the score. The Lake Erie Canning Company makes catsup, processes cherries, but

Unloading coal cars. Sandusky.

the tourist attraction (tours can be arranged here also) is the company's sauer-kraut plant listed as one of the nation's newest cabbage-cutting and fermenting operations. If your taste runs to the grape, take a thirty-minute tour of the M. Hommel Company whose products are—happily—champagne and sparkling burgundy.

West of Sandusky—if you avoid the expressway to Toledo—you cross a long and lonely causeway to Port Clinton where the airport is that houses the world's smallest airline, Island Airline, and its equipment that are museum pieces: old Ford Tri-Motors. With your permission let us dawdle here a moment and sing love songs to the tin goose, one of which seems to be in the sky, leaning casually against a cloud and watching a sea gull soar. This remarkable airline services the five Lake Erie islands of the Catawba Peninsula. The tin goose delivers to islanders everything everyday—from tourists in the summer to a grocery order in the winter. Livestock has flown in the tin goose. Island children consider the old planes school buses and they are; school boards pay the students fare to bring the island small fry to mainland and to school. Although the tin goose is busiest in summer, when the winds of winter howl and the sky is filled with driving snow, the plane still makes its appointed rounds, landing on runways that earthbound esoterics would hesitate to drag their little foreign cars on. Each Ford Tri-Motor has a capacity of thirteen passengers—first come, first served. Each year more than 50,000 people ride these antiques through the sky.

Beautiful, beautiful . . .

The flattened-out peninsula where the tin goose lands is a place of sweet scents: apple trees in blossom, plus baskets and baskets of peaches. Here, too, plums are raised. The peninsula advertises itself as a place where "nature smiles and Lake Erie's cool breezes caress the summer vacationist." Here is a state park, East Harbor State Park, one of Ohio's finest—and longest—beaches. On the eastern point of this finger is the Marblehead Lighthouse. Out there in the drink is Johnson's Island, site of a confederate prison. This is the land of the tin goose, summer breeze, and ice fishing.

And always out there, the lake.

For those of you who collect the homes of Presidents, try Fremont, a handful of miles southwest of Port Clinton and Sandusky. Here you'll find Spiegel Grove —not a mail-order catalogue but twenty-five acres of deep woods, silent paths, and twilight mists. Here the nineteenth President of the United States Rutherford B. Hayes lived out his days, died, and is now buried. Hayes is the President with the Smith Brothers Cough Drop beard. He helped bring normalcy to the South after the Civil War. Civil Service reforms were his baby, too, and after retire-ment, prison reform. "Spiegel"—the family estate is called that because in German

World's *smallest* airline!

spiegel means *mirror*. Around the Hayes place, they say, the water pools under the many trees looked like a thousand reflecting woodland mirrors, trying at night to capture stars. Sandusky County itself was so named because in the argot of the Indians Sandusky means *cold water*. Fremont used to be called Lower Sandusky, but that confused everyone, since Upper Sandusky lies below Fremont, so the name was changed.

If you like sugar beets as well as presidential tombs, you're doubly lucky in Fremont. The town is headquarters for a large sugar beet operation—or rather, a large operation that concerns itself with sugar beets. Utility rates, says the Fremont chamber, are recognized as among the lowest in the state. And on the main street in Fremont an old school has wisely turned partially into a donut shop. *Downtown* Fremont is a hilly little affair. Across from the Fort Stevenson Motor Inn is an old structure labeled simply SALOON. On the east side of town, across the bridge, you'll find Chinese food, well-tended homes, and a few old mansions wondering what happened.

Travel west, though, from Sandusky to Toledo by the lake shore and the magic seems to vanish from the land. The area is lonely and windswept where the clouds—ponderous and close—seem bent on smothering you. Along this lake road is Camp Perry, fenced in and attended by gargantuan warehouses that are silent and no longer loved. As you drive this empty stretch of road you pass many deserted farmhouses. They sit decayed, unmourned, and going to seed. About every fourth forsaken house has in its front yard a rusted and forsaken auto. But farmers do live along here. The farmers who do not have fruit stands before their homes look as if they wish they did. Turtle Creek and Toussaint Creek flow under bridges in search of the sea; they are monster creeks, big as rivers. But the traffic is sparse. Most travelers travel swiftly along modern expressways that have rendered this road old-fashioned, guarded only by deserted farmhouses with broken windows for eyes.

Suddenly, coming at you from the west, is Oregon, Ohio: 28.5 square miles of city of which two thirds is farmland. Oregon is connected to nearby Toledo by one hundred trucking lines, so its chamber says, and four railroads. And a highway few people use. Oregon has Standard Oil's largest Ohio refinery, Big John's Body Shop, and the Sacred Heart Home for the Aged. Vast refineries—crazy mixed-up plumbing jobs—guard the western approaches to Oregon. Round-the-clock orange flames flicker from pipes in the sky, licking at the lowhung clouds. Oregon has traces of suburbia. And somewhere it has 15,000 people. Passed through Oregon three times, stopped twice, but no one was home. But its chamber says—with good will—that Oregon "is young and on the move."

Thus both sides have been heard from. Anyway, soon Oregon will gobble up Toledo. Or soon Toledo will gobble up Oregon. Place your bets.

Which brings us, logically, to Toledo itself. Toledo, like so many Ohio cities, is trying to tear itself down and start over. Yet, much of the old which remains in downtown Toledo is both beautiful and genteel. But let us look at some of Toledo's history. The last time we mentioned the city, if you recall, it had just emerged from Lake Erie and was standing around, dripping wet and looking quite primeval. Toledo, after it dried itself off, still had problems. Both Ohio and Michigan claimed it and, in fact, almost went to war over it. Was ever an Ohio city so loved! Michigan claimed Toledo, as did Ohio, until 1835 at which time Ohio created Lucas County from the disputed territory. The militia of both states lined up, ready for a shooting war, but the federal government stepped in and awarded Toledo to Ohio in what has been called "The Bloodless Toledo War."

The city is the result of the marriage of two towns, Port Lawrence and Vistula, both Maumee river colonies, and Toledo is also the site of Fort Industry.

A grand day for Toledo, among many grand days some still in the future, was in 1818 when the steamboat *Walk Over the Water* tooted into port, having chugged clear from Buffalo with its Christ complex. The first railroad to be built west of the Alleghenies connected Toledo with Adrian, Michigan, in 1836. Then, where the Ottawa, Chippewa, and Shawnee Indians used to play, came the sound of the canal digger's shovel—and the silence of the Indian forests was shattered forever. The quiet fingers of man-made waterways touched Toledo with a wet and wonderful magic. After the canal arrived in 1843, Toledo grew by leaps and bounds. Seven years later came another canal. Now the St. Lawrence Seaway is the ditch that has made Toledo a most important port, the nation's ninth largest, playing host to freighters from just about every country that puts to sea.

But a nice thing about Toledo as a seaport is that Toledo's port does not reflect the anger and danger of a riled ocean. Sure, Lake Erie can get mean, break ships in two, and send them to the bottom, screaming in pain, but to see a great ocean freighter dock in Toledo does not fill one with the same sense of relief that comes from seeing a similar freighter seek the quiet waterways after battling a tormented ocean. Nor do you get the feeling of dreariness that some get when they see the docks that ring Manhattan. Toledo—so far from the wild tides of the Atlantic—is a nautical sanctuary deep and safe in the midwest. Contact the Toledo Board of Trade (Toledo is the fourth largest grain market in the country) and perhaps a tour can be arranged to let you see grains being loaded aboard freighters. Or, perhaps, you'll visit one of the king-sized grain elevators.

37

An ocean port. Toledo.

Although Toledo, so far from the ocean, is an international port of consequence, few youngsters running away to sea head to Toledo. And just think of the sights they miss: in Side Cut Park are old canal locks to gape at, there's always the Toledo Museum of Art, and for something fancier, the pleasant campus of the University of Toledo where leggy charmers stroll on mellow autumn days, kicking leaves.

The east side of Toledo, around East Broadway, is a grimy and melancholy section of the city, but all cities have such neighborhoods. Cross the Maumee River on an elegant suspension bridge, though, look down at Toledo spread at your feet, and you will have to agree that the city has full-bodied and substantial character. Some of the buildings in the business district are old, some are new, and—as we write this—some are missing. As we suggested, a *new* Toledo is abuilding. One businessman told us, "Listen, when we get finished, we're going to have one hell of a city." We believe him. Evidence of that is everywhere, in the steel girders in the sky and in the eyes of the Toledo businessmen. Still, the old buildings that linger along Summit Street like old and rare wine are graceful items from Toledo's more ornate yesterdays. The building that houses the Toledo *Blade*, for instance, catches you by surprise; it has the appearance of a sugary castle, the sort confectioners place in candy store windows and nobody ever buys. Yet, that newspaper building has charm and belongs. If new high-rises that are dispassionate can blossom on Toledo's main streets, surely passionate old stone buildings can blossom there, too. Each belongs because each is Toledo.

And what of Toledo's residential areas? Toledo has any kind you'd like, a few you'll love, and some that should be scraped under a rug. Toledo has mile upon mile of suburbia as well as old neighborhoods near in, great areas of tired little homes of the lower middle class. The streets of Toledo wiggle and wind and leave you wondering—or, if you're a stranger—lost. Toledo also has parkways that go on and on forever—in search of, we presume, well-tended suburbia, which, as we said, Toledo has in spades.

Among other things, Toledo *is* the Jeep, a war baby of the Willys-Overland Company which came to Toledo in 1911 when John North Wills himself purchased the Pope-Toledo plant. Do you remember back to 1922 when the Overland Four came out? Its engine was the great-grandfather of the engine now used in the Jeep. Do you remember the Willys Knight? Until no longer manufactured (1932 was its last year) some 300,000 of them bounced along the highways. In 1940 came the Willys-Overland and in 1941 came Pearl Harbor. The Army selected the Willys-designed Jeep over all other designs offered and thus the Toledo assembly line went to war. The Jeep quarter-ton truck had been originally intended to replace motorcycles and reconnaissance trucks. But as time passed,

Grain storage. Maumee.

the Jeep did everything but make love to soldiers. Perhaps the most famous World War II cartoon penned by Bill Mauldin shows a sad cavalry sergeant standing with his back to his mortally wounded Jeep, one hand over his eyes, and the other hand pointing a pistol at his four-wheeled mount's hood. The sergeant was about to put it out of its misery; no caption was needed. That is the way Jeeps were and still are.

Just south of Toledo is Maumee which, approached by the wrong road, seems little more than a huge intersection through which a six-lane street winds its way. Near its present library was the site of Colonel William Dudley's Massacre but things are quiet there now. Fort Meigs of the War of 1812 fame is nearby in Perrysburg, and here also is where General Mad Anthony Wayne fought 2000 Indians in the Battle of Fallen Timbers, commemorated by—among other things—Bob Finch's Fallen Timbers Meats and Fresh Oysters. Maumee, a pretty community, sits rather quietly on nearly eight square miles that contain 4194 school children, or to put it another way, 500 school children per square mile. The only disturbing item about Maumee, first white settlement in Northwest Ohio, is trying to pronounce its motto, which is "Peh-Kes-Ina-Si-Pio-Ue Tci-Ki-Wi." The motto means either "beautiful river valley" or "the first railroad went through here in 1855."

South of Maumee is Perrysburg, the aforementioned Fort Meigs, and much suburbia.

Then open farm country and, sooner or later, there's Bowling Green blessed with Interstate 75, the Johnny Appleseed Memorial Highway which is U.S. 25, a Holiday Inn, a bunch of car dealers, sandwich stands, a university, and the building that houses the county seat, the county being Wood, named for a general in the War of 1812. Consider, if you please, the Bowling Green State University, which from the street isn't terribly impressive. Its buildings, viewed from that angle, have all the originality of a secondhand Quonset hut. But inside beauty is. At the railroad crossing in town, Wooster Avenue, sits a Burger Chef by which the railroad crews park their engines to sit inside the sandwich place, to eat hamburgers, and to watch—with pleasure and dismay—the coeds passing by.

Bowling Green and the country surrounding it is flatland. On a clear day you can see forever that turns out to be usually more of the same. In that part of Wood County where the Black Swamp used to be, the soil is rich and wonderful and productive. The principal farm products are soybeans, corn, cattle, wheat, and tractors rusting in the distant field. A few flatland miles east of Bowling Green is the metropolis of Woodside: a few frame houses, a gasoline pump, and a railroad track. Woodside is on the north side of the road. On the south side of the road are trees and fields and emptiness—as far as the eyes can see.

World's highest split-level. Bowling Green.

Bowling Green University Campus.

Actually to live in this section of Ohio is the same as being at sea: distant storms announce their approach sometimes hours in advance as dark smudges on the horizon miles and miles and miles away.

South of Bowling Green—a far piece on the interstate—is another town that got its start as the result of the War of 1812: Findlay. Was first a military base. Music lovers will be pleased to learn that a mill on Blanchard River in Findlay inspired Findlay native Tell Taylor to write "Down by the Old Mill Stream," the result being neither Findlay nor barbershop quartets were the same again. Findlay's earliest settler was a French tailor who married a Shawnee lady, but as noted, Findlay didn't really begin until the War of 1812. The discovery of gas and oil helped Findlay to prosper, attracting rubberneckers and settlers by the score. When the gas supply petered out, the settlers stayed on, Mr. Taylor wrote his song, and so there sits Findlay today in the catbird seat, its population well over 35,000, its industries diverse, and its annual rainfall 35.9 inches. Findlay College, established in 1882, is a pleasant architectural offering from the gentler days when college buildings looked sweet instead of austere. The college has an enrollment of more than 1500 students.

The "Underground Railroad" that operated during the Civil War to help runaway blacks find freedom in Canada operated in and about Findlay at a place near Williamsport (now a crossroads of a village with about two dozen houses and a brand new sidewalk) but around there the "railroad" was called "The Grapevine Telegraph and Underground Railroad Through Hancock County." About a dozen blacks a week passed through this area. Now Interstate 75 almost goes through Findlay on its north-south express run between Toledo and Cincinnati. Almost but not quite.

Findlay offers much to see. The Cooper Tire and Rubber Company will show you how it makes truck tires. Eastman Kodak has a big processing plant, you may take a tour there, but—heavens!—no cameras are permitted. This is one of the ten Kodak processing plants from New York to Hawaii. If drain tile causes little lights to light in your eyes, the Hancock Brick and Tile Company—largest producer of drain tile in Ohio and one of the oldest in operation—will be glad to take you on a one-hour tour to see the tile manufactured. Interested in oil pipelines? Visit headquarters of the Marathon Oil Company (advance notice, please) and see the computer area, pipeline oil movements control center, and the company cafeteria. One month advance notice is required for a two-hour tour of what used to be the Krantz Brewing Corporation founded in 1884 by the old mill stream. Now the place is called—hang on tight—The Old Dutch-Frankemurth Division of International Breweries, Incorporated. You can visit the brewhouse where beer is started in a large kettle, fermenting rooms, storage rooms,

45

and the clicketing-clackety-clanking bottle house where beer is canned or bottled.

The next stop, of course, the corner tavern to sample same.

And so we take leave of Findlay.

Northeast of Findlay—seventeen flatland miles away is Fostoria where the Ford Motor Company makes all the spark plugs used in Ford-built equipment. Once connected to Tiffin by trolley, to Fremont (where we just buried President Hayes), Fostoria was connected by a plank road through the forest. Fostoria actually got its start when the Black Swamp caused early settlers to suffer chills and fevers. *The* place to buy quinine was Fostoria's general store. But that was in the dim, dark past. Now Fostoria sits in flatland splendor of a sort, suburbia is rampant, and the Good Shepherd Home has—at first glimpse—the appearance of an auto court. Railroads crisscross the town—four different lines, they say— and expressways through Fostoria have made hash of some sections. But all in all, Fostoria is an active and good-sized town of more than 16,000 good souls plus a marketing area that serves the needs of another 10,000. In 1859 the Lake Erie & Western Railroad first tooted into town—and trains haven't stopped tooting in Fostoria since. Fostoria lies in three counties: Seneca, Hancock, and Wood.

If you have ever stumbled tongue-tied through a historic pageant your community foisted off on the public, chances are the words you mumbled were written in Fostoria. The Rogers Company writes and stages such things at benefit plays and community pageants just about everywhere. The company is no dinky one-room musty office, because on its payroll are nearly a hundred people, and that, as we say in Fostoria, is show business.

Between Fostoria and Tiffin is a rather sedate and somewhat exhausted community called Bascom, its houses bunched together for comfort, and over there a sagging structure—a brick works?—stands in sway-backed glory.

Also between Fostoria and Tiffin—flatlands, empty skies, lonesome winds, and faint memories of a little trolley that once bucketed by, its trolley wires singing at the many, many farms. In summer, little open trolleys hummed along the flatland right-of-way between the two towns, but in 1920, the trolley line called the Tiffin, Fostoria and Eastern Electric Railroad stopped running forever and that, trolley fans, was that. Even before then, in Tiffin, the horses that pulled the cars on the Tiffin Street Railway vanished without a whinny of protest into the nearest bottle of glue. Now jitney buses ply the streets of Tiffin which has five bridges, the Sandusky River, Heidelberg College, and the Octagonal Tavern so named because it is located in a brick building that is square.

Tiffin started life as a saloon—during, of course, the War of 1812. It has since grown to be one of Ohio's more delightful towns. The discovery of natural gas in the area in 1888 helped Tiffin get moving. Heidelberg College was before that, though, starting in 1850. Tiffin is the largest manufacturer of sanitary bathroom fixtures; the American Radiator and Standard Sanitary Corporation there makes johns from scratch or, to put it another way, from raw material to finished product. Thus, Tiffin, having outmoded the out-house, could be called the in-house capital of the world. With forty-four miles of paved streets, sixty-five miles of sewers, and two garbage trucks, Tiffin is in one way typical of small cities in Ohio that, in refusing to die, continue to grow. In 1966 Tiffin was among the first communities in the nation to get Touch-Tone telephones.

To be sure, even Tiffin has touches of the bland suburbia that, to paraphrase Fred Allen, sets mediocrity back ten years. But on the other hand, Tiffin also has many grand old homes and modern new ones that no developer can mass-produce. The public buildings in Tiffin are old-fashioned cupcakes of charm, neat and sweet and fresh from yesterday. The downtown area is a place of narrow streets and substantial brick buildings, both neat and quite healthy-looking. Tiffin looks as if it intends to stick around a long time.

And we're glad.

This—Tiffin, Fostoria, Fremont, and the rest—is *Winesburg, Ohio* land, Sherwood Anderson country dotted with small towns and farm houses, perhaps still peopled with some of the yesteryear characters he created with words and memory and melancholy. In that old house we just passed, the one ringed with wooden porches, perhaps another old man sits in the gloom of an upstairs room, writing his "book of the grotesque." Perhaps, down that township road we just passed on the edge of town—the dirt road goes to what memory?—Anderson's Doctor Reefy traveled in his buggy. And Anderson's George Willard, what of him? He, too, was of this land of county fairs, sulky races, lovers lanes, angry skies, and pools of water lying in wait to capture falling stars. And Sherwood's long-ago railroad telegrapher who sat in the darkness on railroad ties and quietly became a poet? Where? And Seth Richmond's house—showplace of one of these little towns, said Anderson—has it now died or has it grown bigger? And Anderson's Trunion Pike from which a side road led to Al Robinson's farm, which pike was that? For, as we suggest, this is *Winesburg, Ohio* around here, in this part of the state. Sherwood Anderson Country. Each time we passed through or lingered on a village square, we wondered if another Sherwood Anderson now sat in the yellow school bus that went by so noisily.

Or have we outgrown the sweetness that once was this area when the world was a little younger, the winds a little sharper, and the silence of the countryside was not disrupted by the steady hum of traffic on expressways? Clyde, Ohio, *does* exist. So does Camden, where Anderson was born. So does Elyria, where he once

47

worked. But what of the young now racing across the village square that contains only a falling-down bandstand and signs to give traffic directions? And what of those riding in souped-up cars with mufflers that go bang? The young these days move swiftly into the future, too swiftly, and their souped-up cars with mufflers that go bang shatter the mood that was this countryside's yesterday. And so the mood is buried in noise, buried in an unmarked grave in an unattended country graveyard that has for its neighbor a shuttered and deserted country church, also waiting to die.

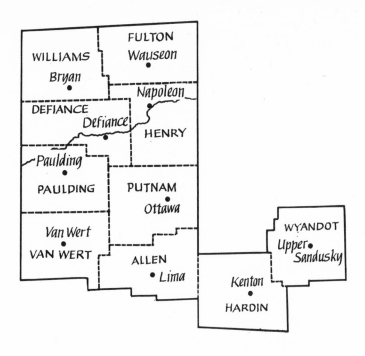

3

Northwest Ohio is a windswept flatland of straight-line roads that proceed without hesitation or curve to the straight-line horizon. The *Ohio Almanac*—best volume about Ohio you can buy—notes that "a headlight on a grade in Defiance can be seen in Antwerp more than twenty miles away." By day these roads shimmer with false wetness as canals which once crossed this land shimmered for real. A car approaches you forever before it passes with a whoosh.

Because this land was long ago a part of the Black Swamp, now drained, the farms are rich and alive with growth. Here tomatoes ripen in fields as far as the eye can see. Here, too, congregate rusted school buses and rickety pickup trucks filled with migrant workers who descend like sad and lonely locusts until the first frost sends them—where?

Although in this flatland of slow sunrises and lingering sunsets there are no great cities, here is where you'll find, of all things, "Chinatown, U.S.A." because Archbold, population 2300, is the world's largest producer of canned Chinese food. Defiance, set smack dab in the center of this billiard table area, has only 17,000 residents. Van Wert, in the southwestern section of this quarter of Ohio, has only 12,000. Metropolitan Toledo is east, up there on the lake. Farther south, 49

Land of the flattened farms.

if you are not too pushy about geography, there's Lima. It has 57,000 people. Mostly, though, this part of Ohio is a wide-open land of big farms, big skies, and strung along the roads like cameo civilizations dozens of little villages, each with retired farmers, grain elevators, Dairy Queen stands, and teen-age girls who dress like Fifth Avenue. After all, we must be reasonable. *All* the tomatoes aren't canned.

Montpelier is in the very northwest corner of the state, a five-mile run from the Ohio Turnpike, and according to its chamber of commerce, "within 500 miles of 60 percent of the nation's consumers." Toledo is closer to Montpelier than that crowd and so is Ann Arbor. If culture is your life's work and Montpelier is your home, consider the town's community playhouse theater group—or get a library card. The town, born in 1845, didn't get going until 1881 when the Wabash Railroad picked it as a division point. Though its population is 5000, Montpelier has a dozen different manufacturing plants. It is also within 35 miles of 50 lakes which means just what you think it means. Montpelier is not the county seat of Williams County; Bryan with 8000 residents is. The entire county, one of the last places in Ohio to be settled, has 32,000 people, 21,000 automobiles, and 1500 farms.

Defiance where the Maumee and Auglaize rivers say hello and compare chewing-gum wrappers, started out as a fort in the eighteenth century; Johnny Appleseed lived in the neighborhood about twenty years; and the town itself contains what's left of the world's largest apple tree. To be honest, all that remains of the fabled tree which they say measured 27 feet around, 45 feet high, and had a wingspread of 60 feet, is a big stump. The tree is said to have yielded each year 200 bushels of apples. Defiance is pebbled with historical markers made from native boulders. One marker tells where Chief Pontiac was born and another where Iroquois Indian Princess Coo-Coo-Che's log cabin was. Defiance also has Defiance College with one thousand students and nearly twenty buildings.

How did Defiance get its name? We thought you'd never ask. It seems that when General Mad Anthony Wayne, who slept in more Ohio towns than Washington ever slept in east-coast ones, looked over the newly constructed fort in 1794, he said:

"I defy the English, the Indians, and all the devils in hell to take it."

General Scott, who was standing beside him, said:

"Hey, that's pretty good." Or, words to that effect, adding, "Then call it Fort Defiance."

In the summer of 1796 the fort was abandoned. Twenty-nine years later at the

51

same river junction seventeen families arrived. They had traveled west by wagon through the Black Swamp and that was how Defiance began.

The canal came—and Defiance, for better or for worse, grew like Topsy.

As far as cities and towns are concerned, Defiance County on the Indiana line is a well-farmed vacant lot. Defiance with 16.564 residents, is the exception. Sherwood, for example, has only 678; Ney, 356; Hicksville, 3422; and that's it. True, you might find places like The Bend and Mark Center on the map, but blink and you've missed them. The rest of Defiance County is flat-out rural landscape populated by complicated farm machinery lumbering along county roads in search of fields upon which to feast. Here farmhouses, huge and shipshape, sit far back from the straight-as-an-arrow roads. Here, winter—that howling madman—hurls blizzards at the unbroken countryside; and here, too, summer—his temperamental spouse—drenches the level land with terrible thunder showers and torments it with lightning bursts. And here things grow that we city people eat.

Little towns like Hicksville in this county come at you slowly from the horizon. Though you drive the legal limit, these towns take forever to arrive. Perhaps from the day coach windows of yesterdays Hicksville arrived as a clang of a crossing bell and a complete surprise and was just as swiftly gone. Perhaps from the postage-stamp window of a mile-high jet, Hicksville and the rest are only toy houses splattered carelessly upon the checkerboard country below. But up close? Listen, there's beauty there. Hicksville—and the rest—are simple and sweet farm towns, each with its one-minute evening rush hour, each with more churches than bars, and each on a hot summer night with its lighted baseball diamond where a frightened Little Leaguer stands at the plate, watches for the right pitch, and dreams of bubble-gum-card baseball heroes. Hicksville is the Hicksville Grain Company, the Hurley Funeral Home, Kenny's Muffler Shop, and a Baltimore & Ohio passenger train that never stops.

Wander southward along the Ohio-Indiana border and you leave Defiance County to travel—whoosh!—through Paulding County, which is only more of the same. The biggest town is Paulding, 4000 people, scene of the tile industry which helped drain the Black Swamp to render the land habitable. Even after the canal came through in the mid 1800s, most of Paulding County was muck and marsh. One of the county's streams was damned to create a canal reservoir, but the resulting lake bred more mosquitoes than Paulding County had people to be bitten. When the state did nothing about the mosquito-breeding lake, the locals did. In 1887 they dynamited the dam—and there went the lake, mosquitoes, and all. Paulding County with its 1000 farms, 5000 voters, and 12,000 cars has been 417 square miles of tranquillity ever since.

Farming. Ohio's first industry.

Seventy miles southwest of Toledo, in the neighborhood of Van Wert County, the Black Swamp kind of petered out. Anyway, years before, Lake Erie itself had reached this far down the state on the Ohio-Indiana line. Mound builders had once lived where the city of Van Wert now is, but their mounds were leveled so the Marsh Hotel could be erected. Long before Van Wert became famous for Liederkranz cheese, the area was forest, swamp, and Indian land. Here in woodland silences warriors left their family while the menfolk went out to shoot arrows at the whites. The city of Van Wert started as a gristmill, really. Then gristmill— and the town—became the county seat. Along came the railroad in 1853 to toot whistles at the Germans, Dutch, and Welsh Van Wert had accumulated. Van Wert was named by mistake and now makes all the Liederkranz cheese in the world, the cheese itself being another mistake, but before you take umbrage, read on.

The county and city were named after Issac Van Wart, an officer in the Revolutionary War. Due to a spelling error the legislature named the county Van Wert instead of Van Wart—and the spelling stuck. As for Liederkranz cheese being a mistake, we call to the stand Swiss cheesemaker Emil Frey, whose New York carriage trade liked Bismarck schlosskaese. Unfortunately the imported cheese did not always travel well from Europe, getting seasick, or whatever it is that disenchanted cheeses do. For two years Frey tinkered with curds and molds and curing processes to duplicate the imported cheese. Instead, he accidentally created a gold-crusted, soft-ripening, spready cheese that was to prove more popular than the imported variety. He named it Liederkranz ("wreath of songs") to honor the singing society to which his boss belonged. The cheese plant came to Van Wert, the Borden Company bought it, and so Van Wert is the Liederkranz cheese capital of the world. Most people think it's imported. A few know that Liederkranz is itself a commercial trade name.

But the Borden people do.

If you like numbers, note that Van Wert, with nearly 12,000 residents, is within 50 miles of nearly 900,000 others—*and* within one thousand miles of 172,193,450 people, give or take a few soreheads. If you collect trivia as well as numbers, note that in addition to being the Liederkranz capital of the world, Van Wert is *also* the peony capital of same, but on the other hand, you can't tell by looking at it. Van Wert used to hold peony parades. It no longer goes all-out. Sorry about that. If you fish, chances are your metal tackle box came from Van Wert. The Kennedy Manufacturing Company on North Harrison Street is one of the oldest companies about to use metal construction for tool and tackle boxes. At which point, ready or not, we leave Van Wert to its dreams and its curds.

Archbold: canned Chinese food capital

But let us continue our international cuisine. Next stop: Archbold. We firmly believe that should evil spirits invade that cordial little community the Beatrice Foods Company's Le Choy Products Division would break out on its employees and hold dances of exorcism—called the "lion dance"—in the streets on Chinese New Year. But Archbold has no evil spirits that we could see, only spirited teenagers, so when Chinese New Year does come to Archbold the residents can mutter —with their midwestern drawls—things like "Gung Hoy Fet Toy" at one another. That's what the Chinese do. Point is, Archbold makes more canned Chinese food than China does, if China does. But its workers are no more Chinese than, say, Izzy Kadetz of that wonderful kosher restaurant in Cincinnati. The Archbold plant keeps outgrowing itself. Each year a new addition is planned and before it can get off the drawing board another addition is needed. One leap forward deserves another. A grand plant exists now. In one top-secret section, bean sprouts are grown. The process is hush-hush. Bean sprouts are harvested there each and every working day. In the kitchen—several acres under one roof or so it seems— are huge vats of this and that, bubbling and simmering and filling the air with delightful aromas. Some of the ingredients for the chop suey are grown in Fulton County, where Archbold is. But from South Korea and Formosa and Hong Kong come water chestnuts, and from Peru and Siam and Burma come Mung Beans. And from everywhere come trailer trucks to load up the goodies and haul them off to market.

Fifty miles southwest of Toledo is Putnam County, which has no cities at all but Ottawa (population 3654) is the county seat. This is rich farming area—flat with a few—too few—slight grades called hills. Most of the people in or around Ottawa seem to work at Sylvania General Electric Products, a subsidiary of General Telephone and Electronics, the Ottawa plant employing nearly 2800 workers to make television picture tubes. If the good people around Ottawa aren't doing that, some are working for Buckeye Sugars, Incorporated, making sugar from the sugar beets the itinerant workers have harvested. The transients, mostly Mexicans from the southwest, give the little flatland town a south-of-the-border flavor briefly—then they vanish in search of another state and another crop.

Ottawa began in 1833, became a county seat at the end of the Civil War, and has—today—one of the most honest chambers of commerce a person could wish for. Said the chamber, "To say that we are a community without future problems and programs would be a misstatement of fact. A community without them is either stagnant or going backwards—we are neither. We are growing, we are experiencing growing pains such that come with annexation and population growth . . . " Who says the New Englanders have a patent on honest talk? We'd be tempted to move our industry to Ottawa on the strength of the chamber's

OHIO
A PERSONAL PORTRAIT
OF THE 17TH STATE

attitude alone. On the other hand, a typewriter and a camera aren't much of an industry.

Six miles up the road from refreshingly honest Ottawa is Leipsic, known as Roanoke until 1857, when the railroad came through, and then it was known as Creighton. But when two entertainers from Leipsig, Germany, passed through and wowed the town, the town repaid the boffo performance by naming the town after the town the entertainers had come from. With fewer than 2000 residents, Leipsic goes full blast during the tomato season. Its streets are a traffic jam of tractors that pull flatbed trailer-trains heaped with bushel baskets of the stuff Bloody Marys come from. Though passenger trains no longer say hello to Leipsic, the Baltimore and Ohio and the old Nickel Plate Road—now called the Norfolk & Western—honk hellos every now and then.

Other villages in this drained Black Swamp county are Belmore, Cloverdale, Continental, Dupont, Fort Jennings, Gilboa, Kalida, Miller City (which isn't), Ottoville, Pandora, and West Leipsic. The Ottawa River through here used to be called Hog River. Seems so many hogs drowned crossing the stream on the way to market the stream ceased to be kosher.

Napoleon, Ohio, where no deaths from smog have yet been reported, is really the tomato captial of the world, the proud possessor of 350 parking meters, 2400 homes, and the Maumee River. The average windspeed through Napoleon in the winter is eleven miles per hour and in the summer, 8 miles per hour. Thought you might be interested. Napoleon is 40 miles from Toledo, 102 miles from Detroit, and about a dozen miles from Deshler. Before the War of 1812 Napoleon and Henry County weren't much to write home about. The area was forest and swamp. But in 1832 the town of Napoleon began, first as a log cabin, then as a log-cabin-turned-inn: a wilderness Howard Johnson. Four years later Napoleon had three frame houses. Then came the canal. Napoleon's first industry was a sawmill. One of its early industries, and one that still exists today, is the Heller Aller Company, windmill makers. Napoleon's first school teacher? Mary Whipple, who in 1837 taught a term in a log cabin four years after the town began.

Since most of these towns and villages in the northwest quarter of Ohio sat where once the Black Swamp was, let us examine one close up, because its history will parallel—almost—the history of the rest. But first, let's sort out this business of the Black Swamp. Technically the swamp—120 miles in length and 40 miles wide—covered eighteen counties of the Maumee River Valley, but in fairness, not all was swampland. Here and there, running east to west, were high and dry limestone ridges that were sometimes a mile wide and in some places separated from each other by only a mile. These ridges later became the east-west roads the settlers traveled. Henry Howe in 1840 described the Black Swamp:

"The perfect uniformity of the soil has given the forest a homogeneous char-

Tomatoes—Ohio's bright crop.

And the lonely migrant who harvests it.

acter. The trees are all generally of the same height, so that when viewed at a distance through the haze, the forest appears like an immense blue wall stretched across the horizon."

Prudence Dangler in a thoughtful and informative booklet written for the Deshler Chamber of Commerce said that one early settler described her Deshler area this way:

"The branches of the tall trees lace together, letting in shafts of dim blue light from above, giving a lonely look to the forest trails . . ."

Deshler—itself located near the intersection of Putnam, Wood, Hancock, and Henry counties and now a village of nearly 2000—started life in the mid-1800s. But first the swamp had to be drained via great ditches one of which (Ditch Number 12) was 37 miles long and in places 8 feet deep, freeing 50,000 acres of farmland. Wood County, knee deep in the Black Swamp, had many such ditches, actually 6000 miles of ditchwork! In 1859 the railroad arrived in Deshler bringing with it cinders, soot, and the promise of growth for the little forest village. A log cabin was built as a rooming house for Portage, as Deshler was called. The town was supposed to have been called Alma and, for a little while, was, until Alma showed up. She was the sixteen-year-old niece of John Deshler, who had laid out the town and named it in her honor. On a visit she leaped from log to log down the muddy main street, growing gloomier with each leap. Her uncle asked her how she liked the place.

"Too much water, too many frogs and mudholes!" she complained. "Why don't you call it Deshler?"

Four years after Deshler was incorporated, the town had 752 muddy citizens, one being Albert Suber, whose small machine shop and foundry had no door. Thus, every chilly stray pig in town wandered in to warm itself by his furnace. But Deshler, like the rest of the communities in the swampy forest, was on the move. By 1900, to curb its flaming youth, Deshler had to ring the town hall bell each night at eight announcing curfew. Deshler had also earned itself the name as one of the wildest little towns the four counties had ever seen.

Prudence Dangler tells it better than we could when she writes that, "the saloon down on East Main spilled forth a noisy group of townspeople. They sloshed through the water which came clear up to the door steps on both sides of the street, stepped up onto the boardwalk, and swung down the street past several houses typical of the location and the time. They were unpainted plank affairs with gaping doors to which screens were unknown. There was derisive yelling and one of them took time to pump himself a drink at the town pump where another fellow citizen had stopped to let his horse drink from the round wooden tub which sat on the ground beneath the spout.

"A couple of women were advancing from the far east end of Main Street. They carried big tin buckets and were on their way to the town pump for drinking water. Everyone from the east end of town came to this pump and those from the west end came to the pump located on the northwest corner of Keyser Avenue and Main Street.

"There were saloons and houses of prostitution on the town's main thoroughfare which rivaled each other in doing a prominent business with the transient population of the period. Men from the canal, woodsmen, teamsters, traveling men, railroaders and farmers from the outlying frontier settlements who came in to do their marketing made up the business customers of the town . . . "

Rather than leave you with the impression that Deshler is still a rowdy place complete with houses that sell services unmarketed by a Sears catalogue, note that in Deshler today the Edwin Library has 20,000 books none of which are dirty, Deshler has a brand-new post office, and in the past ten years, according to its active chamber, 60 new homes have been added to the scene. Deshler, by the way, is now known internationally as a producer of hybrid seed corn, also has an egg-packing plant, and its alfalfa is exported as far away as Europe. Deshler, mature and calm, sits too busy to dream of yesterdays. Other than doing all the stuff mentioned above—like hybrid corn et al.—Deshler manufactures rural mail boxes which are used in all fifty states, and is the proud possessor of two supermarkets, two drugstores, one poolroom, a drive-in ice-cream place, and not one but two funeral homes.

Farther down the state—but still in the northwest quarter—is the largest city this quarter has: Lima, with 57,428 people, 23 elementary schools, 4 drive-in movies, 60 churches, and what seems at first glance a hard-nosed attitude. Second glances then being in order, we'll suggest that Lima, hub of a ten-county marketing area, is, as its chamber says, "A complete and heterogeneous community." Its residential areas offer the full spectrum that the residential areas of most major Ohio cities offer: old mansions, new suburbia, and globs of ordinary homes that time is making hurt. Lima has been an industrial center for more than a century. Five railroads honk horns at it. Truck lines by the score hiss brakes at it. And buses come there from just about everywhere, although the bus station itself is no jewel. Culture in Lima? Well, there's Lima's 70-piece symphony orchestra, basically a volunteer group. If you like the roar of the greasepaint, Lima has the Encore Theater, an amateur conglomerate that can proudly boast of its own theater and full-time director. The Lima Art Association sponsors classes in ceramics and photography. No, Lima isn't a city of dullards.

Lima, as most Ohio cities are, is doing some major reconstruction. But these things take time. The new Hall of Justice in the middle of the revitalized down-

61

town Lima is supposed to be finished this year, this year being 1969. Says the chamber: "Other major improvements are in the works."

We believe them; Lima will have a great city—when finished. They're off to a good start, which makes Lima an exciting place to live or do business.

Lima was called Lima after Lima, Peru, because from Peru came a special "bark" to treat swamp fever. At the beginning, in 1831, Lima was only 160 acres big. The arrival of the Baltimore and Ohio Railroad in 1854 helped Lima get moving—and Lima has been on the move ever since. Actually, we should be fond of Lima for another reason: we are personally fond of trolleys and trains (*passenger trains!*). About the end of the Civil War a lumber man thought up a locomotive to run along rails of wood, a Lima firm turned the engine into reality, and that was the start of Lima as the builder of steam locomotives. Hundreds and hundreds of beautiful, beautiful steam engines—may they rest in peace—saw the light of day in Lima. Doesn't that choke you up?

In World War I Lima developed the Liberty Truck that put our lads on wheels in 1918. Lima is one of the three cities in the United States that owns its own observatory. Also, Lima has two magnificent enclosed shopping malls. The Lima Mall, for instance, has over 500,000 square feet of enclosed and air-conditioned mall. The American Mall, to show we play no favorites, has nearly 400,000 square feet of same. And Northland is a complete shopping center unto itself. The chamber of commerce said so.

Twenty-six miles east of Lima is Kenton, which at one time had the world's largest wire fence factory. And over in Ada is the Ohio Northern University. This about sums up Hardin County, an amiable place of 30,000 good people plus a few others we'll not mention because all counties have them. In 1887 a tornado whistled through Hardin County and nearly blew it straight into Wyandot County next door.

Next door in Wyandot County it would have found Upper Sandusky. Upper Sandusky, population 6000, is the largest city there. It has the Westinghouse Electric Corporation's plant that turns out fractional horsepower motors. Give them a week's notice, if fractional horsepower motors interest you, and they might give you a tour of one of the most highly automated small motor plants you'll ever see. Over in Cary, population 4000, the Roman Catholic Church has a replica of a seventeenth-century Luxemburg miracle statue. In summers this statue is carried in processions, giving Cary, somehow, the reputation as the town for miracle cures.

Or, cures for miracles.

This isn't a religious tract.

62

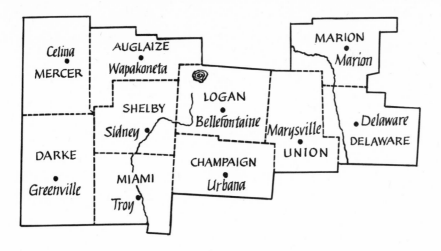

4

As you can see, if you didn't doze somewhere between the mud and the miracle, the Black Swamp made the upper left-hand quarter of Ohio a late bloomer which was a sticky wicket to populate. But now let us wander through the bottom swath of counties this quarter contains. At least some of the terrain will be different. If we start at the Indiana state line, from Mercer and Darke counties, and proceed casually east through a handful of other counties we should, with any luck at all, arrive on the outskirts of Columbus to end our visit to this part of the Buckeye state.

But gone will be most mentions of the Black Swamp; the Black Swamp didn't tinker too much this far south. And gone, for the most part, will be roads that go straight—bang!—into the straight horizon. We shall still be in farm country, but the country will suggest subtle differences: rolling slopes and minuscule valleys to relieve the monotony of the flatland. Also, getting farther from Lake Erie we will not find every other thing not nailed down labeled *Perry This* or *Perry That*, a discouraging thought, really, considering the writer's name, but the photographer whose name is Goldflies is considerably cheered by the prospect. There are no towns in Ohio named Goldflies and the monuments erected to honor that name are difficult to find. You have your problems; we have ours.

Our first stop: Celina, which should be called Salina for its New York state namesake but in the days before zip codes *Salina* became *Celina* to prevent confusion. If Grand Lake St. Marys did not have its western tip where Celina is,

Celina might never have happened at all. Now, though, because the lake *is* there, Celina has become in the summer a quasi-resort town. Or should we begin at the beginning?

Celina is that flattened-out town with 9000 residents in Mercer County, the county ranking seventh along Ohio's 88 for total farm income. Some autumn afternoons Celina has wondrous beauty: the Grandma Moses country town where farmers gather. Then, Celina has charm that won't quit. Unfortunately, the charm does—each summer. Then, summer people, refugees from all sorts of cabins that line the lake, come into Celina. Need we say more? Don't blame Celina. Celina began in 1834 with nothing but a bunch of trees, its chief industry was a sawmill, and by the time the town had a population of 15 good people, the 15 decided to do something about the trees because, as in the case of Deshler, trees and mud and water were everywhere. A "chopping bee" was organized: 70 woodsmen hacked away, shouts of "Timber!" filled the air, and before the Celina Chamber of Commerce could get poetic (later describing Celina as "nestling on the sun-flecked northern banks of Grand Lake"), down came the trees, up dried the mud, and there was the town as advertised and platted. New Celina has a table factory—said to be one of the world's largest.

Lake St. Marys—or Grand Lake—or whatever combination of names pleases you most—started in 1837, was completed in 1845, cost $600,000, and was a man-made reservoir to keep water in the canal between Cincinnati and Toledo. For many years this 17,500-acre reservoir was the largest artificial body of water in existence. Seventeen thousand men, not a poet in the lot, who got paid fifty cents and a slug a booze a day created the pond. When completed, the pond was used by packet boats to bring items all the way up from Cincinnati. When canals themselves went into twilight, the pond remained as a fishing lake. Now the drink is ringed, practically, with all manner of property: ticky-tacky, maudlin, vacationland cute, nice, exceptionally beautiful, and quite expensive. Add to the list a small state park.

To tout the charms of the paradise, Celina—still nestling sun-flecked—built a parade float that featured a fish 30 feet long, 9 feet high, and awfully unreal. This float toured the state, broadcasting the pond far and wide. Rebuilt in 1963, the fish turned out to be 31 feet long, 8 feet wide, and nearly 15 feet high—the perfect example of the bass that got away. In summer, says the Celina chamber, Celina "is a hostess dressed in gay colors and in a holiday mood. There is laughter in her eyes and a song on her lips." Less poetical, the chamber also notes that Celina's sewage disposal plant has a daily capacity of a quarter million gallons, its library has 34,000 volumes, and all units of its fire department are equipped with fog nozzles.

Children's dream world. Fort Recovery.

And so we take fond leave of adjective-flecked Celina which—seriously—seems a good place to live, fish, or cut bait.

South of Celina is the turkey capital of the Midwest plus the world's largest manufacturer of stirrups: Fort Recovery, so named because Mad Anthony Wayne built a fort there after fighting the Indians. A small and serene little community, Fort Recovery still has a fort you can play in, though not the original one. Kids will get a kick out of climbing into the upper floors of the log blockhouse, looking from the tiny windows, and going bang! at whatever Indians are about—which is none. As we said, Fort Recovery isn't big, has less than 1500 people, but on the other hand, they're a friendly lot.

Farther south along the Indiana state line is Darke County. Though the Wabash River originates here, if you cross it, you'll get a surprise. The river at this point is little more than a trickle, hardly sun-flecked because on hot days it isn't there at all, and at best, it's damp, but we suppose it improves as it goes along through Indiana.

Darke County has both rolling hills and flattened farmlands. It has one city, Greenville, and about a dozen small hamlets each smaller and nicer than the other. One of these villages is the birthplace of Annie Oakley or, as she was known in the trade, "Little Miss Sureshot." Her folks were Quakers. Her real name was Phoebe Ann Moses. After her father died she paid off the homestead mortgage by selling game she'd nailed with his 40-inch cap-and-ball Kentucky rifle. The homestead was near North Star. Other Darke County notables: Zachary Landsdowne, a Navy officer whose dirigible fell apart and crashed on Ada, Ohio; Jean Louise Jobes, a graduate of Greenville High School where she played first clarinet; and Lowell Thomas, he being who you think he is, born in Woodington, a few miles from Greenville.

Greenville is where Mad Anthony Wayne held the Treaty of Green Ville to open the Northwest Territory. Greenville's pretty little park contains ponds, horseshoe pits, and a brace of manic-depressive peacocks. A typical county seat, Greenville buzzes with life each Friday and Saturday evening because everyone in town has wheels and if he doesn't drive once down the main street, life has little meaning. On weekdays the stores are active, too. It's no sleepy Rip Van Winkle of a town. The old city hall has been torn down to be replaced by a traffic circle and a water fountain. Duffey's Hardware Company says that it still carries horseshoes and sack needles—plus 47,962 other items.

Once you take a closer look at Greenville the real secret of such non-metropolitan county seats is apparent. Ringed by rich and productive farmland, these county seats are, nevertheless, sophisticated in their own way. Greenville, for example, could have withered on the vine, pitching horseshoes, and wondering what happened to the world. Instead, Greenville made sure the industry it had stayed put. Then it went out and hustled more. Today Greenville buzzes with industry—good industry. There's the American Aggregates Corporation which sells rocks. Add the Buchy Packing Company; it employs 46 people. Corning Glass has 360 on its payroll. The Ex-Cell-O Corporation hires 172. The Fram Corporation hires 750, including Jerry Martin. The General Athletic Products Company hires 120. Hobart hires 97. Inland Steel Container, 60. And the Neff Athletic Lettering Company, which letters athletes, hires 160. But we've hardly scratched the surface. Thus Greenville—and all its Ohio counterparts plunked down in the middle of cornfield nowheres—are foolers. They depend on the rural trade as they always did—but *not* entirely.

Let us proceed gingerly to Darke County's Union City perched astride the Ohio-Indiana border midway between Columbus and Indianapolis. Half the town is in Ohio, the other half is in Indiana. It has two, not one, fire departments, both on twenty-four-hour-duty, which seems reasonable. The tax rate, though, is higher on the Ohio side than it is in Indiana. All told, Union City has about 6000 residents but which state they're in is anybody's guess. It is an industrial town. It is a farming center. It is also a town you must be careful in when you walk young ladies across the street. The good deed could either evoke pleasure or the Mann Act. In Union City it's multiple choice.

To the east of Darke County is Miami County: fifteen minutes north of Dayton and in the Miami River Valley which means that, in addition to flatland farming, we'll see a few hills and valleys. Not *great* hills or *great* valleys; Ohio has those gadgets but not in this neighborhood. But the towns will seem bigger, closer together, and perhaps a little less clean than the towns are in the vast emptiness of the northwest. Some, in fact, will be grimy, dinky industrial towns. Others will be towns that charm the socks off you. In this slightly rumpled terrain of creeks and plains and little valleys, interurban trolleys once bucketed along right-of-way through the trees hurling passengers into Dayton faster than man was meant to travel. Here, too, was the canal to Toledo, bringing life to villages that would have otherwise died on the vine.

Here you'll find Piqua built where once an Indian village stood. *Piqua* is Indian small talk meaning "man born of ashes"; Piqua hasn't changed much since. A bustling city of more than 20,000 residents, Piqua can boast of having the first municipally owned nuclear power plant. Though Piqua, we suppose, has charming thoroughfares and pleasant residential sections, much of Piqua is drab and ordinary and bland. Hence a confession: cities, like rooms and streets and people, evoke within our hearts definite moods. Piqua evoked within us the mood of a factory town. Each time we went there, deliberately to erase this mood, the mood

67

City-owned atomic light plant. Piqua.

returned. Each time we were filled with the same sense of loneliness one gets passing through tired little New England villages and seeing huge and ancient and forgotten factories. We will be the first to admit that Piqua, in total, is not this way. But no matter how often we visited, the mood swiftly returned. We do not deny that Piqua is a dynamic city. Only, to us it seems that somewhere along the line between the first settler and the last carload of sullen teen-agers, Piqua lost something. The fault is probably within us: it may be that we are too shallow and lack the perception to see the real beauty of the place.

Troy is the county seat of Miami County. It has nearly 17,000 residents, suffered the terrible flood of 1913, and is headquarters for the Hobart Manufacturing Company which makes, among other things, dishwashers. Then there is Covington (population 3000), a smaller version of Greenville, twenty-three miles to the west. Covington is residential, rural, and pleasant. A trolley line used to connect Covington with Dayton but no longer. Most of these Miami County towns are more or less alike, West Milton being the exception. West Milton is a cheerful village of 4000 on the Stillwater River. It has little manufacturing. When the Society of Friends built their West Milton Church in 1882, they put a steeple on it and a bell in the steeple. The Central Church disapproved. For a while it was West Milton versus England. West Milton is also supposed to be the home of the first airplane mechanic and the home of the first airplane passenger. Wonderful place, that West Milton. Not as aggressive, perhaps, as Piqua, but . . .

Some 75 miles northwest of Columbus is Sidney. A city of 17,000, it is the county seat of Shelby County, announcing the fact loud and clear via the typical antique courthouse of which Ohio has many. These county courthouses are either grotesque or precious or awful—or, with any luck at all, a combination of all three. Sidney as a town got off to a slow start, but along came the canal and the rest is the same as we've said before. The village of Lockington in Shelby County with now fewer than 400 residents used to be more active, thanks to the canal. Says the *Ohio Almanac*, "The Laramie Summit is 500 feet above the Ohio River water level in the Miami Erie Canal; the canal crossed Laramie Creek via a stone aqueduct . . . " Now there's Laramie State Park and, shades of the past, the Lockington Dam.

About twenty miles northwest of Sidney is St. Marys. Celina, if you recall, is on the western tip of what we shall *this* time label Grand Lake St. Marys. If you don't recall, perhaps *sun-flecked* might trigger your mind. Thirty miles east across the sun-flecked waters from Celina is St. Marys. The importance of St. Marys is due not only to the slow, solemn smiles the high school girls give their boy friends but also to the less alarming fact that the St. Marys River at this point flows north and a few miles south, the Miami River flows the other way. Glaciers caused the rivers to flow in opposite directions. If you want the technical name, try Continental Divide. Indians used to be able to paddle up the Miami from the Ohio River, portage through St. Marys six miles, and paddle north to Lake Erie on the St. Marys River.

St. Marys, now a friendly town of 9000, had dramatic moments in history. Notes the Chamber of Commerce:

"In order to end the Indian hostilities and readjust old boundary lines with the Indians, a treaty was called to convene in St. Marys beginning August 17, 1818. The news was received with great joy. Even before the appointed time the river was swarming with canoes, all wending their way to St. Marys. The Governors of Ohio, Michigan and Indiana, with a large coterie of secretaries, cooks and body guards, were present. The great statesman, Lewis Cass, special representative of the United States Government, came with colored servants and a company of soldiers. Traders from far and near came with packets of beads, notions and trinkets to barter with the Indians. The treaty grounds extended along the west bank of the river as far south as the creek and as far north as Spring Street. Lewis Cass was among the first to arrive and he stationed himself on a gravel knoll. Then came the chiefs of the Shawnees, Wyandottes and the Ottawas, each with his concourse of warriors. And later came deputations from the Miamis, Delawares and Potawattomies. So great was the multitude present that it was necessary to use both banks of the river and temporary bridges were constructed. Three days were set aside to recover from the fatigue of their journey and then the Governors of the three states with Lewis Cass and the Indian chiefs began their deliberations. On October 6, the treaty was signed. It was the last promise of the red man for this treaty ended forever all warfare between the whites and the Indians from the Mississippi to the Atlantic. During this Treaty Convocation a Moravian Missionary named Erwig came and asked permission to preach. This was granted and thus the first 'Church Service' was held. Great festivities followed the consummation of the treaty. There were wrestling matches, jumping matches, foot races, shooting at a mark and a few fist fights besides. That night the Indian chiefs caused 17 bonfires to be kindled in honor of the 17 states and Lewis Cass and the Indian chiefs sat beside them in solemn silence and smoked the pipe of peace."

Although St. Marys is in Auglaise County, Wapakoneta (population 7400, give or take a few Wapakonetans) is the county seat and was once noted for its wooden toys. Because many Germans settled in the county, some German architecture is about, but most of it has dwindled into what might be termed Brick Bland. New Bremen, some suggest, has much of this kind of architecture.

70

Perhaps. But other towns have as much or more. Still, German architecture or no, you'll like the mood of New Bremen if you like small towns, because New Bremen is one of the nicest. The town does have modern homes, but generally the ticky-tacky has yet to dominate.

Around here, wherever that is, we are in the vicinity of the highest point in Ohio, 1549 feet above sea level. The exact point is two miles east of Bellefontaine which has more than 12,000 residents and the first paved street in the United States. County seat of Logan County, Bellefontaine has a drab little business district several blocks long. Its courthouse—no better or worse than the rest—is an antique cupcake with a cream-colored cupola whose paint is chipped. If we seem to look down our noses at Bellefontaine, let us quickly point out that of all the country counties in Ohio, Logan where Bellefontaine is, is about the most active. Everything seems to be in Logan County: hills and valleys, flatlands, industry, railroads, caves, red barns, plus pretty girls in ski pants. Logan County even has two actual castles. Logan County, frankly, is all the nice things in Ohio accumulated within one county. So let the paint chip away on the courthouse roof; Logan County is all right.

Ski in Logan County? Sure, you bet. Surprised us, too, but at Valley High, a quick run from Bellefontaine, is the Mad River Run Slope, 2000 feet; the Sugarbush Trail, 3000 feet; and for beginners and the little old lady from Pasadena, a 500-foot beginners slope. Chairlifts, snow-making equipments, an Alpine Club, and always: a qualified National Ski Patrol guy on duty. Sugarbush Trail is listed as the Midwest's only mountain forest trail designed for the intermediate and advanced skier. Although the hills around Bellefontaine and the ski slopes will not cause Vermont to go bankrupt, nonetheless the hills are steep and winding. Should you slam into a tree—you'll see the same stars they see in the Alps.

Valley High is not the only place in Ohio to ski. To be specific, there are other places, too.

Also in the vicinity of Bellefontaine—three miles out of town on the way to Marysville—is a United States Air Force radar gadget installed at Ohio's highest point. Unless closed on weekends and holidays, the thing guards us twenty-four hours a day from attack. A strange blip, on the other hand, could mean a misplaced skier.

Where's the shortest street in the world? Bellefontaine's thirty-foot-long McKinley Street. Bellefontaine, as we said, also has the first concrete street. It seems that when George Bartholomew came to Bellefontaine in 1886 he found just north of town great marl pits whatever they are. These pits contained almost pure calciuum carbonate underlaid by blue clay that contained silica. He worked with this stuff to find a wet method of making what is now called Portland Cement.

71

Then he convinced the Bellefontaine town council that his stuff would make nice streets, and they said, sure, go ahead, pave some of ours with some of that, but listen, if they don't last four years, we want our money back. At least that was the gist of what transpired. The actual paving involved 1200 feet of forty-foot wide pavement. Cost, $9000. That was in 1891. By 1893 engineers from throughout the world came to gape at the street which lifted America from the age of mud and dust and—almost—the chuck-hole. The street, supposed to last only a few years, lasted more than seventy.

If we seem to be dwelling in Logan County, after having glossed lightly over yours, forgive us, but much is here, like castles. One is called Castle Piatt Mac-A-Cheek; and the other, Mac-O-Chee Castle. You'll find both in Logan County around West Liberty. The Piatts who built the castles were French Huguenots. Building big homes seem to preoccupy them. When Benjamin Piatt in 1817 purchased 1700 acres in one of the Logan County valleys he started right off with a seventeen-room log cabin. One of his sons, Abram Saunders Piatt, built *his* castle down the lane from that Lincoln Log heap. When completed, his castle was a three-story château topped with a five-story tower. Inside were thirty-five rooms. Although some say he built the place so he could entertain properly, most suggest he built the castle to show future generations what the land produced when he lived on it. Stone came from a nearby quarry. Lime kilns burned the mortar. Many of the floors are one-and-a-half-inch inlays of oak, walnut, and wild cherry. The walls? Paneled in ash, pine, or walnut. Or, if not, covered with finished tapestry. The two-foot-thick walls were made from hand-chiseled stone. His brother modeled his Mac-O-Chee Castle after a Flemish one, three stories high, bristling with turrets and spires and towers, frescoed walls and frescoed ceiling, and—scattered casually about—enough antiques to start a museum which, by the way, both castles now are, and open to the public.

Also near West Liberty (population 1684) are the Ohio Caverns, Ohio's answer to Ruby Falls. The caverns, discovered in 1879, are endless formations in underground grottoes that, no matter what the weather is, remain at a constant 54 degrees. If you like thousands of stalactites lighted pretty, you'll agree with those geologists who consider the Ohio Caverns "America's most colorful caverns." Up a few miles are the Zane Caverns, listed as a three-quarter-mile fairyland of many grottoes, one an oval room 132 feet below. Everything—with the exception of the bottom of the bottomless pit—is brilliantly lighted.

On the other hand, if plain old-fashioned girl-watching is more your style, Logan County offers that each summer via Indian Lake, a 6000-acre body of water ringed by hotels, cottages, loud-playing radios, and daring young men standing on their heads. All types of boats can be rented—or bought—but in the areas marked for fishermen, motors must be shut off. Restaurants of every sort abound. The lake itself has a twenty-nine-mile shoreline which is mostly privately owned and commercial. Indian Lake is central Ohio's answer to Geneva-on-the-Lake.

If Logan County begins to sound noisy and crowded, relax, because it isn't. Of the county's 295,040 acres, all but around 14,000 acres are farmland. In Bellefontaine itself Westinghouse makes small motors for laundry equipment, the visiting skiers make funny noises in their funny little cars, and the Carter Steel and Fabricating Company makes steel things, it being one of the largest fabricators and steel service centers in the midwest.

South of Logan County is Champaign County. Urbana—for better or for worse —is the county seat. Although the county is primarily rural, Urbana has diverse industry, as its smokestacks and gloom will attest. Though there are attractive sections in Urbana (as in Piqua), a town of around 12,000, nonetheless the place seems as tired as its tired little traffic circle. The east side of town has charm. Does that help? And there is, of course, the 90-acre campus of Urbana College, tall oaks, walks here and there, stuff like that. New dorms are abuilding: six girls will share a three-bedroom, two-bath lounge complex; each dorm will house seven such complexes plus whatever the coeds themselves bring along. But Urbana itself? Well, let us be as cheerful as we can, noting that in 1811 Urbana had only 225 people. Because as many as 14,000 soldiers were stationed there during the War of 1812, Urbana sort of caught on. Now it has much—and good—industry. The Grimes Manufacturing Company, for instance, is said to be the largest manufacturer of aircraft things in the free world. The Kirby Hatcheries which trafficks with baby chicks and turkey poults is the largest mail-order hatchery in the free midwest. Urbana does have the tasty and the exotic. The W. H. Marvin Company manufactures mincemeat and is the only repacker of imported and domestic dates.

Urbana may look tired, but it isn't. It's going full blast, straight into the future, and who knows? What we mean is, there's always the annual Pioneer Days held in conjunction with the Miami Valley Steam Threshers Association. Then you can see noisy and snorting giant threshers—giants of old, creaking and dripping and panting, shrieking steam-whistle shrieks at all the yesterdays that have gone by; and at people like us who look carefully for the magic of Urbana, know it's there, but fail to see it anywhere.

Mechanicsburg, southeast of Urbana and northeast of Springfield, is a town of 2000. Its business district is small but substantial-looking. It is a hilly town with up-and-down streets, but not *that* hilly, really. The houses are generally clean and sweet and simple, some with beautiful hipped roofs, some with carpentry

73

scrollwork touches, artwork, but not a saw-and-hammer Michelangelo in the lot. An auto graveyard is on one side of town, jarring your senses. Sad, sad. The town itself? A better town to live in than most.

Tombstone readers, please note: at a crossroads called Heathtown we couldn't find lies Richard Stanhope, who was George Washington's valet.

Northeast from Mechanicsburg in the flatland farm country broken visually only by a small hill or a stand of trees is Marysville. In the way, unless you blink, is Irwin whose claim to fame is a three-story brick school building converted into a short-order truck stop. What memories linger in the upper floors is anybody's guess.

Marysville, with its nearly 6000 people, most of whom smile and are cordial, contains the O. M. Scott Company said to be the oldest, largest, and only company that produces exclusively for lawns. Laid out in 1820, Marysville was a seven-acre slice of wilderness that its plotter, Samuel Culbertson, named for his daughter, having better luck at naming towns than Deshler did. Today the pleasant little county seat occupies more than 1200 acres or, to put it another way, nearly two square miles. Its side streets are lined with serene homes, and its business district is unaffectedly old-fashioned, busy, and clean. Wander to the edge of town, out by the Nestlé's plant, turn off on Mulberry Street—a bumpy and sorry road—go beyond the glimmerings of suburbia and soon you come upon a vast tilled field that hides from view the Ohio Reformatory for Women, established 1916. Ohio, you see, is not without its sadnesses.

Our notes on our visit to the prison: "Girls stay in 'cottages' which are really two-story modern brick dormitories in which each inmate has her private room. Is locked in each evening. Each room different, fixed according to taste and ability of girl. On special occasions—Christmas and, perhaps, Thanksgiving—girls can buy cold soft drinks and potato chips. Otherwise, no. Can buy instant iced-tea but no ice. Make tea in room from tap-water. The unfenced prison complex with brick buildings around a grassy quadrangle seems almost like a junior college. But in one building, the laundry, stuffy in the summer, drafty in the winter. In another, a double line of sewing machines extending as far as the eye can see, each attended by a girl. The girls are mostly young. Half of them are white. Half of them are black. Sometimes they wear bluejeans and a sweater. Some wear dresses. During smoke breaks they gather outside the laundry or sit at their machines, murmuring among themselves, and though they pass the time as best they can, they have too much time to pass, and each day is the same as the next. Here and there, perhaps in the basement cutting meat, you'll see a mannish girl surrounded by others not her kind. And everywhere, a sigh below the surface, loneliness seethes— and sometimes hurts so much, it glistens in their eyes. The prison buildings are

School-turned-truck stop. Irwin.

Entrance Women's Prison. Marysville.

in open country with fresh air and sky that won't quit, yet in the quadrangle even on the windiest day, the place seems airless . . . "

Perhaps the most melancholy of all the rooms is the prison hospital delivery room: antiseptic with glistening steel stirrups forever poised and waiting for the next unfortunate. Most babies, we were told, are put out for adoption. As we strolled the grounds we saw one such young lady swollen with child. We could not look into her eyes because we were afraid of the loneliness we might see. Many years before, in a play, we had written words that this girl would soon—in her own fashion—say:

"A woman wants to keep her baby, please. And watch it be born. And watch it get mumps and get measles. And discover fingers and rattles. A woman wants to watch her baby cut teeth and grow hair. Put my baby out for adoption? Hah! My baby will be too beautiful for that! It will be the most beautiful baby in the world. Put my baby out for adoption? Must I? To let my baby live among strangers, pass me on the street and never know, sit by me on the bus—and never know? To let my baby live among strangers? Who will teach it fire? It doesn't know yet about fire. Who will teach it razor blades? It doesn't know yet about razor blades. I will teach it! Do you hear me, God! I'm having a baby. Some guy said making poetry was creative. What about making babies? What's more creative than making a baby? I'll hold my baby through every storm and every heat wave, through every cloudburst and—Please, may I keep my baby? God, I can't say it like the poets do, but I love babies and diapers and midnight feedings and colic and burping and . . . Can anybody get used to a cage? A cage is a cage is a cage. Do you hear me, God! A cage is a cage is a cage . . . "

Beyond the country fields is Marysville. Beautiful. The sun shines on it. The fields themselves are serene. At night the sky is filled with stars that seem so close you can touch them.

But a cage is a cage is a cage.

And the young lady, swollen with child, vanished around a corner.

A pleasanter but bewildering item: a dozen or so miles northeast of Marysville is Raymond, which has a train station—and no tracks.

Marion, northeast of Raymond, is better off (four railroads), bigger (about 40,000 people including Mr. and Mrs. Obal Gearhiser), more historical (Warren G. Harding is buried there), and more likely to succeed (a triangular park contains a machine gun for small fry to practice on). In Marion you will find the Harding Memorial, a not-too-exciting business district, and street after street of one-family houses, many with front porches, all lined neatly in a compact row. The bank looks like a castle. Some sides of Marion, the near-in south, for example,

Industrial growth in Marion.

have seen better days, but here, there, and everywhere the developers have worked their quasi-magic, sometimes creating monotony, sometimes creating beauty. In other words, Marion is the busy, prosperous, ordinary, bland Ohio city that has drive-ins, a sense of history, and growing pains. How much industry? The chamber says 67 different varieties, one being Howard Swink, Advertising, a sharp shop equal to any on Madison Avenue; plus Marion turns out a lot of popcorn, one of the companies doing same being Betty Zane Corn Products, Incorporated. The Houghton-Sulky Company on North State Street makes racing sulkies. The county itself produces an awful lot of hogs and corn, in that order, and its streams are filled—they murmur—with bluegills, catfish, gum wrappers, and bass. Also Marion County is considered a good place to hunt rabbits, squirrels, and pheasants. You might consider Marion as the all-purpose county with Marion being its all-purpose city.

The twenty-ninth President, Warren G. Harding, first journalist to occupy the White House, was born in Morrow County. In 1884 he purchased the Marion *Daily Star*, publishing it until 1923, when he sold it to Brush-Moore Newspapers, Incorporated. In June of that year, on a trip west, he died. His body was taken first by funeral train to Washington, then by funeral train to Marion.

Green Camp, southwest of Marion, is a neat white-frame village of 500 residents. The trim and well-constructed homes all seem to have been painted the same day, giving the village a certain charm that paint could give many other Ohio villages. The Green Camp business district (hardware store, grocery, variety store, dairy-bar drive-in) isn't exactly Times Square in New York but given a choice of the two places to stroll, wiser souls would select Green Camp every time.

Down the road toward Columbus we enter Delaware County, advertised as the county of lakes. That's because the county which already has a couple of attractive lake-reservoirs is at work constructing more. The largest at present is the Hoover Reservoir, eight miles long. Delaware Reservoir is a Y-shaped body of water. Most of O'Shaughnessy Reservoir is in Delaware County, so the county claims it, too. The largest city in the county is Delaware, the second largest is Westerville which is a pleasant dormitory for Columbus toilers, being only ten miles north of Broad and High Streets. Alum Creek—fine for fishing and boating, they say, but we wish they'd do something about its name—flows gently through Westerville. Also in Westerville are the 1500 students attending Otterbein College which is also where the mighty Alum flows. Although Westerville does have some light industry, it is, we suggest, a charming dormitory for many who work elsewhere.

Between Westerville and Delaware are the Olentangy Caves, discovered in 1821 when an ox fell into one, and now a tourist attraction as most Ohio caves are. A million years ago an underground river sloshed its way through the solid

79

underground walls of limestone, forming many passages that visitors today can wander through. Some passages, though, are still unexplored. Four levels down, for instance, an underground river *still* flows to the Olentangy River, a half mile away. The underground river widens into an underground lake whose dimensions are still to be tapped.

Delaware, pretty close to the geographic center of Ohio, is a nice city of 15,000 people. At the Delaware fair the Little Brown Jug Harness Race is the big thing each year, but Delaware is more than that. Ohio Wesleyan University is in Delaware. So are motels, hamburger stands, and little shops. Big shops, too. Delaware with its sulphur springs was once *the* spa to visit to get rid of whatever ailed you. The Mansion House where the elite gathered to sample the waters was even pictured on Staffordshire china. Also, as happened in just about every city and town and hamlet in the northwest part of Ohio, the War of 1812 found troops quartered in Delaware.

On a bright spring day Delaware is especially attractive. This is the moment the young coeds burst from the stuffy dorms of winter to sprawl on the cool lawns of spring, sun-worshiping and truck-waving. To have a university in a town the size of Delaware sets forever the town off as special. Although Delaware is the county seat, dare we suggest that pretty girls with pleasant smiles have more attraction than any courthouse Ohio can offer? Whenever possible on our many trips around Ohio, we would—when the sun was right and the mood was mellow —arrange our travels so that we passed through Delaware. Occasionally we would go ten miles out of our way to pass through Delaware. Once, while going between Cleveland and Shaker Heights, we detoured through Delaware.

And always pleasant smiles from the pleasant young ladies strewn about the lawns.

On the other hand we bypassed Antioch and Yellow Springs a lot. However well constructed the coeds, what's to be glared at analytically?

On which note, we conclude our visit to the northwest quarter of Ohio.

5

The southeastern quarter of Ohio is a troubled land of gentle but skittish hills that turn, almost without notice, into insolent and forsaken ones. This is no longer like the flat northwest where on a clear day you can see forever. In this wilderness land of hollows, abrupt curves, and convoluted grades, on a clear day—with any luck—you can see two miles. This part of Ohio is as different from its northwest corner as night is from day. Straight east from Columbus on Interstate 70, once casual hills become pennywhistle mountains. Once spellbound little valleys become —now and then—temperamental little gorges. By the time the traveler reaches the Ohio line at Wheeling, the flatlands of Columbus are forgotten; he is surrounded by mountains more powerful than prairie sky. If you go south from Columbus toward Ironton on the Ohio River you are in hills most of the way, hills that become angrier as you reach Lawrence County, where Ironton is. The state's entire southern border, which on a map looks drawn by a three-year-old whose mind was elsewhere, is the wiggly Ohio River. River landscape varies here. Some stretches of the river from Ironton northeast to Steubenville are unhurried moments from history filled with silence and uncivilized beauty; much, however, is one vulgar little river town after another, each with soot, industrial ganglia, mills, refineries, and high-reaching smokestacks. Most of these Ohio River towns are industrially inspired but architecturally lacking. In some, where afternoon teas are never held, fresh air comes as a shock and a surprise. But gloomy sandstone cliffs of hanging rock hold industry and towns compressed forever in this river valley—with no time off for good behavior. Now and then the hills move back from the river, permitting the momentary loveliness of a wide valley, but before pleasure comes, the valley tightens again, choking beauty to death with smoke from its great smokestacks.

Consider Ironton which, with its 16,000 people, might be called Ohio's southernmost city. The town gave birth as a blast furnace. County seat and only city in Lawrence County's 456 square miles, Ironton began in 1848 and was incorporated in 1851. Because iron had been found in the hills back from the river, Ironton grew. Today trains still shriek whistles at the memory of Ironton's great industry. But that was long ago, when the railroad connected the river to the pig iron furnaces in the hills and hollows. John Means put up the first such furnace. John Campbell created the "hot blast" method, and thus with fire, each settlement gave birth. Each blast furnace had a name, collected about it homes, perhaps a church, and perhaps a school. But then the iron ore gave out. Some of the villages died. Some didn't. Eight miles north of Ironton is the Lake Vesuvius recreation area—143-acre lake, 200 acres of wilderness—named Vesuvius because that was the name of the furnace. There, beside the dam, one abandoned furnace stands today as a museum piece. Built in 1833, fifteen years before Campbell's town of Ironton began, the Vesuvius furnace first used charcoal and air in the "cold blast method," switched to Campbell's more efficient "hot blast" process, but in 1906—the ore supply dwindling—the fires of the furnace were banked, its ashes hauled, and was closed down for a chilly forever.

The early settlers of Ironton were Dutch and Irish from both Virginia and Pennsylvania; and—hold onto your brooms—many believed in witchcraft. One source said actual witch trials were held. From the looks of Ironton today, one might say the witches won. Ironton is not pretty. We must be honest. And in our honesty, we suggest that Ironton has no time to get pretty; it's too busy.

To those of you who seek only chamber of commerce verbiage and/or poetic beauty, fair warning. Things will not improve too much in this wonderful river valley between Ironton and Steubenville. To be sure, some towns may delight you with elegance, but many others have been too thunderstuck by industry. Just as on a murky day the fumes that trailer trucks spew linger in the air above the expressway long after the trucks themselves have vanished into the mist, so in places does smoke hover over this industrial complex we call the Upper Ohio Valley. Here is not history's gentle valley of yesterday, where throughout the empty land birds sang songs to the west wind's moan. Here, instead, is a hard-muscled cash box. From this dynamic valley come the chemicals and ores which the rest of us, lolling about some less sooty town, need, if we are to exist. This is the valley of hard truths and men who are not afraid to sweat. Coal does not fly voluntarily from the guts of the hills. Chemicals do not blend by themselves—unseen, in distant kitchens. So do not seek pastoral beauty here. Accept this valley for the truth that it represents. Thus, while the villages of this grimy place may not get rave notices, its people and its industries do. Anyway, if pastoral beauty were rampant throughout the land, the land would be silent. America would never have happened.

So let the Irontons and Steubenvilles gather grime. If these people went elsewhere and if each industry locked its door, the valley again would be clean. But when you ran out of gas, there wouldn't be any more.

North of Lawrence County and Ironton—back from the river—is Jackson County where Jackson is and the Apple Festival is. The air is fresher. Is that better? In this county of less violent hills and more tranquil valleys, the little Raccoon Creek flows in search of the sea. Before white men appeared on the scene, Indians came to Jackson's salt wells. The first whites? Primarily Welsh. For awhile, Welsh was the language spoken. Around Jackson are several ice-cold furnaces that are now only tourist attractions. The one just outside Jackson was built by Thomas Price in 1851. A similar furnace, the ruins of which are at Lake Jackson, is said to have supplied the iron plate for the *Merrimac*. Jackson is the boyhood home of Major John Wesley Powell, explorer of the Grand Canyon. Also Governor James A. Rhodes was born here. Jackson—the city, not the county —is a fair-to-middlin'-to-charming little town where you can buy grinder sandwiches, gaze at Little Salt Creek, wonder at its five-story brick building, or just relax, strolling its red brick streets. The Jackson business district looks like something out of the Gay Nineties and also looks bustling and successful. Its chamber of commerce is located in a bewildering little tower right downtown. During the September Apple Festival each year, Jackson is alive with parades, at least two

83

The pain of strip-mining.

dozen marching bands, bingo, street dancing, and all the apple butter you can eat. The town's population? Around 8000.

Nearby, in the same county, is the village of Coalton, home of John H. Patterson, who developed the first cash register, a fact noted in the town by a monument erected by the National Cash Register Company, of course!

Also in Jackson County, atop a hill, is Winchester which at first glance seems to be a convention of all the unpainted shacks the county possesses.

About forty or fifty miles north of the river is MacArthur, with fewer than 2000 people, but it is nonetheless the county seat of Vinton County because it's the biggest town the county has. Peter Zaleski, a well-heeled Pole from Europe, bought land in this county of rolling hills so he could get a town going and have it named after him. Before he arrived in this country, though, the idea fell apart. Today the metropolis of Zaleski has fewer than 400 good people.

In the rolling hills east of sparse Vinton County but still back a ways from the Ohio River is Athens, Athens County, and Ohio University. Athens (population 27,000, give or take a few coeds) is Ohio's second oldest city. Since it was founded principally to support the university that a group of Revolutionary War veterans thought up, logically the town and the university—both along the banks of the Hocking River—have destinies entwined. The nearest commercial airport is forty miles away, in Parkersburg, West Virginia. But the Baltimore & Ohio, New York Central, and a branch of the Chesapeake & Ohio toot through upon occasion. A company in Athens manufactures the King Midget Motor Car seen in airport lobbies everywhere, the company having fewer than two dozen employees. Athens has other industry, but frankly, the largest employer in the whole county is the state because that's where the university and a state hospital are. Student enrollment at Ohio University—fourth largest in the state—increased from 5000 in 1950 to 8000 in 1960. By 1970, the students expect to number 20,000. The school started with a student body of three in a two-story brick building.

Around Athens County, unless you're hard-shelled, you can still see traces of strip mining's tragedy.

Meanwhile, back along the Ohio River . . .

Although many people, with good reason, give Marietta rave reviews as *the* antique river town that has held up beautifully, Gallipolis also fits that category. Gallipolis—pronounce it however it strikes your fancy—with its 10,000 residents is the county seat of Gallia County as well as the county's only city. Located on the Ohio River where the river makes one of its majestic bends, Gallipolis was settled in 1791 by the French, or had you guessed? It can properly be called "the old French city on the beautiful Ohio River" because it's the only French city

85

we have on that waterway. During the Civil War warehouses here supplied the Union soldiers. Camp Carrington was about. And a sprawling gloomy army hospital comforted and cared for 4000 wounded and sick. Although Eastern Avenue is a string of ordinary—and *Americanized*—pizza carryouts, motels, and auto dealers, the town does contain street after street after street of charming little townhouses, each more attractive than the other. These homes are fresh out of the nineteenth century, well-tended and elegant. One is Henry Cushing's 1819 river tavern called *Our* Home, for many years the prime watering hole of Gallipolis, now a state memorial. Here General LaFayette was entertained in 1825. Built of brick in the federal style and containing a tap room, public and private dining rooms, a parlor for ladies, a divided ballroom, three bedrooms, and a separate kitchen in the rear, the place is said to have held ten guests in reasonable comfort —or several dozen in unreasonable discomfort. Why called *Our* House? Because Cushing was invariably inviting patrons to "Come over to our house" and—no doubt—hoist a few.

In Gallipolis, also, is Gatewood, home of the late O. O. McIntyre, journalism's first Broadway columnist. He purchased Gatewood as his dream home, restored it, but before he could return to the town of his childhood to partake of the place, he died.

In the hills behind Gallipolis—steep hills—is Hanersville. With well-built and well-mannered cottages splattered all over the sides of the steep hills, it is little more than a charming wide spot in the road. Farther north is Rodney which is a gasoline pump. Also back in those hills: the agonies of the strip mines. And, at Vinton on State Road 160 is one of Ohio's last water-powered gristmills.

Then, Rio Grande College in Rio Grande, population 500. The college began as a church-supported institution to educate the county's isolated and poverty-ridden youth in the year 1875. Now non-denominational, it has grown, despite limited financial beginnings, into an excellent college, of which Ohio has many.

Along the Ohio River east between Gallipolis and Pomeroy is a mixed assortment of scenery. Now smokestacks pollute the heavens, now—where the valley suddenly opens—are a farm and fresh air. Cheshire is here with its freshly painted frame houses, looking dressed in its Sunday best. Cheshire is a place of narrow streets which are pleasing to the eye, in spite of the nearby power plant with its Rube Goldberg machinery that makes hash of the sky, and in spite of the nearby slag heap which—given a wind change—would have the town in black-face.

Around here, also, is Point Pleasant where the Silver Bridge collapsed, sending people still stuck in their cars into the Ohio River and eternity.

Pomeroy, along this river, is the county seat (population 4000) and largest village in Meigs County. Pomeroy, they say, is the home of Ohio pioneer indus-

86

trialist Valentine DeHorton. When coal was discovered in the hills, Pomeroy was a coal-shipping center. Most of the place seems cramped and dingy, ravines of drab little houses that have seen better days, and dark, high hills that keep the sunshine out. In the back country are the catch-as-catch-can family coal mines strewn along wilderness roads and hidden in shadowy hollows. Here the hillsides and fields are weed-littered and some are drowned in slag. Standing on stilts at crazy angles are the forgotten and abandoned mine structures of rotting wood, collapsing with time. Here, too, are deserted frame houses high on hillsides. They are gray and weathered and windowless. This is the land of the unloved. A land of discards. The only sign of civilization, at times, are the towers of the power lines—up there on the ridges—who, like sentinels keep a death-watch on the silent land.

And more shacks—kissed good-by.

And then, a view of the river.

Then, relax. Marietta is here.

Marietta has been called "Ohio's most historical and beautiful city." True, Marietta *is* historic. It *is* beautiful. As for it being the *most*, well, that's chamber of commerce talk, of course, but in the case of Marietta, the talk is apt. When 48 men led by General Rufus Putnam turned up the Muskingum River from the Ohio River in 1788 and went ashore and settled down, that was the start of Fort Harmar which evolved into Marietta. Marietta, population about 18,000, occupies nearly six square miles of the 637.1 square miles of Washington County of which Marietta is the county seat. Also back away from the river and deeper into the county—and in several other counties as well—are the 113,000 acres of the Wayne National Forest which we shall attend shortly.

You can't help but be pleased by Marietta's gentle streets, serene parkways, and all those historical markers—more markers than anyone but a pure historian could read. Not *all* of Marietta is a valentine, of course. It has some streets and some housing that never should have happened, but at least give the city A for effort. Between industrial Steubenville upstream and Marietta, is much industrial murkiness along the river. It stops just before reaching Marietta which makes Marietta pleasant. As you come downstream and reach Marietta, suddenly the sky is blue and your hacking cough is gone. Marietta does have industry. One huge plant west of the city creates occasional smudges in the sky, but no matter. Marietta is nice.

This town has a sense of history that won't quit. In addition to all those historical markers which we hope Marietta orders wholesale, Marietta has a steamboat-turned-museum: the *W. P. Snyder, Jr.* which was one of the Ohio River's last steam-powered sternwheelers. The beautiful boat—built in 1918, 175

87

feet long, weighing 342 tons—is now tied forever to the Marietta docks, never going anywhere again. In Marietta you can also see a land office, because the town preserved the one it had. Originally located on Washington Street it has since been moved elsewhere but it's still around town. Built in 1788, it is one of the oldest buildings in the territory. Marietta's sense of history and the river includes another museum that contains the pilot wheels, whistles, models, and other momentoes of the steam era on the river.

Marietta College, charted in 1835 and admitting the ladies in 1897, now has a ratio of three men to every girl. A private, non-sectarian coeducational college with a campus better than most, the college began as Muskingum Academy in 1797. Only 30 per cent of Marietta College students are native Ohioans. Most come from the eastern seaboard. The neighborhood where the campus is offers you one of the most beautiful residential districts in the state of Ohio. Trolley tracks still wind around the quiet streets of this section but the trolleys have gone to that Great Trolley Barn in the sky. If Marietta would bring the trolleys back, the town would be perfect!

But Marietta is more than museum, memory, and college girls. Within its corporate limits is a 90-acre industrial park and along the river are eleven industrial sites with 7000 acres. Marietta isn't *all* yesterday.

Woodsfield, back in the hills from the river in Monroe County, has fewer than 4000 people. The entire hilly county has fewer than 16,000. Monroe County is, in reality, 456 square miles of lonesome winds, winding streams, forsaken cabins, and forgotten hollows where there's not a soul to say hello. A few villages are strewn along the river: Sardis, Hannibal, Duffy, and Fly. The roller-coaster hills contain a few others, none with more than 500 people, most with fewer than 200. In addition to the settlers from Pennsylvania, Virginia, and New England, the county was settled by the Swiss who grew fond of the land so much like home. So there many Swiss settled, so far from the maddening crowd that any gathering was cause for celebration, and made watches and Swiss cheese. Woodsfield was on the railroad that Archibald Wood built in 1814 called the Bellaire, Zanesville, and Cincinnati Railroad. But the backcountry geography of the county was so contrary, the little railroad—now no longer in existence—quickly became known as "The Bent, Zigzag, and Crooked." There is coal in those back hills—and man has got much of it out. One of the state's largest coal mines is in this county. So is part of the Wayne National Forest which sits in almost—but not quite—"splendid isolation."

A national forest in Ohio? As we suggested earlier, most Ohioans didn't know they had one. Yet, there it sits: 113,000 acres. The forest, administered by the Department of Agriculture, began in 1934. Before the government could buy any

New railroad on the way!

of the land, though, the state legislature had to pass a special act. Even so, the federal government was not able to get the mineral rights—and thereby hangs a sad tale. First, we'll note that although the place isn't too well known, each year nearly a half million people visit the forest. Three camp sites are available. So are a bunch of signs suggesting you don't burn the place down. But pessimists murmur things like what's the government doing in private business? Seems each year five million board-feet of lumber are cut in the forest by private timber operators whose sawmills ring the forest's perimeter. And, the tragic part, strip mining is there, but not owning the mineral rights, Smoky the Bear can do little about it but suggest the strip miners reclaim the ravaged hills once the goodies have been removed. Does it help to suggest that before the government took over the forest land was in poor condition and that the only purpose of establishing the national forest was, and still is, to bring the area back to productivity? That's what the government says. And so the woodchoppers hack away. And strip miners rip open layer after layer of earth, creating raw wounds, in search of coal.

No matter. Let us be Pollyannas and say the area will someday be good as new. Or else, that nature has been had again.

Back in the hills also is Noble County, which has the dim distinction of being the last Ohio county organized. Caldwell, with fewer than 3000 people, is a bland county seat with a distinction of its own: it doesn't have the typical Ohio courthouse; its courthouse looks more like a high school; and Caldwell, we suggest, is the better for it. Its public square, though, ringed by ordinary stores, is World War Two bland. Olive, a settlement now part of Caldwell, was one of the Northwest Territory's first settlements. Panoramic views—spectacular, breathtaking, powerful—are a dime a dozen in this hilly county. Ava, one of its villages, gained fame of sorts when during a wild storm the dirigible *Shenandoah* fell down on it. Ohio's first oil well was here, drilled in Noble County. Before that, the oil had been considered a nuisance. Settlers, digging for salt, kept getting nothing but oil. But they bottled and peddled the stuff as Seneca Water, listing it as a cure for what ails you. Wolf Run State Park is around this county; its lake is a multipurpose gadget because it helps flood control efforts, plus giving outlanders a place to sail, fish, and swim.

As we head upriver, following Route 7, civilization, as you were warned, does not improve the looks of the land. Bluffs still crowd us. Now and then, more then than now, a clean-looking river village appears. More, though, have been reduced by time to tattle-tale gray. One such grubby place is called Dilly's Bottom in Belmont County. Surrounded by slag, Dilly's Bottom is hardly more than a wide and dirty spot in the road. Industrial plants on the West Virginia shores make certain Dilly's Bottom will never reach top. Then, in Belmont County, there's Bellaire which, although not well-scrubbed, is cleaner than most and thus has the charm that it would lack if it were in a cleaner part of the state. In Bellaire the residents seem to *care*. Flowers grow in gardens. Houses, for the most part, are well-maintained and nicely painted. But east of Bellaire are Riverview and West Wheeling, each outdoing the other in griminess. Both are Little League slum areas of unwashed frame houses planted carelessly on the side of the hill. Bridgeport, with nearly 4000 residents, is on Interstate 70, where Ohio meets Wheeling, West Virginia. But the towns on the Ohio side—Riverview, West Wheeling, Bridgeport—run together. To tell where one stops and the next starts is impossible and hardly worth the effort. Bridgeport does extend a little back up into the valley but not far enough. The smokestacks of Wheeling across the river are too effective. Bridgeport, West Wheeling, and Riverview have nowhere to hide. Also, Bridgeport itself adds to the industrial gloom. The Wheeling Steel Corporation has a sprawling red complex on the Ohio side of the river. On a clear day you can see your way clear to get out of town.

Far back in the Ohio hills—south of Interstate 70—fresh air is. Here roads follow streams to forgotten cottages and a few working coal mines. Here, too, in this valley to Barnesville a new railroad is abuilding—exciting fact!—where no tracks had ever been before. The new rails, at this writing untested by the weight of any train, follow the twists and turns of that dreadful and sweet valley, for, to be honest, there is no escape. Houses that sit across the creek from the road are connected to the road by swinging foot bridges: some freshly painted and in good repair, some other ripe for an episode in *The Perils of Pauline*. But no towns. No tourist cabins. No gasoline stations. Not even a sign advertising Coca-Cola. Only one lonely house, miles of emptiness, then perhaps another house—or perhaps a cast-off log cabin, leaning askew in the weeds, the duplicate of many you'll see in this melancholy valley.

Then from nowhere comes Barnesville—and your sense of loneliness vanishes. Great place, that Barnesville. A civilized, solid, and clean community sprinkled over the top of several ridges. Was once famous for strawberries. Here now, a Friends' Meeting House that gazes serenely down at assorted valleys spread at its feet. Barnesville is an amiable place of no architectural nonsense; roller-coaster streets are lined with good housing; the business district has a substantial and almost metropolitan air; and the Lotus Glass Company, cutters and decorators of American-made glassware, has a plant you can visit any time you're in the neighborhood. That's the way Barnesville is. You can see all the company's operations from decorating, cutting, plate etching, gold decorating, glass bending, color printing, to the Coke machine. Also in Barnesville and in operation since 1862 is the Watt Car & Wheel Company, oldest company in the land making mining cars.

91

Old swinging bridges from yesterday.

Friends' Meeting House. Barnesville.

There's St. Clairsville in Belmont County, too. The town lists itself "a paradise on the hilltop" meaning its 4000 residents are situated reasonably comfortable on one and a half square miles of village. *Well* situated, too. Some of the homes in paradise cost $50,000 but less expensive housing is also on tap. The town, which is Belmont's county seat, is ten miles west of Wheeling and a hundred miles east of Columbus. The county, by the way, is underlaid by Pittsburgh #8 Vein Coal plus six other veins. The county, in addition to paradise, has a couple of Indian mounds.

Cambridge—seventy-eight miles east of Columbus is on both the old National Road which sometimes is U.S. 40 *and* Interstate 70, although, at times, both roads are one and the same. So much for map plotting. The National Road, says the *Ohio Almanac*, "in this county (Guernsey) has several S-shaped stone bridges for which no good explanation has been found." Really, if you like to read about Ohio, you should be reading the *Ohio Almanac* instead of this book. Anyway, at Cambridge, Interstate 77, which runs north and south, intersects with Interstate 70, which runs east and west. This intersection, plopped down in the high hills of Guernsey County, offers you one of the most Mickey Mouse cloverleafs (*not* leaves) ever properly constructed. It is a maze of hills, blind corners, elevations, and wonder. You vanish, for instance, around the curve on one hill; zoom down and around another substantial hillock; cruise under an unexpected bridge you'd not seen before; and, wheee, there you are, on a bridge looking down to another part of the cloverleaf. Frankly, hills crowd your vision so much that as you follow the route through the maze—reading direction signs so you'll not be trapped forever—you have the feeling you're flying on instruments.

For real adventure, navigate the cloverleaf in fog.

Or by car compass.

The county which contains the aforementioned Cambridge was settled and got its name by the English from the Island of Guernsey. Though Indians no longer inhabit the place, some of the towns retain Indian names: Trail Run, Indian Camp, Salt Pork, and Fish Basket. Concord, one of the villages without an Indian name, came in for its share of excitement a while back. In 1890 a 700-pound meteorite fell nearby, just missing the village. While their neighbors from Noble County were palming off oil as elixir, Guernsey County natives with equal imagination cultivated peppermint, extracted oil from same, and presto! another home remedy.

The first business in Cambridge, established as a town in the early 1800s, was Gomber's Flour Mill which operated until 1932, then burned down. At the time of its death it was known as Cambridge Mills. Coal mining was great in the county —between 1850 and 1925. The surrounding hills still carry ugly scars attesting to the fact. Toward the east these hills have been so ravaged by strip mining, they seem in pain.

But a pleasant city is Cambridge. It won the All America City Award from the National Municipal League and *Look* Magazine because as a city it solved its economic problems through industrial development. Cambridge has about 15,000 people. By 1970—not counting those hung up on its S-bridges—it figures to have nearly 18,000.

Where Interstate 70 and U.S. 40 go their separate ways but parallel one another, sadness is strewn along every inch of the old National Road. Route 40—also Route 22—is a beautiful but empty and silent four-lane divided highway that few use. Although the towns along it with motels and restaurants and gas pumps are not dead, they look poorly. Some motels are shuttered for good, their great neon signs gathering dust. Some remain in business, but they are the lingering few. Traffic just isn't there any more. Thus, many little Ohio villages, since the interstates have come, have been reduced to forgotten whistlestops, each waiting for business that no longer drives by. This section of road, to us, is the loneliest stretch of road Ohio has. And the saddest.

But on to more cheerful things. If you like jokes, Zanesville has two, one unintentional. Shall we consider the unintentional joke first? Zanesville—county seat of Muskingum, population about 40,000, birthplace of Zane Grey, and located where the Muskingum and Licking Rivers say hello—is easy to reach from Interstate 70 because Interstate 70 hurls itself swiftly through the town itself. But, on the other hand, Zanesville streets, direction signs, and traffic patterns are so effectively designed that to return again to the same interstate is well nigh impossible. Four different times we left the interstate at Zanesville; each time trying to get back on the expressway, we got lost. True, Zanesville is a pleasant place, charming, et al., but ask yourself, is this any way to increase the population?

The *intentional* joke, of course, is the knee-slapper the locals palm off on strangers seeking directions.

"Go to the middle of the bridge," the locals will say, "and turn left."

And—because Zanesville has a Y-bridge—you can!

The Y-bridge was originally designed to connect three settlements that later became Zanesville. The first Y-bridge, started in 1812, was completed in 1814, and in 1818 collapsed. Their second Y-bridge, built by 1831, went the way of all flesh. The third Y-bridge during the flood of 1832 fell into the river during construction, but they picked up the pieces, dried them off, and completed the bridge anyway. By 1900 the then sixty-eight-year-old bridge quivered each time a trolley crossed, so another bridge was ordered. When the fourth Y-bridge opened in 1902, it was the country's largest bridge—of reinforced concrete. Zanesville locals say

95

State Park near Zanesville.

theirs is the only bridge you can cross and still be on the same side you started from, proof again that getting out of Zanesville is not easy.

Our notes offer one attempt to say farewell to the place: "The south side of town is quite poor. But Zanesville itself? Nice, but tired-looking. Downtown is a prosperous place, but is hemmed in, it seems, by dilapidation. Oops! There goes the interstate again . . . "

East of Zanesville is New Concord, now because the interstate had siphoned business, with less traffic. Hilly country and a wide beautiful valley. Farming. Muskingum College is in New Concord. The school looks like a collection of old three-story red-brick school buildings. Neat and nice. New Concord is also the home of black walnut fudge. And of John Glenn, who left New Concord and earth in a space capsule.

Morgan County—sixty miles southeast of Columbus—is an airy county of hills, great valleys, and the Muskingum River. No cities, though. McConnelsville (population 3000) is the county seat of the 421 square miles of limestone hills, fertile valleys, and signs that advertise Zanesville motels, and Zanesville has some good ones. Here is where cows are. Some say the Ohio Polled Hereford industry began in Morgan County. Also, the finest Merino wool was produced here. Now this is lamb chop and buttermilk land. This is also potato land.

Says the chamber, "The Muskingum River has long been famous for fine fishing, boating, and water skiing. A new boat dock for launching and landing will be found just up the river from McConnelsville. At the old locks the island has been leveled off and seeded and with repairs of the dam completed, fishermen are assured of excellent facilities for this sport. The Muskingum River, its locks and dams—being no longer considered a navigable water course by the Federal government—were deeded to Ohio in 1958. Department of Conservation officials, realizing the enormous potential of 11 sets of locks and dams whose pools actually form 11 separate lakes, are repairing and beautifying the river for recreational purposes . . . "

The river was once a wet highway north and south. Most boats in those days stopped at McConnelsville or Malta across the river. Because the Muskingum River drops 100 feet, dams were needed. That's why Muskingum River pilots were known for their skills.

Personal pride in a namesake requires us to look with more than the usual degree of affection at Perry County. Unfortunately for this book's photographer no counties have been named Goldflies, an oversight which causes him depression, but on the other hand, no Goldflies shot bullets at the British during the Contretemp of 1812, although a Goldflies used to hang around the army camps a lot, selling postcards. Anyway, where Perry County is concerned, our affection ends

97

up tattered and torn. Perry County, forty miles east of the penitentiary at Columbus, has no great cities. Its largest is New Lexington. Only 5000 people call it home. Somerset, with about 1400 residents, looks fresh from the pages of Tom Sawyer with its pleasant cottages, church steeple, water tower, and town square that has a statue. You'll like the inscription of the Somerset courthouse. Because the stone carver didn't have room to carve *though* in the inscription he arbitrarily changed *though* to *if* which fit. Thus the inscription reads, "Let justice triumph—if the heavens fall." Does it help to mention that hilly Perry County has coal? It's hilly in the southern part, kind of level farther north. Also, for real drama, in 1884 a bunch of disgruntled miners near New Straitsville started an underground coal-mine fire—and the fire is still burning to this day. Perry County has about 28,000 people in its 409 square miles. Perry County has no zoo, no civic theater, no lecture series, no museums, no art galleries, nor anything like that.

But in November 1950, it snowed a lot; over two feet fell that month, to be exact.

Next door to Perry County is Hocking County, Logan (population about 7000) the county seat, and everything mentioned herein is about forty-eight miles southeast of Columbus. Like Perry County, Logan is sparsely populated. The county got going on coal and the Hocking canal enabled the coal to reach market. But when its Perry County neighbors set that coal mine afire, twilight came to the coal industry. Hocking County now has a population of little more than 20,000, five parks whose combined acreage is ten acres, and six—count 'em—six state parks which attract 750,000 tourists each year. The Hocking River runs through this county and—until the Wyandots executed him for witchcraft—so did Chief Leatherlips.

Lancaster was founded by Wheeling's Colonel Ebenezer Zane, merchant-trail blazer-pioneer-soldier who after the Treaty of Greenville decided the middle part of Ohio was someday going to fill up with people so he wanted part of the action. He petitioned Congress for a contract to hack a 266-mile road through Ohio's forests from Wheeling to Limestone, Kentucky, in return for three land grants near river crossings. And so Zane's Trace, the first important Ohio road opened by 1797, creating Lancaster as well as Zanesville in the process.

County seat of Fairfield County, Lancaster is located in the hill country in the southern part of the county fifteen miles southeast of Columbus. Although Lancaster with a population of about 35,000 has glassmaking as its main industry, should the glass break, the city has diverse industry to fall back on. Factories are about—many of them—but they do not tinker with Lancaster's charm, which is one part history, one part modern, and one part ordinary, all parts being nice. Here and there Lancaster has cobblestone streets and beautiful old homes. Also

County Fair Grounds. Lancaster.

middle-class dwellings of little architectural consequence. Some of the older homes along the main street are hiding their magnificence as commercial buildings. On one side of town—far out—is the three-story red-brick children's home, a great and lonely building that seems to be sitting under a bluff upon which a huge boulder teeters. On another side of town, located in the shadow of another huge and wild bluff, are the fairgrounds, the site of the oldest county fair in continuous operation in Ohio. Its antique wooden grandstand is curved to match the curve of the race track. After gas was discovered, the Fairfield County Fair was world famous for racing by gaslight, but they don't do that much any more.

When the first canal boats loaded with stone coal arrived in town on the Lancaster Lateral Canal, the natives watched with wonder; they had never seen stone coal before. When, in 1854, the first two trains whistled hello to Lancaster, the town greeted the trains with band music, cannon shooting, and lots of shouting.

Lancaster is the center of a rich agricultural region that is mostly swine, dairy, and cattle. The industry, as noted, is glass, including the largest producer of table glass anywhere.

Elsewhere in the county is Lithopolis with fewer than 500 people. But it has a library that cost a half million dollars. The library was a gift of Mabel Wagnalls Jones, daughter of the Wagnalls of Funk and Wagnalls Publishing Company.

A sampling of other Fairfield County villages finds Oakland a collection of cottages, with antique stores, gas pump, grocery—dearly beloveds—a wedding service. Coalfax, as noted elsewhere, has the Make-Believe Motel. Unfortunately, there doesn't seem to be a town to go with it.

And over there is Broad and High, which means we have again arrived in Columbus.

Now, let's join hands and explore the northeast quarter of Ohio, where, if history serves us correctly, Cleveland will be.

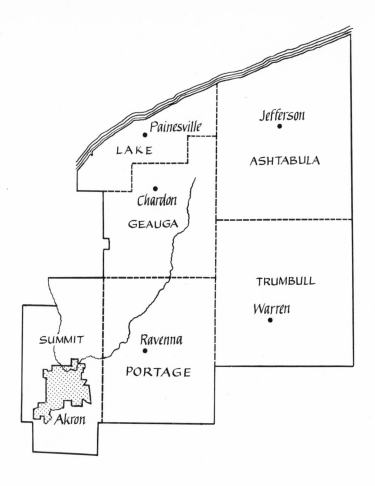

6

Had there been no Revolutionary War or boundary squabbles afterwards, the state of Connecticut—thanks to King Charles of England in 1662—would have extended from the Atlantic Coast west through part of Ohio to the Pacific Ocean. The hot question in 1872 was this western territory. Except for Connecticut, the other eastern states relinquished their claims. Connecticut, instead, created the Western Reserve of Connecticut, then turned right around and peddled it to the Connecticut Land Company.

Originally the entire Western Reserve was called Trumbull County. Warren was its county seat, but as the population increased, the present Ohio counties were formed. So now in the northeast corner of Ohio—or, as geographers say, the upper right-hand corner—we have Ashtabula County.

The county is named for the Ashtabula River, which flows through it. The

101

county is Ohio's largest. Ashtabula is Indian chitchat for *fish river*. Along Lake Erie, of course, the terrain is reasonably level but south are scrublands, rolling hills, farms, forests, and dramatic ravines. Conneaut and Ashtabula are the county's big cities. Farther west along the lake are Geneva and Geneva-on-the-Lake. Conneaut is in the very northeast corner of the state, a stone's throw from Erie, Pennsylvania. Although it can claim itself a resort area (safe ocean swimming, lifeguard-protected beaches, fishing, leggy girls) Conneaut has more than that going for it.

The town was started on the Fourth of July, 1796, by Moses Cleaveland, who had come west as the Connecticut Land Company's leader to see what could be made of the territory. Conneaut with nearly 16,000 residents is now a collection of workingmen's homes, some of which are huge and old-fashioned, trimmed in wrap-around porches and bay windows. On Liberty Street is an octagonal frame house—private! On Center Street you'll find another made of brick. On Depot Avenue where the New York Central Depot used to be is a great steam engine—its fires banked, its boiler cold—trapped forever on a fenced-in siding as part of a museum. Inside the depot is a wooden scale locomotive that actually operates by compressed air.

In 1892, the same year the first ore dock opened in Conneaut Harbor, the last spike was driven on a railroad that connected the city with the south. By November of that year, first as a dot, then as a reality, the first ore boat said hello. The whole town turned out to greet the steamer *Charles J. Kershaw* with 1130 tons of Minnesota ore in its belly. Conneaut has since become one of the world's leading ore-handling ports. Lumbering sausagelike in from the lake, freighters make hundreds of visits to Conneaut each year, some of them carrying as much as 22,000 tons in a single load. Thus the city docks are a beautiful and clangorous place of giant Tinkertoy machinery rearing up into the sky. Five electrically operated Hulett unloaders reach deep into the guts of each vessel, extracting ore in seventeen-ton handfuls. This ore is either dumped directly into waiting railroad cars or carried through the sky by conveyor belt to storage piles and saved for future shipment. Conneaut can store 500,000 tons of ore each hour. Even when the lake ships hibernate each winter, Conneaut still ships ore to the waiting mills. When these great unloading machines—the Huletts—were first installed, they operated with steam—adding a hiss and drip and soot to the scene. Now, all is electric. Iron ore that once came only from Minnesota, now arrives at the docks from as far as Labrador and Venezuela.

West of Conneaut along the lake to Cleveland is Ashtabula. Between Conneaut and Ashtabula—unless you wish to be a spoilsport and take the interstate—you can travel Lake Road beside Lake Erie. This is a curious area where mostly sum-

mer cottages line the lake side of the road and year-round houses line the other.
You'll see an occasional big home on this stretch, but not too many of them. Around North Kingsville, where Camp Luther is located between the lake and the road but hidden from view by trees, you'll see scrub wilderness. Sometimes traveling beside the lake, sometimes drifting inland away from it, the road winds up and down little hills, crosses little bridges, and finally wanders lonesomely through unattended forests. Civilization is less here. It is hardly here at all. But near Ashtabula the marsh wilderness gives way to a cottage or two; then, all too soon, the sky is marked by smokestacks of Ashtabula, where the Ashtabula River runs.

This river was the line that divided the hunting grounds of the Senecas, Cayugas, and the Delawares from the Chippewas, Ottawas, and the Wyandottes. All tribes fished in the stream and partook of the wilderness shopping center that contained fresh berries, nuts, elk, deer, bear, and turkeys. The shopping center was a stilly place of water trickling, birds singing, and the rustle of the beaver meadow and the marsh grass. Now, this is gone. In its place is Ashtabula.

Some say that the Battle of Gettysburg was planned in Watson's Ashtabula home—he being Assistant Secretary of War Peter H. Watson and his home being on Park Street in a building that later became the Hotel James and after that, a home for aged women. Secretary of War Edwin M. Stanton himself is said to have spent two weeks there, connected to Washington by military telegraph, planning the battles, one of which was Gettysburg.

The township of Ashtabula, organized in 1888, was located on the east side of the river and known first as East Village. Later the west side joined the town and there is Ashtabula. The city is a mixed assortment of good and bad. It has serene middle-class surburban sections, some little streets of empty stores, and a whopping industrial complex that is its reason for being. Ashtabula has about 26,000 people and a city income tax. The chief industries of the entire area are manufacturing, agriculture, dairying, fishing, and—of course—the shipping of coal, iron ore, rubber, and other products via the St. Lawrence Seaway. Like Conneaut, Ashtabula has Hulett unloaders too.

An old-time vaudeville house in the city is today the Ashtabula Playhouse, presenting about a half-dozen professional performances each year and also housing a group called the Community Players who present several rather excellent programs of their own, too. Thus, although Ashtabula seems heavy-handed and grim, it has more going for it than industrial muscle. In addition to unloading an ore boat, you can slip into your tutu and have a go at an *entrechat* at the Ashtabula Fine Arts Center, ballet being one of the items on its agenda. Here, as another cultural added attraction of importance, is a branch of Kent State

Ore unloaders. Ashtabula.

University located in the vicinity of the Elks Shore Club whose sign graffiti-bent urchins occasionally reletter. On the west side of town is pleasurable suburbia and the Ashtabula Country Club which, when we last looked, had a FOR SALE sign out front.

Between Ashtabula and Geneva-on-the-Lake, however, is a collection of small and somewhat oppressive little summer cottages, most of which are for rent. They huddle together for whatever comfort their society offers, while, now and then, across the road from them are the typical year-round homes of ordinary suburbia. But consider Geneva Township, which seems to lack rentals and therefore has a relative calm. The township says that it is "zoned for your protection," which we suppose means it won't be going the commercial way Geneva-on-the-Lake has gone. Next door to it, Geneva-on-the-Lake seems to be a summer resort town that has everything—and everything seems to have a price. Only forty-seven miles from Cleveland—translated that means forty-seven minutes—Geneva-on-the-Lake has a permanent population of only eight hundred—plus a half-hundred motels and hotels for rent. And 13 bars and restaurants. Can you guess what the town's chief industry is? Also available is an eighteen-hole municipal golf course which the chamber calls "sporty and in excellent condition." On its main street you can hire a pizza, a ferris wheel ride, a speed boat, a room for the night, and a horse. Geneva-on-the-Lake seems to us to be a wearisome collection of pancake houses, penny arcades, carnival rides, and dirt roads that lead to the lake. The roads all seem to be lined with unpleasant little cottages with cute little names, each advertised by a sign bigger than the rest. At night in the height of the summer season the fulsome main street is as noisy and as purposeless as Times Square. No matter where you choose to stay in this town—and to be fair, Geneva-on-the-Lake has several beautiful and cheerful hotels and motels whose charm goes on forever—you are always within sound of the sea (call it Lake Erie) and a transistor radio tuned to a Cleveland rock-and-roll station. The beach water is tested for sanitation.

In winter—off season—Geneva-on-the-Lake is a ghost town dotted with FOR SALE signs. Shuttered is the midway booth where you can knock over stacked milk bottles, gone the hawker of raffish jewelry, closed the steak house, empty the pizza parlors, silent the side streets, and lonely the lake. This, to us, in when the town has beauty, which shows how we feel about things. Lest you take umbrage, let us suggest that in Ohio we all don't like the same things, because Ohio would be dull if we did. Certainly if Geneva-on-the-Lake had no reason to be, the place would not exist, but there it sits, existing—and quite well. As all the little cottages pressed together attest, on weekends and for quickie vacations this is where a lot of Ohioans come. Nor it is a rowdy town; the officials chased one fellow out because he looked like a hippie. As we said at the beginning of this

105

book, to like Geneva-on-the-Lake you have to like that sort of thing. To be more than fair, in season, when going full blast, the town is noisy but clean. You don't have to worry about seeing a middle-aged Tinkerbell leaning against a lamppost, asking young men if they believe in fairies. So take your kids to Geneva-on-the-Lake. It's a family place. Although we can't take fond farewell of the town, if we are to be honest, we do suggest that we're glad it's there and we wish it well.

Down the road a piece is Geneva itself, back from the lake. Here's where P. R. Spencer lived, he having created the Spencerian Method of Penmanship that has rendered our handwriting forever intelligible.

Along the lake between Geneva and Painesville, where U.S. 20 still is, the roar of the east-west traffic isn't. Since most of the drivers prefer Interstate 90, U.S. 20 has been relegated to a wide and vacant thoroughfare with many sections where the restaurant signs say NO TRESPASSING, motels—if open at all—are seldom used, and the highway advertising signs are things of peeling paint and messages from sweeter days. True, some of the businesses are active, but many others are not. Considering that Lake County being the smallest can be traversed in twenty-five minutes via the interstate, see how much you miss when you travel the interstate? Perry Township is a place of truck farming and many nurseries. Farms line each side of the road but so do ticky-tacky dwellings, automobile dealers, gasoline pumps, billboards, and trailer parks.

Happily, Painesville is a good scene. Painesville is a gratifying little town that is a thing of beauty. Here is where, in 1857, Lake Erie College was founded. On the east side of town, which a sign labels a high accident area, is a collection of two-story frame homes that are as welcome as the roses in May. Some are painted an Elysian yellow. Doesn't that inspire you? The Painesville courthouse, because the town is the county seat, is a genial and ornate cupcake in the best tradition of Ohio county courthouses. Though the Painesville business district is a hodgepodge of different kinds of architecture, the chamber smiles and says, "Relax. We're working on that."

The west side of town where Lake Erie College is has some apartment complexes, but mostly the streets are lined with orderly and agreeable homes with great cool lawns to make the setting satisfying. Says Painesville, "Variety is the word which describes (our housing) best. The regimented atmosphere of the solid allotment living is absent. Occasional allotments exist, but not row upon row, mile upon mile. In many neighborhoods there is a balance of new and old houses; of young and old people; and the residence you may want may be on a city lot, suburban plot, or farm. Scenic, wooded homesites are plentiful." Painesville, which could be considered a Cleveland dormitory since expressways can hurl you into Cleveland fast, is thirty miles north of the Public Square in Cleveland.

It is in reality a town that has an engaging New England atmosphere—and that means Painesville is bent on being more than a Cleveland dormitory. It seeks, in addition, self-sufficiency. They say that thousands of acres are available in the county for industrial development as well as much commercial land just sitting there, waiting to be developed.

Next door to Painesville is Mentor. Mentor, also, has many beautiful and rambling old homes, a few of which have been turned into commercial establishments. Nurseries abound. Mentor is where our twentieth President Jame A. Garfield had his splendid home called *Lawnfield*. Everything in Mentor—with the exception of its business district—is high, wide, and handsome; that which was not antique, has been antiquated. But the business district is a heavy-handed commercial section, relieved by the beauty that lines the side streets in the form of genial old houses, some of which have widow's walks. As you go west on Mentor Avenue there are smaller houses—modern two-story items—which seem small only when compared to the older and more ornate houses. The spell of Mentor is broken completely around the Great Lakes Mall: shopping center plus. The streets on either side of this commercial wonderland look the same as any other shopping center, lined with satellite businesses: hardware stores, trailer sales, gasoline pumps, and one place advertising itself as a nursery for children. The sign's emphasis is on children, but you must remember this is nursery country (farming under glass) and there are only a few nurseries catering to children; most cater to shrubs. This is America's nursery capital.

Then, there's the Chargin River—and before we know it, we're in Willoughby, whose business section is a wide thoroughfare lined with ordinary shops, World War One vintage. Here is where you can pick up Euclid Avenue, which meant, before expressways, Cleveland was a thousand traffic lights thataway. Willoughby is a place of winning homes—many downright beautiful—and losing apartment complexes—most downright new. Anyway, as far as towns go, around here they blend because Cleveland has reached out to mix them all up together.

So before we visit Cleveland itself, let's look around some more in the northeast corner of Ohio. For instance, anyone for Warren? Warren is over there, near the Pennsylvania border.

Warren, with about 66,000 people and a clutch of skyscrapers some of which are almost a dozen floors high, has many sections of agreeable homes, especially around the country club area. There, gracious and expensive-looking dwellings sit back far from the road, an expensive-looking lawn the buffer. But for the moment, downtown Warren itself will not get rave notices from the garden clubs. The business district is bustling and prosperous, but also an unalluring collection of buildings which have, for the most part, seen better days. Business districts in

107

many Ohio cities are the same, so let's not give Warren gloomy stares. Rather, let's look on the east side of town on that grand boulevard which would carry us quickly into Pennsylvania. There, as noted, is a cordial and clean and cheerful Warren, pretty as a picture, as subdivision follows subdivision, each outdoing the other. Turn north from that road when you're out a distance, head to Brookfield, and be pleased all over again. Here gentility is rampant—and so is fresh paint. Here is a nicely mannered town square that is more like a New England commons than a commercial stopover. And all around—this way and that—twilight hills that are gently rolling hills, casual grades, good roads, many stately trees, and an occasional farmhouse transplanted from New England.

Trumbull County itself is smack up against Pennsylvania about forty miles southeast of Cleveland. Until 1900 coal was mined here. Founded in 1799 and named after surveyor Moses Warren, the town has a steady growth. President Thomas Jefferson appointed Simon Perkins as postmaster. Perkins owned so much land that he paid one seventh of all Ohio's real estate taxes. Warren has several claims to fame. The Packard brothers, before going on to Detroit to make automobiles, made lamps in Warren. Some say that in a Warren stage-coach inn Stephen Foster started to write "I Dream of Jeannie with the Light Brown Hair," but they never say what interrupted him. For culture of sorts, the Kenley Players each season, operating in air-conditioned Packard Music Hall, bring in such luminaries as Ethel Merman, Noel Harrison, Izzy Kadetz, Martha Raye, Arthur Godfrey, foreword-writing Hugh Downs, Juliet Prowse, Robert Cummings, and the wonders of Dagmar. But basically Warren is in the murky and gloomy industrial steel district of eastern Ohio, which is called the Ruhr, but not the Ruhr you're thinking of.

Near Warren is Niles where the Mahoning River as well as a brace of creeks flow, a fact that attracted the Indians because the waters made their canoes go fast. One of the first Niles settlers was Ruben Harmon. Others came; coal, iron ore, and limestone—the raw ingredients for steel—were discovered; and along came James Heaton, who built a foundry in which he forged the first iron bars in the state of Ohio. In 1806 Heaton started the township of Heaton's Furnace, which was changed to Nilestown, which was changed, by the post office, to Niles, Heaton hired a foundry man named William McKinley to run the store. McKinley ran it so well he became President of the United States.

Down in the lower righthand corner of Trumbull County, a stone's throw from Pennsylvania, is Hubbard, part of the Warren-Youngstown-Hubbard triangle. Hubbard has 9000 residents. Iron works are here; so are steel plants. Originally, though, Hubbard was a mining town full of Welshmen who dug soft coal. The biggest employer in Hubbard these days is the Valley Mold & Iron Company, employing about 2000. Youngstown is thirteen miles one way and Pennsylvania thirteen miles the other.

In Kinsman, also in Trumbull County, the criminal lawyer Clarence Darrow lived. Born in Farmdale, he was raised in Kinsman, where he learned his father's trade: carpentry and cabinet-making.

Around thirty miles south of Cleveland in Portage County is where Kent State University, Revenna and Hiram College are; and—until in 1832 when the good folks tarred and feathered them—the Mormons were. Ravenna, with a population of nearly 11,000 and a National Guard Armory that doubles as a community center says, "We're proud of our tree-lined avenues of homes. The stately trees which have caught the eye of many a visitor are planted and cared for as a free service by the city government." Other than trees, Ravenna also has industry: one, the making of molded baby-bottle nipples; and another, the making of huge earth-moving machinery.

Kent, too, considers itself the "Tree City." Kent is the most populated of all the cities in Portage County, having in 1968 30,000 people—a 70 per cent increase over 1950. Kent also has industry, 75 to be exact. Its biggest are the university and servicing the needs of same. Kent has 36—count 'em!—bars and restaurants. Kent State University is Ohio's second-oldest state university, ranks thirtieth among the nation's public universities, and has an enrollment of about 24,000—18,000 on campus and 6000 in academic centers in other Ohio towns.

In Hiram, where Hiram College is, James A. Garfield and Vachel Lindsay were.

As you look about this over-all area—bounded by Cleveland, Conneaut, Warren, and Akron—you can almost sense the presence of unseen cities and unborn crowds of people waiting in the wings. True, great swarths of wilderness linger in this land of rolling hills that flattens at the lake, but around here—in the forest silence—you can feel the glacierlike approach of Cleveland, soon to replace this growth called wilderness with growth called suburbia. Except for the industrial complex along the Ohio River, southeastern Ohio is still in the clutch of mountains that refuse to let go. Little cabins like lost kingdoms rot in forest weeds. In the northwest part of Ohio—flatland and the wide sky—cities are few and far between; the land is still that new. But here, in this upper right-hand corner of our state, big cities, a few dozen miles from one another, are a dime a dozen. So some parts of the state, at the moment, do not need park districts, but this part of Ohio does. And has them. In a decade or so subdivisions will breed subdivisions where now trees and gulleys are. In a decade or so, except for the park districts here, you will never be more than a mile from a stop sign, drugstore, beauty shop, or funeral home.

And so Ohio's wilderness dies that Ohio may grow.

109

Witness the twilight of forest silence.

And hear the mating call of bulldozers, snarls of sweet hellos.

No matter.

Fifteen miles east of Cleveland is the hilly Geauga County where Fred J. Gould wrote the poem *Remember the Maine*. Years ago, when this county was only hills and forests, few villages could take root, but agriculture did. Creameries were everywhere—sixty of them, making cheese. Charles Martin Hall who invented processed aluminum, panicking spellers the world over, was born in Thompson in this county. Because the county leads Ohio in the production of maple products, Geauga is called, usually by its chamber, "the sweetest county." If you like to ski, try the Mont Chalet Ski Area or the Apline Ski Area. Also, there's an Olympic Sports Camp. And if you've already broken your leg, when June comes, hobble to Middlefield and attend the Swiss Cheese Festival.

Burton is the festival-happy town: in June, the Butter Churn Festival; in September, the Rug and Craft Show; and in October, the Apple Butter Festival. When April comes to Chardon and the sap is running, there's a Maple Syrup Festival. But in spite of its sweetness and its many festivals Geauga County has no cities to speak of, in fact, none. Chardon, with 4000, is its county seat and largest village. Altogether 62,000 people live in the county, though. But not altogether.

When James A. Garfield was not allowed to speak in a church in Geauga County's Newbury, the town built a chapel for him to talk in. He later dedicated the chapel to free speech. It became the scene of early hippies, including radicals advocating temperance and woman suffrage.

Southeast of Cleveland is Akron, and halfway between the two is the Blossom Music Center, summer home of the Cleveland Orchestra, George Szell its musical director and conductor. In Akron itself in October Iacomini's Restaurant holds its annual clambake—all Little Neck clams—and year round, tire companies make tires. The Goodyear Air Dock—world's largest building with no interior supports—is equal in height to a twenty-two story building, large enough so ten football games can be played simultaneously, and is so constructed that it creates its own atmospheric pressure, which means it can cloud up and rain on cue. Akron also creates its own atmospheric pressure from its various industries, but don't cloud up and cry, because although this may come as a surprise to many, Akron is one of Ohio's more beautiful cities.

But first things first. Although it is now called the Rubber Capital of the World, until 1807 Akron wasn't there at all. Joseph Hart was first on the scene, selecting a spot two miles east of Akron on the river. In 1825, when there was talk of a canal from Cleveland to the Ohio River, men cocked their heads thought-

Akron—for great restaurants.

fully and looked at where Akron is now: a bump, really. Downhill both ways from Akron. The eyes of Simon Perkins glittered at the thought of the canal possibilities and the need for locking through Akron. Perkins hurried over to see his neighbor Paul Williams, they combined their lands into a partnership, plotted Akron, and when the canal opened in 1827, Akron was born.

In 1870 along came Dr. Benjamin Franklin Goodyear, who had been lured into making a housecall to Akron because of a brochure touting the place. He came from Melrose, New York. Once here, he got the support of nineteen locals who subscribed one thousand dollars each so he could start a plant manufacturing, among other things, fire hose. By the end of the nineteenth century most of the Akron names we know were on the scene: Firestone, Seiberling, Goodyear, Diamond, Miller, Star, and Swinehart. By 1900 Akron was bursting at the seams, a wonderful rubbery boom town.

Between 1910 and 1920 Akron's population went from nearly 70,000 to over 200,000. It annexed territory like crazy, making Akron today Ohio's fifth largest city. Its 413-square mile metropolitian area includes eight city parks and a 400,000-acre metropolitan park area. Also, Akron is a trucking center: headquarters for 113 freight lines and 58 carriers. Its Rubber Bowl seats 36,000. Akron has, in addition to 27 public and private golf courses, the American Golf Classic and the World Series of Golf. Don't forget the small fry who participate in Akron's American Soap Box Derby, though few recall what a soap box is.

Downtown Akron? Hilly, tightly packed, but rebuilding itself into something brand-spanking new.

Yet, even some of the locals of Akron look hangdog and say, "Listen, Akron isn't really a cultural city, but we have some of the greatest restaurants. People come here from Cleveland just to eat and . . . " We agree Akron has more fine restaurants than any city should have, but we quarrel with the Akron attitude that seems to say, "Pardon us for being so commercial with tires and stuff like that."

Listen, Akron old buddy, to be sure you have industry that puts your city on top of the heap, but why get embarrassed about that? You're not a one-industry town. Oh sure, tire-making plays an important part. Should the tire-makers pack up and go—where?—your over-all payroll would be less, stores would sell a few less trinkets, but Akron would still be there. The Rubber City wouldn't die. Akron, you have over 700 manufacturing concerns—and they don't *all* make tires. You're one of the country's largest producer of books and toys. And you're a bunch of other nice things—in addition to restaurants and snow tires. Culture? You have that, too. And don't kid yourself that you don't. Listen, Akron old buddy, you should see some of these university towns where university is *the* main industry. They don't come near you when it comes to culture. And, besides that, they can't make tires worth a darn. Retreading is their business: retreading yesterdays to palm off to today as Great Truths. Snow tires last longer. If making tires and money are dirty words, so is making poetry.

What other city has the Stan Hywet Hall and Gardens? Here, with a little imagination, you can drench yourself in Tudor luxury. For those not in the know, which until we visited Akron included us, this is the sixteenth century-styled heap built in the twentieth century by Frank Seiberling, a kin of his by the name of Judy later attending Oberlin College where she had the nicest smile which, however nice, has little to do with this paragraph. This mansion has halls of hand-carved oak and ash, sunken gardens, and, on the tower, a gargoyle. Here the greats, near greats, and occasionally ingrates gathered: from Will Rogers, who never met a man he didn't like, to a few famous females of the same inclination. The mansion had—and still has—a music room of Palladium proportions. Four Presidents were entertained here. But all was not sweetness and light for the Seiberling whose vision created this place. Big men, as well as the rest of us, can come upon hard times—and he was no exception. Five years after he moved into the place, then being in the hire of Goodyear where he developed cordless tires and dirigibles, Goodyear was near bankruptcy. Seiberling lost the chairmanship of the company plus about $20,000,000. Nonetheless he maintained the Tudor mansion and didn't can the two dozen needed to keep the place operative. When he was in his sixties, he started the Seiberling outfit, amassed another fortune, and there you are. He died in 1955, leaving the place to his six children, who, one supposes, blanched at the generosity. The original 3000 acres of the estate had by then been hacked to only 65. The children quickly signed a contract with a bunch of civic leaders who formed a foundation to operate the place as a public spectacle, one of the nicest sort. The crest over the front door—NOT FOR US ALONE —became, as they say in Akron, a kept promise.

Akron also has the State University of Akron, an agreeable plant that contains nearly 12,000 students as well as nearly 2000 others in the college's special program. Many charming girls attend.

Near Akron, in fact next door, is Barberton, which finds itself surrounded by Akron, Norten village, and both Coventry and Franklin townships. Barberton is called "The Magic City" because, the story goes, of its growth at the turn of the century, the same time Akron was growing. Located about thirty-five miles from Cleveland, Barberton finds itself contained in nearly eight square miles of reasonably rolling hills some of which are dotted with attractive subdivisions and others of which are dotted with industry. Actually, Barberton got its start when Ohio Columbus Barberton, who sounds as if he had been named by a train-caller, bought 640 acres around a lake so he could make matches. He named the lake for

113

Anyone for Lovers Lane? Akron.

his daughter Anna. When Barberton—the man, not the city—got in a tiff with Akron over taxes, he picked up his match factory, moved everything over to the lake, and founded Barberton, naming it after himself. The Barberton match factory—first in Akron, then guess where—later became a part of a huge match empire that earned Barberton the title "Match King." As for the lake, Lake Anna is a ten-acre pond of spring-fed "clear blue water charmingly set in a garden of flowers, lawns, and trees," so murmurs the chamber. "In the springtime Oriental cherry trees blossom along the winding paths that line her shore. For generations, men have tried to fathom Lake Anna's origin . . . her why and how. No one yet has discovered her true source or depth. Lake Anna lies today amid industrial spires . . . " and on and on and on.

The original Barberton place in the town was a huge streetcar barn of a building made of brick. It had many towers, corners, and stuff like that. Happily for the esoteric, the building has been removed to pave the way for a shopping center.

The first settlement in the county where Akron and Barberton are was Hudson, which had a college until 1882 when an interesting thing happened and the college moved bag and baggage to Cleveland, changing its name en route to the Western Reserve University. Hudson with about 4000 people was a Western Reserve village settled in 1799 by Deacon David Hudson whose house still stands. Hudson, both in the chamber of commerce brochure and in real life, is a typical New England village as pictured by typical Ohioans. Though Hudson has industry, the town keeps the industry like a maiden aunt hidden from view. The Flood Company, for example, produces paints and additives in the buildings of what seems to be an old farm so picturesque that its employees should join the 4-H Club. Other industries in Hudson—equally disguised—are the Euclid Division of General Motors and several fabricators of plastic, wood, and steel who are so well hidden, one wonders if they are about at all.

Hudson's fetish for the Grandma Moses stuff is such that its chamber says, "Come visit us someday. Choose, if you will, some get-together on the village green, our ice cream social in the summertime, or on a crisp winter evening, join us and our children for Christmas caroling, later to tramp through the jeweled snow to the church parlors for a cup of hot chocolate . . . " Since a cup of hot chocolate is not our cup of tea—that doesn't sound right but you get the idea— the chamber notes that in the village there is a state liquor store for those who need grog to enjoy the snow, jeweled or otherwise. Seriously, and we have always been, you will like Hudson. Today Hudson has dozens of homes left over from the past. Here you will find examples of colonial architecture, Greek revival architecture, New England farmhouse, and flowery writing that someone should

115

have edited. Hudson is approximately twenty-five miles from Cleveland, fifteen from Akron, and a few steps from the nearest public library.

Then there is the city of Tallmadge started in 1809 by the Reverend David Bacon as a community for Presbyterians and Congregationalists. His daughter Della enters the scenario as author and lecturer. She is said to have been the first to have blown the whistle on William Shakespeare when she wrote a book attributing the authorship of Shakespeare's plays and Hudson's brochures to Sir Francis Bacon, no relation. The county is named Summit because, of course, it is the highest point on the Ohio Canal and the reason Akron began.

Akron, like Hudson, has a lot of jeweled snow, but it gets kind of dirty before you can get a setting for it.

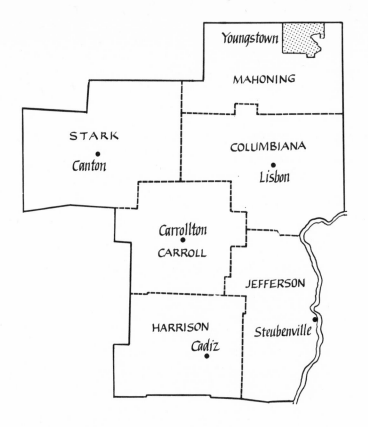

7

In the northeastern quarter of Ohio—or at least the way we have sliced up the state for the purposes of this book—the Ohio River flows. Thirty-nine miles west of Pittsburgh, which should give you an idea of the terrain and mood, is Steubenville, the biggest city in these parts. Bezaleel Wells founded the city in 1797. He called it La Belle. It was an offshoot of Fort Steuben built in 1786 to protect geographers from the Indians. Once Steubenville was the wool center of the west. Gone, now, are the sheep herders. Today industrial Steubenville with about 35,000 residents has more electricity than it knows what to do with. More steam electricity is generated within twenty miles of the place than anywhere else you can name, so please don't.

In addition to kilowatt hours, titanium and ferro alloys, and steel, you'll find that Steubenville makes and peddles tin plate, wood and paper products, clay, tile, and brick.

The city was named for Fort Steuben which was named for a Prussian nobleman who helped out during the Revolutionary War. His name—hold onto your hat and watch out for the wet spots—was Aron Frederick William Augustus Henry Ferdinand von Steuben. A soldier since he was fourteen years old and later a drill instructor at Valley Forge, he came from a noble family that produced generations of long-named soldiers.

The Jefferson County Historical Society, Jefferson County being where Steubenville is, now has as a tourist attraction the nation's first land office, the land office having been in Steubenville. Steubenville's first industry was Benjamin Doyle's tannery. Back in the early days the town was hip-deep in sheep, wool mills, and gristmills, plus distilleries. The first steamboat made there was a classic. Built in 1820 and called the Bezaleel Wells, its smokestack was brick. Back in the dark and lonesome hills behind Steubenville can be found all the coal anybody would ever want. Deep mines bring it up from the earth's darkness and strip mines ravage the wilderness in search of same. By 1854 the coal shafts were first sunk. Some, once they got underground, tunneled every which way, some as deep as 200 feet below the sheep herders, and some actually sneaking under the Ohio River itself. Thus Jefferson County became one of Ohio's foremost producers of coal. Then the Steubenville Pottery Company began.

But ten years into the twentieth century found the chief reason for Steubenville's existence: steel. As the Steubenville poets say in their brochures, "The status of steel is a gauge of Steubenville's economic health. At night the eye takes delight in the lights which dot the sloping black hills of its residential district and in the glow of the steel converters, red in the night skies. For these sights are the badge of Steubenville, city of steel . . . " Which means, unpoetically, that parts of Steubenville are the land of the grimy and the unwashed because that is the way steel mills, if they are to function, must do to the communities in which they operate. Up the sides of hills—and back in the valleys they contain—away from the river valley's earthy commercial rumblings—you can find great swarths of suburbia which, if such delights you, are satisfying, agreeable, congenial, charming, cordial, amiable, and friendly. But Steubenville's business district, reasonably dusted and clean, is basically a brick conglomerate of two and three story buildings, some dirtier than others. An excellent shopping area, nonetheless.

The two railroads that rattle through town are the Penn-Central and the Norfolk & Western. More than ten dozen trucking lines add to the evening rush hour. Adding to the traffic are five different bus lines: Greyhound, Trailways, Lake Shore, Pittsburgh-Wierton, and the Steubenville bus company itself. Along these streets, but we trust not at the same time, marches the Steubenville High School "Big Red" Band. One of these streets, by the way, has been renamed for native Dean Martin, but the street name was not available as we write this.

Smoky giant of the valley. Steubenville.

This, then, is Steubenville, land of the eighty-inch hot strip mill—which is really next door in the Wheeling Steel Corporation's Mingo Junction operation. This is the land of power: the Cardinal Power Plant in Brilliant, eight gloomy miles downriver, Ohio's largest power plant, feasting each year on three million tons of coal to create nine billion kilowatt hours. Here, too, is the land of culture. Founded in 1948, the College of Steubenville is an attractive plant offering four-year liberal arts degrees. Here is nature ready to nail you: where the river valley narrows, great rocks teeter on the edges of cliffs, waiting for the right breeze so gravity can have its fling. But travelers don't seem to mind. They take these "falling rock" areas in stride. One reason is, on a rainy day or when the river fog is heavy, you can't see through the gloom to see the size of the boulders.

Next to Steubenville, as we suggested, is Mingo Junction. Here, after the Indians left, frontiersmen used to assemble, gathered for expeditions against the retreating natives. Although George Washington visited Mingo Junction, no one is certain exactly where the father of our country bedded down. Complains one historian, "If it were possible to locate (his) lodging spot in Mingo Town, a memorial might be erected . . . " Anyway, note that Mingo Junction's first post office was built in 1879 and that its first postmaster was Robert Turner. Note also that while much of Mingo Junction's residences are frame houses—some neatly painted, most not—plastered to the sides of hills, a dreary lot of Mingo Junction is in the river valley in dreary little houses.

Upriver the other way from Steubenville is Toronto, Jefferson County's only other city. Its population is about 9000. It began as a flattened-out place along the river because it seemed right to settle there. George Washington when not sleeping in at Mingo Junction said that where Toronto is, was a plateau three miles long and one mile wide. The town started in 1818; first as Newburg; later as Sloan's Station; and finally as Toronto, so named because one of the town's first businessmen was from Toronto, Canada. Because the city sits on a bluff looking slightly down at the Ohio River, floods that plague other river communities leave Toronto mostly alone. And if Toronto strikes you as a cleaner community than the rest—it is—remember that all values are comparative, especially when Mingo Junction is within hollering distance. Some of Toronto's streets—most, in fact—are paved with red brick from the valley's yesterdays. Here you can see where trolley lines once ran because their rails still glisten in whatever sun that shines, but—alas—the trolleys have died. These brick streets run everywhere throughout Toronto's cramped little downtown section. Always—up there—are the dark mountains frowning down, adding to the sense of melancholy strangers feel in river towns.

120 The village of Costonia—with mountain bluffs on one side and railroad and

A cobblestone and trolley memory. Toronto.

the river on the other—is a hemmed-in little place one can hardly take a deep breath. The village, what there is of it, is cleverly hinged to the side of the hill. Also upriver from Steubenville is Empire and Stratton. Here, like the rest of the busy valley, the trees seem to be gasping for air, suffocating in the industrial drippings that fall like powder from the sky. Great heaven-tinkering smokestacks dwarf these villages. Huge docks with huge machinery overpower them. Everything in Stratton and Empire and the rest is oversize, too big for the villages, out of proportion, including the Ohio Edison plant and the great industrial heaps too gargantuan to all but giants. For a quick moment one gets the feeling here in this valley that man has not won but lost; and that it is machinery and not man in control of the sky and the valley's destiny. Then, just as quickly, one sees a man move a handle or press a button. We watch as towering Erector sets—high as the sky—do man's bidding the same as a dog comes when his master whistles. We feel better, rub the cinder from our eye, and move on. This is not a valley where poets thrive. These people are doers and not dreamers.

But nonetheless they dream. Those great machines did not spring to life by themselves. They are the poetry of the valley. They are the valley's grimy sonnet.

Now, though, for some peace and quiet.

Back deep in the hills and mountains of this river county, many twists and turns and trees away from the lapping water, is Mount Pleasant, a town of only 700 residents. Here a Friends' Meeting House—made of brick, 92 feet by 60 feet, with auditorium and galleries that could hold 2000—stands silent, preserved now as a state memorial. Erected in 1814 for what is called the Ohio Yearly Meeting (composed of quarterly meetings in Ohio, Pennsylvania, and Indian territory) this wonderful building was the first such meetinghouse west of the Alleghenies. From the meetings in its great auditorium, Quakerdom for the rest of Ohio sprang. The greatest Quaker migration to Ohio was around 1800. Nearly a thousand Quakers from the east, sometimes entire congregations, moved through forest paths by wagon trail and on horseback, driving before them their livestock. First because they had no meetinghouse they would gather for religious worship under the great stands of trees that turned noon into twilight. But quickly the Quakers built the town of Mount Pleasant. Jesse Thomas and Robert Carothers plotted the place in 1803, calling it Jesse-Bob's Town. Here the Quakers farmed, raising wheat and hogs. They ran grain mills and they operated stores. For nearly 100 years the serene and cool brick worship building was the center of Quaker faith in Ohio. But in 1909, the last regular meeting was held.

And silence reclaimed its galleries and its auditorium.

Farther upriver from Steubenville is a collection of tight and narrow little streets, old buildings, and a business district that has seen better days—the whole

New dams harness the Ohio River.

shooting match being Wellsville, a fooler of a town because it keeps getting bigger and better and more attractive with each passing day and each passing riverboat. About 8000 people work and live here, making things like pottery for milady and fraternity paddles for fledgling masochists. In Wellsville are giant and clangorous river terminals operating full blast, manhandling every kind of cargo from industrial fuel oil to liquid sulphur to lime products, all of which sweetly scent the air with industrial fragrance. The town with many of its narrow streets seeking the river has the appearance, at times, of an abandoned railroad division point someone forgot to bury. The town, though, does have a sense of humor. In one two-story frame that hasn't been painted in years is located the Magic Mirror Beauty Salon. Along the south side of Wellsville—in the vicinity of Clark Avenue —the town improves considerably. Here are nice and pleasant neighborhoods which, all things being comparative, would in other parts of Ohio be considered depressed areas. Wellsville began in 1797, was named for early settler William Wells, and became a city in 1889. In 1817 John Kountz started Wellsville's first pottery.

Next door along the river is East Liverpool, founded in 1798 by Quaker Thomas Fawcett. In 1834, when the town was inundated with English potters who showed up for work, the place was renamed East Liverpool. Although the town seems mostly *in* the river valley itself, many frame houses—discolored gray—hang to the side of the steep hill where roads, like terraces, line the hill in layers. Because of the availability of native clay and coal, the pottery industry boomed. Now the area houses forty-six ceramic and allied plants in which thousands of people are employed. East Liverpool is national headquarters for both the United States Potter's Association and the International Brotherhood of Operative Potters. The high school team is called, logically, "The Potters." The first potter was James Bennett, an Englishman who started his business in 1840. Although recognized as "the pottery center of America," East Liverpool is also a regional hub for an expanding steel industry.

Far back from the noise and smoke and karate chops of the river valley are wild and angry hills—mountains, perhaps—an area of gorges and streams and emptiness. Here the Beaver State Park is. Here are the ruins of the Sandy and Beaver Canal and its forty locks, one of which—having been abandoned for nearly a hundred years—is nevertheless still intact. Here is Gaston's Mill. Built around 1837, it was first operated by water power, then by steam, then by gasoline engine, and—for the benefit of sightseers—operated again by water power. Gaston's Mill was the last of a half dozen around there. Corn, oats, wheat, corn meal, buckwheat flour, and something else was made here, ground by the millstone.

Also back in these hills are several villages and towns. One is Lisbon. It has about 4000 people. It is the county seat of Columbiana County. A historic spot 58 miles from Pittsburgh and 73 miles from Cleveland, Lisbon has a clutch of older buildings, including the Old Stone Tavern on East Washington Street. Built in 1805 by Lewis Kinney, the Old Stone Tavern was restored as a historical museum —and no liquor license—in 1851. It is said to be the oldest building in Ohio. The oldest *stone* building, that is. Should any other community quarrel, we shall say it is at least the oldest stone building in Ohio in which you can't get a martini. Lisbon also has—here we go again—the oldest *brick* building in Ohio, the building now being Hamilton's Drug Store. It was built in 1806. The back of it, which isn't there any more, was even older, having been built in 1803. Also, suggest the good people of Lisbon, this is probably the oldest store in Ohio: the Nace Drug Store, established in 1848, has been doing business in its new location since 1888. Listed as the second oldest community in Ohio, Lisbon was originally laid out as New Lisbon in 1803, the year the county itself was established and Ohio was admitted to the Union. Nearby is where General John Morgan's raid into Ohio came to a screeching halt. This is where he surrendered.

Up through the hills from Lisbon is Salem, which is called the second largest city in the county. Listen, every city has to be something: Salem was established in 1803 by the Society of Friends from Pennsylvania and New Jersey. Now it is a collection of nice homes where most read the *Salem News* and many of the homes have bridges because there is a creek between them at the road. In Salem is where the first Women's Rights Convention was held, not a water pistol in the gathering. A place of factories and some housing that is not too spectacular, Salem is a town of narrow streets. Its business district is a bunched-up clutter of stores, both old and new, plus a litter of signs. The over-all effect, simply put, is gray and dismal. But go out around North Lincoln Street and the mood of the town changes to charming. Farther out, not-too-expensive one-family dwellings and apartment buildings are the order of the day. Farther out—and the city ends.

The town of Salem was laid out in 1806 by Zadock Street, John Strawn, and Samuel Davis. Approximately twenty miles south of Youngstown and sixty-two miles from Cleveland, Salem has about 15,000 people living supposedly in the climate the Quakers created for them. But it has, in addition to not having that, all sorts of industry: American Radiator & Sanitary Corporation does sheet metal stampings and assemblies there. The Cherry-Hill Corporation makes upholstered furniture. The Church-Budget Envelope Company makes collection envelopes and church calendars. And the Electric Furnace Company makes just about any kind of electric furnace your heart desires. Because strip mining is about, the Paxson Machine Company furthers this cause by making strip mining machinery. So does the Salem Tool Company. The town, in other words, has sure changed a lot since the Quakers got there.

Over in the hills east of Salem are several villages. But they are not too exciting

125

because, to be fair, this is not the richest part of the state. Between here and the river a change has come over the land. The hills have become even more pronounced. This is a forest area of valleys and ridges, of twilight mists and morning fogs, of woodland loneliness and little villages. The village of Rogers? Well, it has a railroad running through and an ordinance against mufflers. Rogers is a casual gathering of frame buildings, some of which still seem white, but generally the village looks exhausted. Its dreary business district along Depot Street has some stores so ancient they seem unreal. The village, at best only several streets wide, sits cramped in a tight little valley, hills dominate, and the village can't escape. Beyond the hills: civilization, wilderness, and the noise the strip miners make.

North from Rogers is East Fairfield, a scattered farm village of two or three dozen houses, a red brick building, a pottery that peddles to tourists, and—well, that's all. North of East Fairfield is Columbiana—the city, not the county. Columbiana is famous for many things: Harvey S. Firestone of that tire company was born on a farm in the vicinity, the town hasn't had a Chinese laundry since Lee Soon closed up shop about fifty years ago, and—oh yes, the town is 750 miles from Boston. By the time you've traveled this far through the violent hills from the Ohio River, the anger of the hills lessens and you can sense the beginning of prairie country. To the east, and quite close, is the Pennsylvania border. To the north and to the west: smudges in the sky, the outcroppings of the area called Ohio's industrial Ruhr. To the north is Youngstown. To the west, Canton and Alliance.

Youngstown, biggest city in Mahoning County, was settled by and named for a fellow named John Young who came from New York State. Iron ore deposits being there, quickly Youngstown blossomed gray as a brawling manufacturer of steel. The first steel mill—Ohio Steel which began in the 1890s—later became part of the United States Steel Corporation. Then came more mills and more workers. Today Youngstown covering thirty-five square miles is in the heart of the nation's fourth largest steel-producing district. But Youngstown is much more than steel mills, noise, bustle, and a bottle of cold beer. Here is where the Monday Night Musical Club, which has been in existence since the invention of Mondays, brings in nationally known artists to sing at the people. The Youngstown Symphony Society sponsors a trio of cultural items: the Youngstown Philharmonic, the Junior Philharamonic, and—of course—the Philharmonic Chorus. The Youngstown Playhouse, says Youngstown, is one of the nation's better community theaters. And you can always join the gang at the Mahoning Valley Polo Club, which does polo things at the Canfield fairgrounds. Also, there's the Youngstown State University with nineteen buildings (five others leased), an enrollment of 13,000, and nearly 700 teachers. Point is, Youngstown is more than a hot furnace,

though, to be fair, steel is a big item there. So what kind of place is Youngstown—
this assemblage of polo, drama, music, and mills? Well, we must be realists.
Because it *is* an industrial city, parts of it are not beauty marks.

The 1960 census gives Youngstown 166,689 residents—many of whom have
parents who were foreign-born. Where from? Most came from England, Germany,
Poland, Slovakia, Hungary, The Ukraine, and Italy. In case you think Youngstown
has a one-track mind industrially and manufactures only steel, you can also
purchase in Youngstown: a church altar, burlap bag, ornamental iron balcony,
venetian blinds, mailbox, casket, catalog, box car door, envelope, fire escape,
safety goggles, mattress, house paint, potato chips, baby rattle, burial vault, and
—of course—smokestack, of which Youngstown has lots. You see: you can't say
that Youngstown, although dominated by mills, is a one-industry town, but on the
other hand they do cause smudges in the sky.

Youngstown is also a place of suburbia, tea rooms, and tenements. Most of its
churches are so modern, however, they have the appearance of building & loan
establishments. One of the city's more bewildering sights architecturally is the
Child Guidance Center, located in a cantankerous old frame building bedecked
with more cupolas, spires, and porches that any structure in its right mind
would ever require. Youngstown's outer business districts—leading to the square—
are strictly business: six lanes wide and loaded with car washes, soft drink places,
and big signs that advertise this and that. Much is there that used to be residential, but commercial fronts tacked on obliterate that memory fast. Then,
into the downtown area itself. A long bridge leaps high and gracefully over grubby
valleys—deep and wide—that are littered with mills and river and railroad tracks.
The town square? Impressive. Beyond, up the hill, is the aforementioned Youngstown State University established in a collection of charming but antique old
buildings. Nearby is the Women's City Club, itself in a similar old and beautiful
structure, ornate and painted pink.

Directly south of Youngstown is North Lima, a one-street wide community or
so it seems, the proud possessor of cottages and a shut-down railroad station.
Beyond there, to the south, flatland, semi-flatland, and the faint hint of hills.
But, always, you can sense greater hills waiting just offstage, for the right cue, to
smother you and the land.

Southeast of Youngstown is Canfield—polo country—for years the home of
Northwestern Normal College. Canfield now advertises itself as one of the nation's
"cleanest villages." Five thousand people clean there. It may well be one of the
cleanest villages but the several times we visited there were scraps of paper blowing
down the street, blowing by several houses whose paint was chipped and whose
porches sagged. In fairness, Canfield *does* have a serene and broad street that

127

Antiseptic antiquity. Youngstown.

has a park in the middle. But on the Canfield-Niles Road north were straight-from-the-catalogue sections of suburbia which, clean or unclean, are abundant in Ohio. No matter. Around here is an area of ten thousand pleasant valleys, far more than Louis Bromfield dreamed of either in his philosophy or his book.

Berlin Center is a nearby village that is a wide spot in the road. It possesses a school and an unhappy frame house which has not been painted in years. The house is deserted. Whether people live there or not isn't the issue here. Around here also is Damascus and its toboggan slide. Also here you'll see several operative coal mines: huge frame buildings standing on stilts. On the side roads housing is generally as tired as the adjectives we have been employing. Tired and disenchanted.

Canton, as Akron and Youngstown are, is an ambivalent place of time-clocks, municipal culture, and cleanup campaigns. An industrial city which manufactures 1500 different products besides anchovy pizzas, Canton is picking itself up by the bootstraps, dusting itself off, and—practically from scratch—starting all over again. As we write this, the rejuvenation is still going on so, reasonably, there exists in Canton much that is murky and much that is embarrassing. But change as well as smog fills the air. Although from one side of Canton—the south side—the city appears to be little more than power plants, bumpy roads, and factories; and on Cleveland Avenue especially the traveler can become depressed; take a look at downtown Canton and save your depression for cities in need of same. First consider the plaza in the heart of downtown Canton: a colorful parkland and well-benched respite surrounded by trees and flowers. There, in winter, you can ice-skate; and—because the rink converts to a reflecting pond—there in spring you can hoist a few in the outdoor saloon they call a cafe. In addition to skating and hoisting, the Central Plaza offers an illuminated water fountain and an indoor exhibition area.

How did Canton get its name? Well, an Irish trader, Captain John O'Donnell, named his Baltimore (Maryland) estate Canton because he brought to Baltimore the first freight ever delivered there from Canton, China. To make a long story even longer, when Steubenville's Bezaleel plotted Canton in 1806, the Baltimore captain—hero of the Steubenville surveyor—died. Bezaleel Wells read of the sad event in the paper the day he was recording the plot, so he named the plot Canton and aren't you sorry you asked?

In 1843 William McKinley, who was not born in Canton, passed the bar and started his law practice there. Two years later he was elected county prosecutor. He was later shot, you may recall, when as President he was attending Buffalo's Pan-American Exposition. His body now rests forever in a Canton mausoleum 97 feet high and 75 feet in diameter around the base.

Traffic circle. Youngstown.

Ohio is coal mines.

Seat of Stark County and center of a large trading area, Canton has many old buildings plus many new ones that will surprise you. One new piece of architectural drama is the Wells Professional Building. Elsewhere in Canton is the Loretta Home for the Aged operated by the Sisters of the Divine Spirit. For colleges Canton has the Malone College affiliated with the Ohio Yearly Meeting of the Friends Church. Its campus is brand spanking new. Also there is Walsh College operated by the Brothers of Christian Instruction. It is ten years old in 1969. And in Canton if you can't go to church, perhaps the church will come to you, as in the case of the spectacular St. Haralambos Greek Orthodox Church. It was moved—bodily and spiritually—from one section of Canton to another, remodeled, and glued back together again, better than new. For industry in Canton there are Republic Steel, Timken Roller Bearing, Ashland Oil, Ohio Power, and a bunch of other things.

Culturally Canton takes a back seat to no Ohio city. The Canton Art Institute in addition to permanent showings presents nearly six dozen exhibitions each year. The Canton Symphony Orchestra has each year four subscription concerts. The Civic Opera Association presents opera. And each season, beginning in September, the Guild Players put on Broadway plays. Also, there is the National Football Hall of Fame. Although its structure may be described architecturally with mixed feelings (one Canton native remarked he had seen better-designed used-car lots), nonetheless the million-dollar home for football heroes and artifacts was dedicated in 1963. Situated along the interstate where you have to shut your eyes to not see it, there the building is with its 52-foot-high dome, which is supposed to be an architect's rendering of a football looking up and saying hello to God. Inside is Jim Thorpe's Bulldog blanket, Knute Rockne's helmet, and other things of that nature, properly deified. Press a button—there are many to press—in the rotunda, pick up a telephone, and the football greats—by recording—will talk at you. On a clear day you can hear the voices of Jim Thorpe, Red Grange, Jack Samuelson, and Whizzer White. Via modern technology and tape banks it is easier to reach Jim Thorpe in Canton than the long-distance operator in Oxford. Well, so much for the sport of kings or some such.

Between Canton and Alliance is sprawled a place called Louisville, not the one you're thinking of, but a spread of suburbia, and not too spread at that.

Alliance, a city of Quaker origin and now with a mixed assortment of architecture and moods, began first as a crossing where two divisions of the Pennsylvania Railroad intersected. Alliance is called the "carnation city" because William McKinley always wore one in his lapel for luck after an opponent, whom McKinley later defeated, stuck one in his lapel while both were in Alliance. Now, other than history, Alliance manufactures traveling cranes, mill machinery, drop

133

Football Hall of Fame. Canton.

forging bricks, anchovy pizzas, bathroom fixtures, metal stampings, electric motors, cheese pizzas, paint, pipe organs, pottery, and rubber bands. With about 30,000 residents in the city and 100,000 books in its beautiful Rodman Public Library, Alliance covers about eight square miles of Stark County. Different parts of Alliance evoke different moods. The east side, for instance, to some seems one huge industry mishmash that goes on and on and on. To others, the south side around Union Avenue is, in places, an assortment of tranquil homes and townhouses. But as you get closer in, they murmur, tranquillity goes down the drain, commercial takes over, and that's all. North of the tracks is a section of workingmen's homes, neighborhood after neighborhood of nice people and just what you'd expect.

Alliance's Mount Union College, founded in 1846, is a Methodist affiliated heap that began at a town meeting where a bunch of people decided the town needed an institution where men and women could be educated in science as well as the humanities. The college was not established by church efforts, everyone is quick to say, but its founders and early faculty members were dedicated Methodist laymen who, one might suppose, set the tone of the college. The Pittsburgh Annual Conference (now the Western Pennsylvania Conference) endorsed "heartily" the new college and, in 1884, granted full patronage. The college sits attractively on seventy-two beautifully landscaped acres which contain twenty-two major buildings. The "Old Main" dates back to 1864. Cope Music Hall is a hundred years younger. Thus the college is a happy accumulation of old and new. The college library, in addition to sixteenth-century Bibles and special collections of Greek and Latin classics, has 120,000 books.

Fifty-four miles south of Cleveland is Massillon, named for a French Catholic bishop. The town was started by James Duncan, who came from New Hampshire. He once grazed sheep on the "plains" where the Indians grew corn and where now the Massillon State Hospital is. Kendall, an early piece of Massillon, was founded in 1812 by Thomas Rotch of Massachusetts. He brought a bunch of Merino sheep with him and opened a wool factory north of Massillon's State Avenue.

When the Ohio-Erie Canal opened, Massillon became "Port Massillon," the principal export being wheat and football players. The arrival at Massillon of the first canal boat, the *Allan Trimble*, from Akron was cause, of course, for celebration. People gave speeches, led band marches, built bonfires, and shot cannons. Today Massillon is an industrial town, part of Ohio's Ruhr, where in addition to steel items you can load your shopping cart with neon signs, plastic coin holders, cooking utensils, funeral supplies, surgical gloves, anchovy pizzas, grain silos, and door sashes. The Massillon City Planning Commission says it best: "Both large

135

and small urban communities find themselves with areas that contain obsolete and deteriorated structures, traffic congestion, inadequate recreation areas, mixed land uses, stagnant vacant land. These areas, which are often social and visual burdens on a community, are usually also financial burdens. They require extensive public services, but due to their dilapidated condition, have low assessments and pay relatively few taxes." Having said that, the Massillon Planning Commission took a hard look at itself and decided the city needed tinkering with. So a new Massillon is abuilding—and more power to it.

Of course everyone in or out of his right mind has heard of the Massillon Washington High School *Tigers*—that high school football team which some in Massillon as well as elsewhere look upon as a football talent factory. Well they might, because Massillon is renowned for producing not only fine football players but football coaches as well. One of the first professional football teams was from Massillon. The high school stadium seats 22,000. Massillon also has a public library. How many seats it has, no one will say.

South from Alliance and southeast of Canton industry generally dwindles and there, rubbing their hind legs together, the crickets sing love songs at one another in the fields. One of the many towns in this area of easy hills and great valleys is Minerva which has narrow streets, mixed housing, and some industry. Minerva is, in places, a clean village that is neither terribly pretty nor terribly ugly. It is more like the girl next door. But one of its train stations has seen better days; its ramps are loaded with plastic outboard boats for sale. Part of Minerva business district is gloomy, old, and touched with melancholy.

Minerva had its beginning in 1813, when Isaac Craig settled along the Little Sandy in the Muskingum land area. In 1789 the Pennock Brothers, who invented the steel railroad coupler, made railroad cars in Minerva; but later they sold their patents, and the industry moved bag and baggage elsewhere. In 1863, long before Cleveland had electric current, Thomas Edison—friend of the Pennocks—helped establish Minerva's power plant which, operating until 1966, was the oldest municipal power plant in the world. Minerva's industry today is diversified: from hand-molded brick made the slow-motion century-old way to space-age components using the latest computerized methods. In between: laminations, color pigments, paper tubes, forging, and precision machinery.

South of Minerva are both Carroll and Harrison counties, the most beautiful sections of real estate that Ohio has. Occasionally you'll see ancient smokestacks of old kilns in little villages like Oneida, the villages being little more than wide spots in the little traveled road. Oneida, for example, has a few stucco houses, a railroad crossing, and a deserted school with broken windows for eyes. Nothing else but the wind's moan. Yet, as you climb one of the many high, high hills you can see in the distance perched on still another high hill the county seat of Carrollton. It takes a long time, up and down many hills, before you actually reach this town of fewer than 3000 residents. But no matter. You'll be glad you got there. Carrollton has enough charm and grace for a dozen towns. It is a clean and open village, fresh as a breath of fresh air, windswept, and wonderful. Most of its homes are freshly painted gray frames, vintage pre-World War Two. Its downtown streets, though narrow, are light and airy. The over-all effect: beautiful, beautiful . . . The town square, small but sweet, is ringed by stores that are almost Disneyland antiseptic. Though the Norfolk and Western toots through, it leaves no grime behind—or perhaps the townspeople dust after each train passes. On the north side of town, logically, are traces of bland suburbia, but not enough to detract. In the village itself are several huge old homes, magnificent memories with the artistic touches some carpenter-artist added from his soul. Sitting on top of the hills as the town does, panoramic views are everywhere. You could sit on your porch at night and watch lightning—miles away—rake the dark hills. And never once hear thunder. And never once feel rain.

Below Carrollton—over rolling hills that twist and turn in and out of deep and beautiful valleys—the countryside pitches at times like waves during a storm at sea. Down here, in this vast loneliness, is a place called Petersburg: no more than a half-dozen houses, gasoline pump, and that's it. Not even a chamber of commerce. South of Petersburg is more hilly wilderness and more valley emptiness. Here and there may be a cleared field but quickly, as you pass, trees take over again. This is the area of Camp Muskingum which is the Ohio FAA camp. A huge lake is somewhere beyond the next hill. From the top of each high hill you can still see more high hills crumpled in the distance, almost as far as the eye can see. Where Carroll County and Harrison County blend, the blending is impossible to fix.

But Carroll County, like Harrison County, is marred with strip mining on the backside of hills, painful views we never see. Harrison County is more of the same. Located about eighty miles southeast of Cleveland, it has hills and forests and strip mining. No cities here. Cadiz with 3500 people is the county seat and largest village. Bowerston with about 500 people in a gully is a scattering of houses graying on the sides of hills. A railroad runs through. Then the hills take over again. But strangely, suddenly the hills are devoid of trees. Have trees been hacked away? Or what? This is the Tappan Lake Region south of Leesville Lake Region, both lonely and beautiful areas. In 1803 Cadiz began as the point the road from Pittsburgh crossed the road from Virginia. Around 1880 no other Ohio county had so many sheep per square mile. Now the entire county has only 17,000 people. One of its early residents was General George A. Custer who was born in New Rumley, which is no longer on the map. Custer went west where a terrible thing happened that we'd rather not talk about.

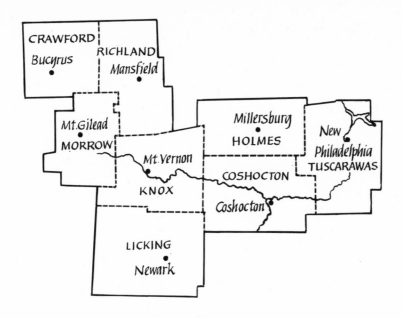

8

Back in the abrupt hills of the Muskingum Valley a hundred miles northwest of Columbus and eighty south of Cleveland, is the yesteryear world of the Amish. Before your eyes glitter with glee at the prospect of one of the commercialized Pennsylvania Amish areas right here in Ohio, heed this warning: you'll have to look far and wide—perhaps the nearest dime store—to find counters filled with "cute" Amish trivia. But in this land of cultivated foothills—in the vicinity of Sugarcreek, Walnut Creek, New Philadelphia, and Millersburg—are real honest-to-goodness Amish "family" farms. But the quaintness, if that is what you label such, and we're sorry if you do, is not for sale.

Here, also, a lot of Swiss cheese is made. Sugarcreek's annual Swiss Cheese Festival in September, for example, is several crowded days of pseudo-Swiss carryings-on during which the non-Amish of the community dress funny, hold erzatz Swiss events like wrestling and stone-heaving contests, and listen in stylized wonder at the music festival. But all year round Sugarcreek looks more Disneyland than Swiss. Still, if you like that sort of thing (many Ohioans do), more power to you and Sugarcreek. We hope you are both happy together. Meanwhile back in the hills the unpretentious Amish look upon Sugarcreek with a mixture of curiosity, bewilderment, and affection. But let us approach this area of commercialized gaiety and unpretentious living in a logical manner.

139

We are looking at Tuscarawas County and those parts of Holmes County where the Amish are. Other items are about, too. In southern Tuscarawas County is Newscomerstown which began with a name you hiccup: Gekelemukpechunk. Because Chief Eagle Feather got the seven-year itch, the town changed its name. Seems the good chief got fed up with his first wife—a child-turned-shrew who had been captured by Indian raiders—so he went out and got himself a later, younger, and newer model: another captured white lady. As wives will, his first wife got jealous of the "newcomer," the next thing you saw on Peyton Place was the first wife running through the village screeching her husband had been murdered, and also she screeched that "Newcomer" had taken off like the wind. Since the accused was pursued and captured in that funny-named town, the town was thereafter known as Newcomerstown. In 1827 a canal went through. To quote verbatim the chamber, "By 1880 the traffic on the canal was at its height. Each lock had a tender and nearly every lock had a strange story connected with it. It was a strange and interesting period in the life of the community of Newcomerstown." To which we can only add, that must have happened a lot around there.

Six years after the railroad opened in 1855 to connect Newcomerstown with exciting places like Steubenville and Coshocton, the railroad went bankrupt. Now Newcomerstown, with about 5000 good people in the city limits and another 5000 out there in the surrounding hills and valleys, is connected to the world by nearly two dozen Greyhound buses each day. An industrial and a savvy community, it makes many things other than non sequiturs. The Heller Tool Company makes files, saws, and abrasives. The Seilon Plastics outfit makes extruded plastics. High-grade face brick sees the light of day in Newcomerstown as do brass plumbing fixtures, power hammers, fabrics, and burial vaults.

Uhrichsville and Gnadenhutten in the central-eastern part of the county are within shouting distance of one another. The area around here is called the clay center of the world, more tons of clay products being shipped from here than anywhere else you might care to name. Gnadenhutten—a train caller's testing ground—was where long ago ninety Christianized Indians—men, women, and children—were done in and scalped by the militia; but things have calmed there since. Uhrichsville is the largest producer of clay products: pipe, brick, pottery, china, and tile. In Uhrichsville they say that once clay pipe is put underground it is the most durable of sewer pipe. It is supposed to be guaranteed for a century. First the canal, then the railroad brought stuff in and out of this area.

Since everywhere in these parts is called the Muskingum Watershed Conservancy District, let's look into that thing here and now. What is the district? Well, it is a political subdivision and a public corporation combined. It is a thing everyone glued together in 1933 for the purpose of flood control, conservation, and recreation. The first waters to form the lakes were made from the ten dams put up in 1938. A year later the flood control part of the district was handed over to the United States Corps of Army Engineers. The division of wildlife—with the approval of the state—is responsible for all the hunting and fishing in the district. All told, around 52,000 acres of both land and water in the district are available to the public. A taxpayer's burden? Relax. Since the district's formation, the district *itself* has paid more than a half-million dollars in taxes to the counties in which it owns land. The district itself, also, has not levied any direct taxation for its operations. Headquarters for the whole shooting match is in New Philadelphia.

Because New Philadelphia and Dover are side by side, to tell where one ends and the other begins is a wasted exercise. New Philadelphia (population about 50,000) has a branch of Kent State University that, in its air-conditioned quarters, can teach things to 2000 students. But New Philadelphia, on the whole, is a rather ordinary community with a fetish for labeling every other object by the name of *Quaker*. Thus, in New Philadelphia the movie house is called the Quaker. A restaurant is called the Quaker. And stores give Quaker stamps. In the heart of the business district stands a forlorn and immense three-story yellow-brick building decorated with scrollwork. But it contains only the lonesomest of stores: a collection of sad little businesses like Goodwill Industries, discount houses, and things of that sort. On one side of New Philadelphia is the railroad depot, deserted and forgotten. Through the town are many wonderful old-fashioned houses of brick and frame, each festooned with wild trim and wrap-around porches.

Out beyond New Philadelphia is the Schoenbrunn Village State Park, a reconstructed Moravian Indian settlement originally established in 1772. Fine tourist spot. The Ohio Historical Society is rebuilding a scaled version of the original for us tourists. The Moravian Church started early to teach Indians about Christ. After seven such mission villages had been established in Pennsylvania, an Indian chief invited the missionaries to try their hand at Ohio. So here came David Zeisberger with more than two dozen Christian Indians, they settled down, they called their settlement Schoenbrunn, they cultivated the land and erected buildings, and you know the rest. The locals didn't look kindly upon the Indians, something terrible happened at Gnadenhutten, and thus instead of a people we have a historical site.

Dover intermingles with New Philadelphia so corporate entities of these Siamese communities get lost. Both began in the early 1800s. Early settlers were Swiss and German from Pennsylvania and the New England states. The canal livened the area commercially and because of the abundance of clay, so did the potteries. The area's first metal-working industry began around 1850. Thirteen years later the New Philadelphia Foundry and Machine Shop was among the

141

largest makers of sowing machines and reapers the country (or, at least, southern Ohio) possessed. Located as the two cities are in the Tuscarawas Valley, where floods can tinker every time someone upstream spits, important to their dryness is the Muskingum Watershed Conservancy District. Since the completion of the many dams and lakes by 1939, the river has been sufficiently harnessed so that Dover and New Philadelphia are now relatively unwashed.

Ernest "Mooney" Warther, a Swiss of Swiss parentage, which seems reasonable, is in Dover. He began carving in 1913, has carved ever since, and is now world-famous. The New York Central Railroad—now the Penn-Central—has shown exhibits of his models around the country. Grand Central Station, for instance, held a three-year exhibition of his efforts. He has appeared on such television programs as "Tonight" and the "Mike Douglas Show." A gentle man with the most adept hands in the trade he is a master carver, now operating the Warther Museum in Dover, the museum containing hand-carved and operating miniature steam locomotives. He has also carved a Lilliputian steel mill complete with a sleeping worker and a somewhat disgruntled foreman. His largest effort is a steam locomotive that contains more than 10,000 different carved parts. This one model took him 367 hours to carve. His wife, by the way, has a collection of buttons— 50,000 buttons!

Up the valley from Dover is Strasburg, where you'll find the Garver Brothers Department Store, once called the "world's largest country store." Strasburg was named for the Pennsylvania village of Strasburg which was, they figure, named for Strasburg, Germany. The village's early expressways were Indian trails, one of which evolved into U.S. 21. Here in Strasburg Colonel Henri Boquet met with a bunch of Indian chiefs, demanding the return of captured white children. Right after the Civil War Philip Albert Garver of Fort Wayne, Indiana, came here to join relatives in the Tuscarawas Valley and started a drugstore which became the red-brick building listed as that large country store. Even today the store has those little baskets that operate as trolleys to send your money rattling through the sky to the cashier somewhere high up and out of sight. Also, to break the spell, the store has cash registers here and there, the penalties of progress. Strasburg, which covers less than two square miles and has a population of fewer than 2000 people, nonetheless has five gasoline stations, two restaurants, four drive-in restaurants, a place to buy goat-milk fudge, and, on the edge of the village, a potato farm.

West of the valley communities of New Philadelphia and Dover and up in the foothills beyond are the aforementioned Sugarcreek and its annual Swiss Cheese Festival, the latter being an immense and manufactured undertaking that warms the hearts of both the locals and the assorted bumper-to-bumper hordes of tourists who invade each year to partake of same. During the event Swiss delicacies, most

The master carver. Dover.

The simple life. Walnut Creek.

of which are made in the area, are served. Service clubs operate a great open-air cafeteria. By the time the festival ends, tons of Swiss cheese, 9000 halves of barbecued chicken, 25,000 apple fritters, and 12,000 hamburgers have bitten the dust. Logically there are parades. They say that Swiss people come from everywhere in Ohio—and from elsewhere—to wear colorful costumes and enjoy the moment. Musical groups are varied: yodelers and accordion players. Ample parking in Cleveland and Cincinnati is available, but nearer Sugarcreek traffic gets a bit more sticky. The noise of the organized gala even seeps back into the hills and valleys of Sugarcreek. There are, within yodeling distance of the Sugarcreek Hotel, twenty Swiss cheese factories. Here the Swiss cheese industry in Ohio began and, if the buildings of Sugarcreek get any cuter, here the industry could end. Sugarcreek, you see, doesn't take off its costume when the festival is over. Its supermarket, plus other stores,wear year-round false faces to make them look fresh from the Swiss Alps. The bank, similarly decorated, even has a toy train chugging about its upper Swiss structure.

But enough of Disneyland. Let us go up into the back hills where quiet valleys are, the Amish work, and reality is. In such hills the hard-surfaced roads soon give way to gravel ones. Horse droppings indicate exactly what you think. Here the high and slender buggies of the Amish, like little beetles, scurry through the back country—now with horses clopping, hoofs flashing, swiftly down a steep grade; now with horses tugging, harness leather creaking, plodding up the valley's other side. In the back of each black buggy glows the familiar bright-red triangular farm sign to indicate farm machinery in slow-motion. In each buggy is a bearded Amish farmer, his wife, their children—or any well-scrubbed and thoughtful combination of the three. But as their buggy passes, a sense of sadness consumes us. In this world of souped-up cars and stereo, where dare the Amish and their buggies go? And what, even as they pass, is happening to their world?

The Amish are mostly a hard-working and forgiving lot of people surrounded by the rest of us who are mostly neither. One Amish farmer—a blue-eyed melancholy realist—said, "We realize that history is against us. People tend to go from the simple farms into another life. And when they get there, into industry, they are liable to adapt themselves to you people . . ." More and more Amish youth are finding work in factories.

But to be fair, there are Amish and there are Amish. The "house Amish" have no churches at all. Each Sunday they meet in one another's homes, each member of the congregation being host about once a year. Also, there are "church Amish"— and a diverse group they are. There are Amish who do not own automobiles. There are Amish who do. The Amish who own cars are not supposed to get highfalutin about the fact: no car newer than three years. In some instances, the chrome is painted black. Some Amish smoke. Others don't. Thus, there are divisions within the churches which result in splinter groups and another church arising. Do they leave this or that church because of tobacco or a car? "That's not always the real reason," said an Amish farmer. "I'm sure it isn't. And that's the only thing I don't agree with some of these people about. I like them and they are my neighbors and I don't hold one thing against them, but you have to be honest. That's the only thing I don't like about them . . ."

Amish farms can never become the industrial conglomerates of other Ohio farms because instead of machines, Amish farmers rely mostly on horse- and people-power Milking machines? Their milking machines are their sons and daughters and wives and grandmothers and themselves, each capable of milking a half-dozen cows each moring. Thus there is a limit to the amount of land an Amish man can reasonably farm. So the Amish farms can with logic be called "family" farms in the purest sense.

"I don't want to give the impression that we are starving," the Amish farmer said. "We live comfortably. And every year we're making money. But as far as lots of money, few farmers do that." About credit? "I'll tell you frankly, I believe in credit—if you borrow to make an investment to give you a return. But to borrow on the installment plan for things you don't need? No. Today's luxuries become tomorrow's necessities." Note here and now that the Amish don't talk cute or quaint. True, among themselves they may speak a German argot, but when they speak with others, from their lips ordinary conversation flows. In other words, the Ohio Amish do not make a habit of saying clever things that would look precious painted on an ashtray and sold in Pennsylvania Turnpike gift shops.

Some of the Amish have diesel engines on their farms; some don't. How can this be justified? Explained the Amish farmer, "Well, about the only way it can be justified is as the Bible says, 'Not to be conformed to the world but to be transformed.' So now it comes down to a thing like a diesel engine which is modern. Some people have convictions against electricity. In order to have peace in your church, if that is the case, you go along with their conviction. In other words, let's say from the Scripture—" and here he launched into German, smiled, and said, "I can't translate it word for word, but it means 'Serve one another with love.' If a man has convictions against this or that, like machinery, we want to serve him out of love. We can do without machinery in order to have unity amongst us . . ."

And the Swiss Cheese Festival in Sugarcreek? "Well, our people don't partake much of the festival. Two days before it, I might go look at the antiques. I like to see how people lived years back. But the festival is highly commercialized. Anyway, I'm happier here than you fellows who are all the time gadding about down there. Joy comes from within. It doesn't came from without. If your happiness has to depend upon having this and having that, soon you tire of it."

Will the Amish last? We wish we could say tune in tomorrow, but already the

147

Small "family" farms. Sugarcreek.

handwriting seems to be on the sides of every hill and valley of the Amish communities. As one Amish mother said, staring from her kitchen window to the house across the way, "Do you see that home over there? The big one with the little one next to it? The grandmother lives in the little one. In the big house is the next generation. The Amish in the big house have a car now, an old model, but any day I expect to see a new model in their drive. And the house, instead of white, will be painted some pretty color . . ."

And some day when we drive along these gravel back roads, power lines will run from every pole into every house. Color television—that awful flattener—will have with laugh-tracks reduced the Amish to the everyday. Horses will no longer snort in barns on ice-cold winter nights. Amish carriages will decorate the lawns of suburban antique stores. And the idea of these Amish and their land will have evolved into a plastic tourist attraction, touted by billboards and brochures. The valley will become a quickie spectacle with a thousand roadside stands. No matter. The history that is against the Amish is against all of us; and so we live in the wonderland of the supermarket. One day, all too soon, an Amish grandmother and grandfather will wait with sweet patience for fellow Amish to come, sing chants at God, and worship. But they will wait in vain. The others will not arrive. They will be in New Philadelphia, attending the flicks. Sugarcreek—and the outside world—will have won.

Millersburg, which is the county seat of Holmes County, has about 4000 residents. This is Amish land, too. The county was settled by the Amish from Germany and Switzerland. Around here you'll find more Amish and Mennonites than are in Switzerland. The terrain is hilly. Some of the hills upon which little villages sit rise 300 feet above the great valleys spread below. Here are produced cheese, bologna, bus seats, addressograph machines, sausages, and wool—as well as fine Amish buggies made in the buggy works. The county has a half-hundred churches scattered about. Each fall Millersburg, not to be outdone by Sugarcreek, holds a festival of its own: an antique festival that, they say, turns the town into a Main Street museum. And, of course, there are parades. Began in 1963, this antique festival features beauty queens, organ music, a firemen's parade, more organ music, and—on the courthouse lawn, the Brewster Clown Band. In the home of Mr. and Mrs. Thomas Lea, nearby, are 131 mustache cups. One of the few places in Ohio that weaves nylon cloth on industrial looms is Millersburg. They make specialty items like Geodesic domes—self-supporting structures—one of which appeared in the New York World's Fair.

In the county also is Winesburg, a cheerful hilltop village, and though it was the title of Sherwood Anderson's book, it was not the setting. As we suggested earlier, Clyde, Ohio, was.

The Detroit of Amishland.

Coshocton—a far piece away—is announced by smudges in the sky in the hill-and-valley land. With the Muskingum River potting around one side of Coshocton, the place spreads out on a flatland plateau protected by two dams that keep the town from getting too soggy. Coshocton is 72 miles from Columbus, 100 miles from Cleveland, and 80 miles from Wheeling. And you'll find no other town so named. The name comes from three different words: one, *Goshachgunk* which means *where the river is crossing*; two, *Koshocktoon* which means *river crossing device* or *ferry*; and three, *Cush-og-wenk* which means *place of the black bear*. Put them all together, they spell *mother* or *Coshocton* or *Goshachgunkkoshocktooncushogwenk*. In 1802 the town was laid out, called Tuscarawas, but in 1811 was renamed the above, which we'd rather not go through again. In 1833 the town was incorporated. In 1863 its first paper mill started. In 1878, a cigar factory turned out smokes. Meanwhile, back then, over the Walhonding River was an aqueduct via which canal boats used to leap the river, but in 1913 the flood nailed the bridge, and that was that.

Probably one of the most attractive physical settings for any Ohio college or university exists in Granville where Denison College—taking full advantage of the fact—sits like a red-bricked ivory tower atop a huge hill that looks down on the serene little village strewn artfully below. Both college and village are in Licking County about twenty-seven miles east of Columbus. Established in 1805 in what are called the foothills of the state is beautiful beautiful Granville. What other village with red-brick streets has The Old Colony Car Wash? Quarries about; some are now swimming holes on a grand scale. The college itself occupies about 800 acres upon which more than a thousand fellows and 800 girls learn things. Thirty per cent of the students are Ohioans. The rest are from about thirty other states and ten foreign countries. As you approach Granville and the college, first the chapel spire announces the presence of civilization and culture. The Swasey Chapel can be seen for miles. Dedicated in 1924 the chapel was named for Dr. Ambrose Swasey, its benefactor. As you wind up the steep and curved drive to the campus the village swiftly falls away. The educational plant is a delightful accumulation of old and new brick buildings, leggy coeds, and handsome lads, all bunched theatrically together on the hilltop with crosswalks, underpasses, overpasses, and sky. Its roads seem to wind in and out forever among the buildings—snaking around hidden curves and unseen drives. A beautiful beautiful setting. The village itself, even if it lacked that place on the hill, would have all the charm a village should have. One ounce more—and the whole shooting match would be precious.

Sixteen miles east of Granville is Newark. Cross Raccoon Creek and there you are in an area of Indian mounds and attractive homes where—happily—sub-

Forsaken farms . . . forsaken barns . . .

One of Ohio's nicest towns: Granville.

divivions have yet to take root, thus each home has character unto itself. West Church Street varies, changing gradually from residential to commercial as you approach the business district. The beauty of downtown Newark suffers only by direct comparison to the nearby village of Granville. In its own right, Newark holds up well. Near downtown, though, the residential houses along the main street seemed bunched and crowded, begging for elbow room. Farther out to the east—a land of expressways and workingmen's homes—several factories are. Newark occupies fifteen square miles gracefully. It has 90 different manufacturing plants that produce together more than 300 different products. Newark has more than 47,000 residents, 16,000 of whom work in area industry. Close by are several parks including the Historical Mound Builders and Octagon Park.

To show that Newark and its residents both have good taste, we call your attention to the left ring. Here, on the east side out of town a distance, is a huge automobile graveyard that in most places would be a first-class eyesore, but not around Newark. The place is so well fenced and screened you hardly consider it a lonely place where autos die.

In the country east of Newark you'll see an occasional oil well. Many of the hills here are not hills at all, but great masses of rock that give you the mood of the Palisades in New York. Hanover, one of the little villages in this stony land, seems little more than a wide spot in the road. It has a railroad siding and a shale plant. And that's about all. As you head east more and more, oil wells take over. The hills rear up higher. Some of these oil rigs, by the way, are only rusting memories that keep watch with the wind over the land—until weather, time, and perhaps a lightning bolt hurls them—pow!—into eternity.

Knox County, where Mount Vernon is, is a geographical hybrid: its eastern half being the rolling hills of southeastern Ohio and its western half being like Ohio's northwestern plains. This is farming country. More than 1500 farms are in this county, each farm averaging about 150 acres. There are woods here, too. Of the county's 330,000 acres, 24,000 are wooded and another 112,000 are silent woodland pastures filled with animal droppings. Where the trees have been chopped down, corn and wheat and hay are grown. Also, the county has about 800 acres of orchards. In Gambier, a village of around 1500, Kenyon College is.

The county seat is Mount Vernon (population about 14,000). Mount Vernon was laid out in 1805. It is supposed to be the Greek Revival Capital of Ohio but some of the structures which assisted in that claim have been destroyed by time. *Look* Magazine and the National Municipal League in 1966 named Mount Vernon, however, as the All-American City. The man who wrote "Dixie"—he being Daniel Emmett—was born here. Jack Samuelson being part Indian, the first white man to locate in Knox County was Andrew Craig from Virginia. He

Ohio, one oil boomlet after another

built a cabin where Center Creek runs into the Kokosing River, which used to be known as Owl Creek. This is on the southeastern side of present Mount Vernon. The town itself was laid out by Joseph Walker, Thomas B. Patterson, and Benjamin Butler. The town has good industry. Coke bottles are made there. There, too, you'll find the Continental Can Company, the Cooper-Bessemer Company, the Chattanooga Glass Company, and a fistful of others equally as fine. Mount Vernon is also the home of the nationally famed Mount Vernon Sons of the Union Veteran Fife and Drum Corps, a claim no other town disputes. As noted, the town is supposed to have millions of dollars worth of colonial architecture, but as we said, some is now missing; nonetheless intentions being honorable in Mount Vernon, public buildings, places of business, and many homes try to carry out the theme. Thus, the effect even today is dramatic. And for dog lovers, note that Mount Vernon has planted thousands of dogwood trees. Says the chamber, one day all of Knox County, thus beautified, will have gone to the dogwoods.

Morrow County, west of Knox County, is the same geographical hybrid of hills and plains. Its farms, though, are smaller. Each farm averages about 120 acres. Also the county is in the midst of an oil boomlet. In the summer of 1961, three miles west of Mount Gilead, oil was struck. Two other wells drilled on the same farm were also producers. Three more wells drilled within a one-mile radius also, as they say in the trade, struck oil. And so now a great portion of all the oil land in the western and southern part of Morrow County is under lease, and everyone says a large oil pool—if not a major pipeline—has been tapped. Historically in 1821 Morrow County built its first sawmill and gristmill. Cardington, today with about 2000 residents, was once a great carding mill for the sheep industry. The county's largest village is Mount Gilead (population around 4000). The county has no cities. But on the other hand, says the *Ohio Almanac*, are several barns in the county upon which are remnants of landscapes painted by itinerant artists depicting the specialty of the farm.

North is Bucyrus, county seat of Crawford County which once was a silent and empty land of prairie and dark forests. Now farming abounds—and a few little villages. Its city, of course, is Bucyrus where each August is held the Bratwurst Festival. According to Bucyrus locals some people may still call this event Colonel Crawford Days to honor the soldier that Indians burned at the stake. However the popularity of the bratwurst as opposed to peoplewurst won out and thus the festival. During this event, which last several days, German "fun and games" are scheduled for all, drill teams do things, folk singers sing stuff, and bratwurst is peddled. Bucyrus started not as a bratwurst factory but as a stage-coach stop that rapidly became the marketing center for the area's villages and

156

farms. Among its early industries were brick works, tanneries, sawmills, wagon shops, and one knitting machine company. Now Bucyrus, located 90 miles southwest of Cleveland, makes a bunch of other things: women's clothing, rubber hose, anchovy pizzas, tractor booms, custom truck bodies, copper kettles, locomotive cranes, and brass castings.

On the surface Bucyrus would seem a drab little city riddled by industry and painted gray. But its town square is a splendid place if you like town squares. Its business district is typical of small Ohio cities that have lived and worked hard: commercial buildings made of brick, some having modernized false fronts and some having bay windows on the upper floors. On the north side of Bucyrus is the Galion Iron Works and Manufacturing Company, which makes huge road machinery that you see scattered along the highway construction areas. Go farther north on Sandusky Avenue and the housing, which wasn't great to begin with, is even less.

How did Bucyrus get its name? Well, it was named by its surveyor, Colonel Kilbourne. The prefix *Bu* means beautiful and *Cyrus* was a Persian general who, one supposes, was a beauty. Bucyrus has around 14,000 people.

The only other city in the county is Crestline with about 7000. Crestline began as a railroad junction and division point. And in the county you'll find little villages like Chatfield, its population less than 300, its chief preoccupation watching the action at the Standard Oil Station and wondering why the place is—in most places—only one street wide. It has some pleasant residential sections—a few houses, that is—on the north end of town. In town where, if it had a business district, its business district would be, is an old frame building that advertises itself simply as LUNCH, LIQUOR, BEER.

In adjacent Richland County are Mansfield and Malabar, the latter being the farm where Louis Bromfield lived after he made a bundle typing. This is the land of sweet valleys and gentle hills. The main town, of course, is Mansfield with about 52,000 residents and a courthouse that seems to have angered every pigeon in Ohio. Mansfield was named for Colonel Jarred Mansfield who, sent to the area to correct surveying mistakes, noted with melancholy that Ohio was "a place of wolves and Indians." Mansfield, filling one great valley, is a city dominated structurally by the Westinghouse plant. In the older sections of Mansfield's downtown are many two-story white frame houses crowded side by side, almost seeming at times to overlap, but most are well-tended, freshly painted, and have about them the aura of a workingman's gentle touch. Also, in the same vicinity, is a poorer section which—if it had eyes—would cry. On the south side are the better homes, complete with lawns and high mortgages. Then, over a hill, down a valley, and you're out of Mansfield.

157

The Louis Bromfield World. Pleasant Valley.

Louis Bromfield was born near Pleasant Valley. Right after World War One he published his first novel *The Green Bay Tree*. Then, after publishing a bunch of other successful books, he found himself with more than a million bucks loose in his jeans, so he turned his attention to Pleasant Valley to see what could be made of it. He purchased four exhausted farms and made them one. Having seen the trouble that soil erosion, floods, siltation, droughts, pollution, and women wearing high heels can cause the land, he decided to do something about the matter. And so he poured money and energy and love into his farm, it loved him back, and its fame soon spread throughout the nation. Some love affairs like that have happy endings: we're glad his did. Robert Douglass, a farmer in Butler County, was equally successful with a window box.

The county's only other city is Shelby with about 10,000 people. It calls itself, rightly, the birthplace of the seamless tube industry, dating the event as 1890. The town was settled in 1828 as Gamble Mills, but in 1834 changed its name. Shelby is a pleasant place of both amiable residential areas and noisy industrial ones. Much industry is there, several companies employing more than 500 workers each, many employing more than a hundred. Some of the industries? Well, there's the Ohio Seamless Tube Company for one. The Shelby Mutual Insurance Company, another big employer, has home offices there. In Shelby, actually, you'll find them making everything from seamless tubing, insurance, and television towers to—of all things!—bubble gum.

Lexington, with only 3000, is one of Ohio's more attractive little communities. Just outside of Mansfield, it bills itself as being in the center of Ohio sports. Here is a proud and friendly little village plucked fresh as a daisy from yesterday. Though a railroad runs through the town, and though its train station is painted neat and nice, grass grows on the station platform where, we suppose, ghost passengers wait for trains that never stop. The town with its many great trees that turn its streets into leafy tunnels is riotous with color in autumn. This is hill country. And this is beautiful country.

Beyond Lexington? Nothing. You fall off. The world is flat.

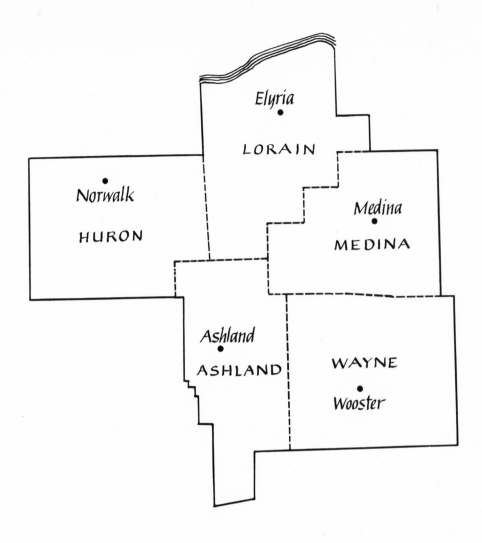

9

Compared to the area immediately around it, Wooster, which is forty-five miles southwest of Cleveland, is the granddaddy of all the other communities. Also, Wooster represents that happy combination that few small towns do: a smorgasbord of university-rural-and-industry.

But first things second. Wooster is the home of the nation's first Christmas tree. In 1847 to join his family, German immigrant August Imgard came to Wooster from Bavaria. Because there was no Christmas tree, the custom of his homeland, Christmas in Wooster saddened him and made him lonely. So he went to the woods, chopped one down, obtained a tin star from the village tinsmith, made paper decorations, and there—in the Imgard home—was a Christmas tree!

161

The following year all—well, almost all—Wooster glittered with such. The custom quickly spread through Ohio and the land. Now at the tomb of August Imgard at the Wooster cemetery, as a tribute each year a Christmas tree is lighted.

Though Wooster (population around 19,000) got an early start as a community, it was, nonetheless, a late bloomer of a city. During and after the Second World War, Wooster's population expanded from 14,000 to whatever it seems to be at this moment. What triggered the expansion? Babies, of course, and also Wooster went shopping for businesses. Now the city is the home office of Rubbermaid. Also, Wooster has the College of Wooster. It has the Ohio Agricultural Research and Development Center. Thus present-day Wooster is a cheerful please-don't-eat-the-daisies kind of community hip deep in pleasant homes, many with colorful gardens. A clean town with well-tended lawns and slim, attractive coeds, Wooster has a main street business district that is long, wide, and active.

Three years after Ohio became a state, the first Wooster settler arrived in Wayne County where Wooster is. He was William Larwill, originally of Kent, England. First he explored the silent wilderness, and liked what he saw, so he went back and got his brothers, Joseph and John. In 1808 Wooster was platted, becoming Wayne County's first community. Larwill named the new village for General David Wooster, a Revolutionary War hero who, when dying, was supposed to have gasped, "I am dying with this strong hope and persuasion that my country will gain her independence." They used to talk like that a lot back there, or so history tells us. Things are less formal now. Anyway, when Wooster first started, it didn't have a mayor, it had a president. That lasted until 1853 when Wooster locals decided to call their chief officer the mayor, feeling that a country should only have one president at a time. The first house in Wooster, occupied by William Larwill and Abraham Miller, was built the year the town was laid out. Larwill and Miller stocked the place with powder, blankets, homilies, lead, and tobacco with which they traded with the Indians. The second house was a tavern that Benjamin Miller built so hunters could wet their whistles in the wilderness. He was also the first *married* man in the county and father of the first white girl to be born there. But the honor of naming her Tillie Miller fell to John Bever for reasons history does not list. We will add only that deer used to be so plentiful around Wooster that when Benjamin Miller had a customer who ordered venison, Miller would got out and shoot one fresh. Also in the Wooster area were lots of wolves, bears, and rattlesnakes. When Yale graduate Carlos Mather came to Wooster to practice law, there was so little to practice that he became, instead, the town's first schoolteacher.

One of the many touches that makes Wooster attractive are the aforementioned coeds from the College of Wooster, a coeducational liberal arts college founded in 1876. When it first opened it had only 5 teachers, 34 students, and high hopes. Since then more than 15,000 men and women have wandered through its halls, learning stuff and trying to relate. A residential Presbyterian-affiliated college, it has a present enrollment of 1500 students, the lads outnumbering the lassies. The student body comes, disassembled, from not only Ohio but 40 other states as well as 22 foreign countries. The college's 35 attractive buildings are strewn about 300 acres of campus, here and there, places like that. In reality the college is one of Wooster's major industries. Each year nearly $5,000,000 is spent by the college in Wooster. The 500 faculty and non-academic personnel have a payroll that comes to roughly $3,000,000—and the students, not the sort to sock it away under the mattress, spend at least $300,000 in Wooster. That's an awful lot of pizza.

Another enterprise that fills Wooster's cash registers is the Ohio Agricultural Research and Development Center, one mile south of the public square. The center occupies nearly 2000 acres there as well as 4000 more acres in nine outlying districts and at Ohio State University. Simply put, the center is more than a window box. It has on its payroll around 7000 people, of which 250 are on the scientific staff. Organized in 1882 the center is one of the most outstanding research facilities in the world. It has total assets of over $20,000,000, not counting the take from the Coke machine. Financed by state and federal funds as well as industrial grants and special contracts, a big portion of its more than $6,000,000 operating budget each year is spent—Wooster is pleased to note—in the Wooster area. Sooner or late, someone is bound to ask, "Yeah, but what does the place do?" So let us solve that matter here and now.

Simply put, whatever God has wrought agriculturally in Ohio, the center tinkers with the wroughtings. To do this, the center has a whopper of a main campus—as it is called—that does things via research and sunshine for the state's 126,000 farmers. Also us city dwellers benefit because of better food and better lawns. Lawns? Sure, you bet. The center not only fools around with food but with things like grass and ornamental plants which means those petunias that gave you such a fright last year. The center, you see, looks into hundreds and hundreds of consumer products that contain one or more ingredients originating on an Ohio farm or in an Ohio forest. The institute is concerned with the development of an agricultural product from the germination of a seed or the development of an embryo through to what goes on your dinner table or in your flower pot.

In the center near Wooster, for example, you'll find everything from graduate student housing, perennial flower gardens, and test lawns, to an electron microscope laboratory. You'll find horticulture greenhouses up to their ears in research of tomatoes, flowers, and a bunch of other greenhouse things. The Vector Virus

163

Laboratory does biological studies of insects and mite vectors of plant viruses. In the Thorne Annex laboratories and greenhouses, researchers dabble with the control of insect pests. There's even a coroner's office for dead plants: the plant pathology greenhouses which does research on plant diseases. Bessie the Cow is not ignored. The animal nutrition building studies the nutritional value of beef and sheep. Here is the home of the fistulated steer—a steer with a window in its side. Experimental livestock rations are mixed and tried out in the building marked Grain Storage and Feed Processing. A turkey research unit researches turkeys. Seven acres have been set aside in Walnut Hollow for rhododendron and azalea cultivars. In the 115-acre Secrest Arboretum, research is done on trees and shrubs. Twenty acres are devoted to seeing what kind of shade shade-trees can offer. And the Veterinarian Isolation Building, we presume, is where they isolate veterinarians. All told, about 350 research projects are being conducted in 14 different departments, so how come your neighbor has a nicer lawn than yours?

Insofar as Wayne County is concerned, it is among the ten top agricultural counties that Ohio has. It is first in total cash receipts from dairy products, fourth in income from cattle and calves, and fourth in poultry and eggs. With around 2500 farms in the county, each farm averaging about 124 acres, the county has nearly 300,000 acres in farm land: 59,000 in corn; 50,000 in hay; 28,000 in wheat; 18,000 in oats; and nearly 5000 in soybeans. If you like to count animals, Wayne County has 3000 milk cows; 65,000 cattle and calves; 47,000 pigs; and 629,000 chickens.

But as they say in Wooster, while the town's early economy was based on the rural, that's not the true picture today. Though Wooster does rank fourth in the state for cash receipts from farming, which means farming is not to be sneezed at, nonetheless Wooster has some good industry, too. The Rubbermaid Corporation, mentioned earlier, employs nearly a thousand. The Gerstenslager Company, which makes custom-built truck bodies, employs more than 400; and so does Timken Roller Bearing, Incorporated; Buckeye Ware; and the Warner Motive Division of Borg-Warner. The Baltimore & Ohio Railroad has a freight connection with Wooster. The Penn-Central serves the town directly. So do all those bus lines which operate from the bus terminal. Between them—Eastern Greyhound, Ashland City Line, Ohio Trailways, and Lentus Lines—nearly three dozen buses arrive and leave Wooster each day.

In nearby Millbrook is Guy Kister's Grist Mill—or, Guy Gister's Krist Mill— one of the last of fourteen operating water-powered mills in the state. In season at the mill they saw lumber, grind corn, press cider, and pose for snapshots. Wayne County has a potpourri of little villages and two other cities in addition to Wooster. Rittman, with around 7000 residents, is one of the cities; Orville, with around 8000, is the other. Orville has a pleasant main street, a branch of Kent State University, industry, farmers, and a public library. The main—and only—city in the eastern part of Wayne County, Orville can boast of thirty-five manufacturing and processing plants in its area. Some of the county villages are Apple Creek, Burbank, Congress, Dolton, and a few others. Though you'll find Amish here and there in Wayne County, you'll find more of them in Holmes and Tuscarawas counties. Also, the little villages here are, at times, little more than crossroads. Consider, for example, Burbank. With fewer than 300 residents, its business section is hardly Times Square, but it does have on one corner some kind of store that has on the second floor a porch extending over the sidewalk, creating a sense of calm and a touch of shade, an ideal place to stand, should ever a parade go by.

If you're the sort who wants to know what time the balloon goes up, go to Ashland and ask. Ashland, so they say, is the balloon capital of the world, which, depending upon your age, attitude, and religious persuasion can create within you any number of interesting responses. Ashland is also the only city and county seat of Ashland, another one of those geographically mixed counties, being hilly in the south but in the north the slopes are either mild or not there at all. Located sixty miles southwest of Cleveland, the county with only one city has many villages: Bailey Lakes, Hayesville, Jeromesville, Loudonville, Mifflin, Polk, Savannah, and Perrysville which—we note with pride—was once ringed with liquor stills. On the other hand, in Loudonville was born Charles Kettering who headed the research department for General Motors, developing items like ethyl gasoline; diesel motors for trucks, railroads, and buses; and the automobile self-starter. Because of John Kennedy's *Profiles in Courage* Ashland has become known as the original home of Senator Edmund Ross, whose vote saved President Johnson—not *that* one, the *other* one!—from impeachment in 1868.

Although at one time Ashland was connected with Cleveland and the universe by the Cleveland & Southwestern Interurban Electric Railroad, the beautiful beautiful interurbans are no more which is a shame. In the days of interurbans one seldom heard of terrible jetliner crashes. Now the interurbans have gone and—well, you've seen the crime rate in the land. And how many interurbans were ever hijacked to Cuba? Hardly any. No matter. The interurbans are gone; and now we have juvenile delinquency. Things have certainly changed, including Ashland, which—though—says of itself, "Unusually high ownership keeps the old established neighborhoods fresh and green and well-manicured." You'll like Ashland. Everyone else does. Johnny Appleseed did.

There was a character: an early American hippie, doing—as the young sometimes

165

say—his thing with apple trees. Johnny Appleseed whose real name was John Chapman wandered about Ohio planting apple orchards wherever he could. Born in Massachusetts, he was later seen along the Potomac in 1789 and a year after that was seen potting around Pennsylvania. Then, about the turn of the century, he came into Ohio. In 1805 he established apple orchards where Ashland is today, some of the trees now in their third and fourth plantings. Easy to recognize from a distance because he wore no shoes on his feet but a pot on his head—which when not a hat was a cooking utensil—Johnny Appleseed was an Ohio character. In 1915 the Johnny Appleseed monument was erected in Ashland by children of that county to commemorate the hundredth anniversary of Uniontown, which Ashland used to be called.

You see, Ashland began right after the War of 1812 when William Montgomery got a tract of land later known as Montgomery Township. Here he established the village of Uniontown—now Ashland—which he named after the Pennsylvania town that had been his home. But when in 1822 the postmaster was petitioned to grant Uniontown a post office, the postmaster said, Listen a minute, will you, we already have one and that's going to mix up the mail, so do you mind terribly getting some other name because it will be years before someone invents zip codes? Or, at least, words to that effect. Congressman John Sloan came to the rescue. He suggested the town be called Ashland after the country place of Henry Clay in Kentucky. To make a long story short, the name was changed. About that moment in its history, Ashland had only a tavern, blacksmith shop, shoemaker, tannery, wheelwright, two distilleries, one doctor, lots of squirrels, and the Graham general store. But when in 1838 Ashland Academy was established, the village blossomed.

Actually with a little luck, Ashland might have become another Detroit. In 1836 John S. Studebaker and his three sons—Clement, John, and Henry—settled there to make Studebaker farm wagons, some of which are still about, but only as museum pieces. However in 1851 the father and sons moved on to South Bend, Indiana, still making wagons, and later making the Studebaker automobile. Though Ashland doesn't have an auto industry, it does have a statue on the Studebaker farm two miles east of town.

Today Ashland's largest industries are the F. E. Myers Brothers Company, which makes water systems, pumps, and items of that nature; Faultless Rubber Company, which makes drug and surgical rubber goods; Union Malleable Manufacturing Company which makes malleable iron pipe, fittings, and castings; and the A. L. Garber Company doing letterpress and offset things via printing. And, of course, Ashland manufactures toy balloons and rubber products, like rubber toys, which brings us—somehow—to Ashland College.

Founded in 1878 and affiliated with the Brethren Church, Ashland College is a four-year college serenely spread over sixteen acres in Ashland. In addition to the main campus, a few blocks away the college physical education plant stands. Since Ohio has more than forty private colleges and universities as well as a dozen state-supported educational heaps, we should look into this business of higher education. Some will be touched upon when we try to explain Yellow Springs and Antioch to the world, but for the moment let us suggest that Ohio State University with nearly 43,000 students, most of whom drink beer, is the largest state-assisted establishment. The University of Cincinnati (1967 enrollment 27,259) is the second largest. Based on the same 1967 enrollment figures, the smallest private college in Ohio is Boromeo Seminary, with 203 students; followed by Hebrew Union College-Jewish Institute of Religion, with 268; and Western College for Women, with fewer than 500 but all charming. The biggest private facility is the University of Dayton, with its 1967 enrollment of over 10,000 including Ralph Vines, who attends on the sneak. But are these places really any good? Hard question. And we mean not just the ones mentioned here but all the rest as well. Rather than inundate you with catalogues which are as uninformative as most chamber handouts, let us look into one particular segment of these ivy-covered places and see for ourselves. Since all teach spelling and finger-painting and since all are involved in the tedium of academic make-work, at times creating courses out of thin air because they look nice in catalogues, let us examine one particular area of teaching. We'll pick *theater* for two reasons. It is more of an intellectual art than, say, business administration. And, standing in the wings is Dr. Ronald Kern who has tasted the teaching of theatrical arts in both the huge impersonal university and the small intimate college. How does he sum up the educational shooting match?

"For almost two and a half decades, colleges and universities in Ohio have grown from tranquil communities of higher learning, untouched or undefamed by the outside world, to subsidiaries of the largest industries," Dr. Kern says with a quiet smile. "As the years have passed, the ivy on the buildings has been torn away and the cloisters have been filled with fluorescent tubes. Armies of bulldozers are now clearing trees, pushing over houses, and digging cavernous holes for more and more buildings which will serve larger and larger enrollments. Administrators spend a lot of time with architects to determine the use and location of the next building, with efficiency experts to decide how buildings and personnel can be occupied during the working hours of a five day week, with statisticians to investigate if professors are working enough hours in courses, committees, public relations, and community projects. As the IBM machines flick away, teachers who once lived in a placid and reflective world of basic black and

167

who preached the doctrine that the individual was paramount, must nowadays publish or perish, seek titles to protect their status, and leak their virtues to a disinterested press.

"Parents, taught in the old racoon coat and freshman beanies, are perplexed at the behavior of their offspring and do not understand why administrators and teachers do not take more interest in their children. On the other hand, students in this area know that TV classes and mechanical teaching devices can be compared to the housewives who wish to take back the ice man because there is no love in the refrigerator. To the parents' eye, what started as a masterpiece has become a synthetic product manufactured by electronic and computer techniques. To the student, except in the small schools, such as Ashland college, higher education in Ohio and elsewhere is a mechanical and impersonal experience.

"Among the courses taught in colleges and universities, the dramatic arts, although ancient and honorable in history and literature, are often relegated to subordinate positions. Theater history and research, stage literature, writing, dramatic criticism, and teacher training fit neatly into the curriculum of a library-centered college with a faculty of good lecturers. The practical art of the drama, however, is difficult to pigeon-hole. Acting, directing, stage design, and its technical application require a theater and many laboratory hours, which, unlike the sciences, are irregular and often without lesson plans. Reflective and creative thinking cannot be adapted to the waking hours, a five day week, or the sterile thump-and-say method. As a consequence, many administrators in Ohio, unable to force college theater into conformity, emphasize only the wholesomeness of the drama as a leisure-time activity, praising the cultural effect on the individual as he works backstage. Teachers, therefore, weaken themselves with attempts to mesmerize the administration into spending large sums of money for what is regarded as mere recreation then rely too heavily on television cameras, tape recorders, and records of professional productions, as their principal training devices. Parents, thinking the road to the stage is the way to hell and/or impracticability, may, by sending their children to college, delay a decision for four years, but the undecided position of many Ohio institutions toward practical theater makes the choice of a school difficult to make. The machine-oriented students often set their standards from movies and television and have their teeth capped, pulled or pushed and their hair covered, tinted, or woven before they have hardly begun to train as performers."

Dr. Kern—drumming his fingers—goes on to say that even if a theater building is built on campus, other people come in to lend a hand and suggest the shape and size of it—a camel being a horse that the committee designed. Some of the

168

others are the ones involved with band, orchestra, glee club, and artist's lecture series. "Unfortunately," says Dr. Kern, "a few college directors sell their programs by faintly tainted means. Sitting on pompous perches, they issue catalogues and play announcements which read like an 1880 ad for some golden elixir; the statistics sent to the administration are falsely impressive, their relations with the radio station managers of the area and the local newspaper editors are of family proportions, and the thorough orientation of drama critics insures nothing but kind remarks for the production and the directors. One should see, in this case, in order to believe and to decide for oneself whether or not the *Insect Comedy*, for instance, needs a bug bomb.

"In this dark world, Ohio can boast, fortunately, of some excellent schools in the various theater specialties. Ohio State is outstanding in history and research, Bowling Green State University can be recommended for its educational theater program, and if students wish to combine the academic with professional approaches, Western Reserve University has both a good curriculum and an association with the Cleveland Playhouse. For a student who wishes to specialize, Ohio University offers an extensive and yet specialized curriculum which is coupled with imaginative teaching. Denison should be noted for its teaching of the individual and for its active summer theater. Marietta College, another small school, is important in the field of scenery building and design."

And to that Dr. Kern should have added Ashland College is a good place for theater—because, simply put, he is there.

So much, for the moment, for higher education. Time for a stroll.

When we stroll the streets of Norwalk we are—if we pick the right streets—in for a pleasant surprise. Norwalk is in Huron County, which means we are in the flat Lake Erie land again. Norwalk, called the Maple City, is a town of about 15,000 residents, equidistant from Cleveland, Toledo, Akron, and Marion. These are the "Firelands" or "Sufferers' Land" granted to Connecticut residents whose homes the British burned. Norwalk is a combination of graciousness from the past and—sorry to say—the aggressiveness of the world today. Here you'll find, in a tender building that has beauty, the Firelands Museum. The Huron County courthouse, of course, is the typical Ohio county courthouse, long may they wave. Some of Norwalk's streets have tasteful colonial homes full of gentility and fresh as a daisy. On other streets is suburbia. Actually Norwalk has over 4000 homes; 80 per cent are owned by the occupants, but modern times have come to town: apartment houses are also taking root. A town which is a blend of past and present, Norwalk has thirty-five different industries which produce things like furniture, fire extinguishers, rubber products, anchovy pizzas, cotton products, automobile accessories, and surgical equipment. More than 1800 people are employed by Norwalk's industry. Norwalk is served by both the Penn Central and Norfolk and Western railroads—and thereby hangs the tale of Milan.

Milan is an antique and antiqued village of winners and losers. It is a place of tree-lined streets filled with hush, history, ancient homes, some trying to be, and—here and there—thoughts of the city that got away. The aging shops, so says its chamber, with false fronts surround the town square which makes up most of Milan's business district. Antiques and historical signs abound. Unfortunately hints of bland suburbia are beginning to line the roads into the village, but no matter. Milan could have been a dramatic city, full of vinegar, but its long-ago city fathers had the perspective that many of our politicans today possess. These ancients decided the town (then) was making so much money from the canal business, it had no need of a railroad, chased the railroad to Norwalk, and thereby signed its own commercial death warrant. Curtains for commercial Milan. Nine out of every ten Milan locals moved away, leaving the town sitting there, becalmed, wondering what happened. The parents of Thomas Edison even moved on. Tom had been born there.

Probably Milan's greatest—and only—boom was around 1847 when the town fathers built their city into a grain export center equal at the time only to Odessa as the leading grain port of the world. After much bickering the Milan city fathers got a canal built, linking the Huron River with the lake, and the town was off and running. From 1841 to the mid-sixties the shipbuilding industry flourished. One year saw over 35,000 bushels of grain loaded into canal vessels each and every day. At the height of the wheat harvest in 1847, nearly 800 wagons lined an old plank road to town, waiting to load grain into one of Milan's fourteen granaries along the canal. Now, gone—all is gone.

Now the town is filled with memories and some old homes. Everything in Milan is either quaint, historic, or precious. It is a self-contained antique village that has grocery stores, plumbing shops, hardware stores, a drugstore, restaurants, and the usual, including a delicatessen. Plus a bunch of real estate offices, feed mills, and four local industries which employ about 200 people. But its chief industry seems to be tourism. Each year hordes descend upon the town to see the home where Thomas Edison was born: the house on the side of a hill overlooking the canal upon which silence has fallen. In restoring the Edison home, the restorers found that the floors were locust wood—things of great beauty and sweet colors. Then, there's the Milan Historical Museum at 10 Edison Drive. It was the home once of Dr. Lehman Galpin who assisted in Edison's birth. Inside the museum you'll find an old-fashioned kitchen, complete with fireplace, and an old-fashioned parlor. Here, too, are the ledgers and records of the Milan merchants of yore, when the city was going somewhere important. Behind the museum: a blacksmith shop of other days and a carriage shed containing a surrey with the fringe on top. Around 1893 an electric interurban trolley used to move serenely through the streets of Milan. Connecting Norwalk and Sandusky it was, at the time, the longest trolley line in the world. But it, like Milan, bit the dust.

A nearby town is Bellevue, which was settled in 1815 as Amsden's Corners. It was named Bellevue in 1839, when the first Mad River and Lake Erie Railroad train tooted through. Now with a population of around 10,000 people, it has forty-seven industrial establishments which turn out everything from paper balers to boat hoists and from steel safes to showcases—and *that* should give you an idea of the town itself.

Another community is Willard, located in the southwest corner of Huron County and covering nearly two square miles with industry and houses. Willard, which calls itself The City of Blossoms, blossoms with the car dealers on the west side of town. The main highway actually bypasses the place, but the bypass itself is a litter of places that will sell you anything from a tractor to a room for the night. Willard in sections is split-level bland, out there is Hartenstein's Supper Club (or is it?), and that's Willard. Then, there's New Haven, which is little more than a traffic light, a handful of gasoline stations, a school, a church, a few white frame houses, and that's it. Delphi is another such crossroads, this one lacking the amenities like traffic lights; it has a church, though. On the outskirts of Greenwich (population 1500) everyone and his brother has put up a horse country fence, the sort Kentucky has many of, but as you get into the town itself, the town sucks in its breath, the streets narrow, and the houses—two- and three-bedroom homes in reasonably good repair—line the street like Coxie's army. In the business district is an old three-story yellow building with a wrap-around second-floor porch whose pillars form sidewalk obstructions; it might have been a hotel at one time. Greenwich has, scattered about, many huge old homes decorated with yesterday's styles. One of the several octagonal houses to be found around Ohio—built for what reason no one knows—is in Monroeville, a village of 1500.

While Medina County doesn't have any record of Indian settlements to list in its historical memoirs, locals do say that actual Indians went through a lot, on the way to somewhere else. Medina County was part of the Western Reserve, all its land having been divided into townships five square miles each. Medina, the county seat, with now about 10,000 residents, got its first courthouse in 1820 and a new one in 1840. The first industries in the area were sawmills and cheese factories, about every township having one of each. Medina City was laid out in 1818, named at the time after Mecca in Arabia. The population in 1820 was only

171

113, which wasn't bad considering the first settler had arrived only six years before. In 1835 the name of the town was changed to Medina after another Arabian city. An interurban trolley line from Wooster to Cleveland clanged through Medina around 1901 to link Medina with the world. Medina has many industries now, but one of its most famous started in 1865 when A. I. Root started his company—the original and largest in the field of bee-keeping supplies. Says the Medina chamber with justifiable pride, the town is a combination of the old and the new, and on Friday nights during summer band concerts are still held in the courthouse square. The town, by the way, is 18 miles west of Akron, 29 miles south of Cleveland, and 112 miles southeast of Toledo.

Around 20 miles south of Cleveland and 20 miles northeast of Akron is Brunswick, now with 17,000 to make it the largest city in Medina County. Brunswick, though, had been dozing in reasonable contentment until the mid-1950s. It had been a sleepy gathering of a few farm homes, a dab of suburban life, a few small groceries, a saloon or two, an out-of-date telephone system, and a school system that served the needs of 671 students. But then came the bulldozers. And then came the developers. And whoops! Before Brunswick knew what was happening, nearly 6000 additional residents popped up, suburbanites, and they brought with them the problems of the city. Now the schools of Brunswick cater to 2700. There are thirteen churches. There are two—count 'em, two—fire departments. The area has a full-time police force and a pair of shopping centers. Brunswick, for better or for worse, woke up. The sleeping princess had been kissed by a bulldozer.

On the other hand, consider the *un*bulldozed Lodi, first settlement in Medina County, though its name at the start was Harrisville, having been named after Judge Harris and his good wife Rachel. In 1810 Lodi township was surveyed into 100-acre lots. Families arrived, and so there we are today in Lodi, a town of serenity and calm with only 3000 very fine people. Lodi's houses—all well-maintained and sitting back from the crisscrossed roads in the hilly little village—exude charm. So does the creek that sloshes through the village. So does the gentle town square around which a most relaxed business district sleeps on warm summer afternoons.

How did Lodi get its name? Well, indirectly Lodi owes its name to Napoleon. As we said, it started out as Harrisville but another town had first dibs on that name, so a new one, said the post office, was in order. The Lodi citizens held a town meeting in the school house, now the feed mill on Harris street. As such meetings go, this one went: everyone talking at once, comparing names, babies, crops, wives, and one other thing not important this time of the year. In the midst of the general confusion—so the story goes—someone jumped up and started to recite *Napoleon at the Bridge*, a stirring poem having to do with Napoleon, Italy, and the Battle of Lodi, little to do with anything else, but committees were ever thus. Some of the locals said, "Hey, that's pretty good. Listen, why don't we call *our* town Lodi? I mean, really, why don't we?" The quote is probably not accurate, but the mood is, so there you are. And, according to William Dunlap, the former editor of the *Lodi Review*, that was how Lodi was named. Unless, he suggests, you consider the other version: Lodi being named Lodi because of its location on the *Low Divide*. No matter. When the first passenger train rattled into town in 1881, the villagers turned out, held a picnic in the woods across from the depot, and got rides to Wellington, which, really, is as far as anyone in his right mind would care to travel. Also the Cleveland Southwestern, which was actually the Cleveland Electric Company, built a most pleasant trolley line through Lodi in 1901. But after twenty-two sweet years the trolley cars rolled over and played dead; too many autos honked at them. Embarrassing.

Consider now Wadsworth, host to the Ohio Match Company. In a nearby village named—of all things!—River Styx, experiments in sulphur took place. Wadsworth now with around 13,000 people evolved from a pioneer farming town to a coal-mining town. Then when the mines went the way of all flesh, Wadsworth evolved again, this time into an industrial town. Between 1814 and 1865 Wadsworth came of age. Its first families were farmers and because so many trees were about a sawmill was established in 1825. Five years later the first gristmill was built. Then came blacksmith shops and assorted stores. Coal mining dominated the town from the Civil War to the turn of the century. The area around Wadsworth today is still honeycombed with abandoned shafts and tunnels and mine entrances. Wadsworth is in the southeastern portion of Medina County, 14 miles from Akron, 35 from Cleveland, 109 from Columbus, and—should ever anyone from Wadsworth get elected President—425 miles from Washington. The town occupies about six square miles, it has a volunteer fire department, your dog needs a license there, and for higher learning, Kent State University has one of its many branches there. From 7:45 a.m. to 6 p.m. Mondays through Fridays the town has telegraph service. All of which gives you an idea of the place. You can even buy food for your mink in Wadsworth. And as for the Ohio Match Company, the poor little match girl would never recognize the business. Automation has crept across the land, hanging up in Wadsworth.

In nearby Seville are buried Captain V. Bates and his wife. Before they retired to Seville they traveled with the P. T. Barnum Circus. They were both eight feet tall. They no longer are.

The only other county we've not visited along Lake Erie—with the exception of Cuyahoga where Cleveland is—is Lorain County: a mixture of summer cottages, quarries, colleges, foundries, coastline, and that pretty city hall in Wellington, which was once a leading cheese-producing village and the home of Archibald M. Willard, who painted *The Spirit of '76*. Also in Lorain County is Pittsfield, which in 1966 a tornado almost blew away. In this diverse county you'll find all types: farmers who don't understand the Oberlin College students who don't understand the farmers. Here also is Vermilion—and how anyone understands that town is anybody's guess. But let us approach the county with cool heads.

For the moment we'll avoid the lake shore. We'll look at Oberlin College in the village of Oberlin, because where else can you pass a gymnasium and hear—instead of a basketball thumping—someone tooting mournful toots on a French horn? And where else but Oberlin College can you see a bunch of students gazing at a strobe-lighted go-go dancer and trying to resolve her as if she were a mathematical question? Unlike his counterpart at Antioch College in Yellow Springs, the Oberlin student is well-scrubbed and friendly. But like his Antioch counterpart the Oberlin student is used to getting dirty looks from area locals beyond the basic area of the campus, the locals considering all the students childlike upstarts who go around rocking boats. It is true that both Antioch and Oberlin students travel the same curious route, both sets are thoughtful and reasonably intelligent children, but as noted at Oberlin the students are friendly, whereas at Antioch they are not. A sense of friendliness pervades the Oberlin campus. A visitor doesn't get the feeling the student body is about to froth at the mouth at the approach of a stranger. At Antioch, on the other hand, the students seem to distrust everyone, including each other as well as themselves. Chilly. At times a most lonely place.

What of Oberlin College, though, and the village of Oberlin itself? Well, just as Oberlin students have mixed feelings about the world they're supposed to inherit, so does the campus have about its architecture. Whether the over-all architectural effect is good or bad is anyone's guess, all guesses being subjective, but Oberlin does point up a basic problem. For instance around Tappan Square, the village commons, are all kinds of college buildings. There is Cass Gilbert's Allen Art Museum, a structure left over from another architectural era. It has an enclosed courtyard that contains an iron dragon that squirts water from its mouth—and some suggest wistfully the dragon is a bewitched math major. Next door is the Hall Auditorium which Wallace Harrison designed. A lavish and modern facility that in a proper setting would be a thing of airy beauty, there it stands, architecturally becalmed. Meanwhile directly across Tappan Square is an even stranger heap called Peters Hall—that outlandish and poorly conceived but beloved old stone building which has towers and turrets to spare as well as bay windows where no bay windows should be. Next to this beautiful bad dream is

Minoru Yamasaki's Conservatory of Music—the new structure being in direct and shattering contrast to the ill-proportioned Peters Hall. But put them all together, say some Oberlin faculty members, and "under the softening shade of Oberlin's magnificent elms, they (these diverse buildings) reflect the inherent unity of a remarkable educational institution."

Anyway the question is: should a campus be designed (packaged) as a satisfying architectural unit, the twin of planned suburbia and poetic industrial park? In other words, should the style of building A be in harmony with building B and so on, as new buildings are added? This dilemma can be seen both at Oberlin and at Oxford, where Miami University is. Oberlin has let each building stand on its own architectural merits whether it blends or not. Miami University, on the other hand, starting out with a sweet campus of red brick buildings, maintains the red-brick motif to the dreadful point where too much has become too much. Instead of looking like the university it once did, Miami University has the appearance of a vast industrial complex—with trees—proof that any half-truth, even an architectural one, embraced completely to the exclusion of other half-truths makes the one who embraced it grotesque. So there sits Miami University, an educational brickyard, and there sits Oberlin College, an architectural hodge-podge that surprises you with charm.

But a college or university is more than its buildings—much more. Oberlin College started in 1832, when two Yankee missionaries—advertised as "without liberal education, unendowed with more than ordinary intellectual gifts, and wholly destitute of financial resources"—got together to help the world spiritually. Their names: Reverend John J. Shipherd and Philo P. Stewart. Well, after they talked, read, and prayed together, they decided to start a colony of Christian homes and a school to give the benefits of education to both sexes, there being only two in those uncomplicated days. So the first log cabin was built in 1833. When Oberlin College—then called the Collegiate Institute—opened that year, it opened with 44 students: 29 men and 15 ladies. Oberlin got the name Oberlin from Alsace-Lorraine pastor John Frederick Oberlin, who inspired the frontier with his preachings. In 1853 Oberlin College voted to admit students regardless of color, being the first college anywhere to adopt this policy. It was also the first to let the girls graduate with the same degrees the men got.

Opening first was Oberlin's theology department, which in 1916 became the graduate school of theology and which 50 years after that was spun off—as they say in the *Wall Street Journal*—to merge with Vanderbilt Divinity School—and that was that. Although Oberlin College has never had any formal denominational ties, it has always been—murmurs its catalogue—of a strong Christian heritage. Perhaps best known of all Oberlin activities, other than its Big Ten football team,

175

Saturday morning chores. Oberlin College.

Saturday evening chores. Oberlin College.

which plays usually to half-empty stands, is the Conservatory of Music, founded in 1865 as a private school but merging with Oberlin College two years later. Today Oberlin College has about 2000 students in its college of arts and sciences, plus around 450 in its conservatory.

When we get to Yellow Springs—and Antioch College—we shall look deeper into the matter of whether such colleges as Oberlin and Antioch should justify themselves to Ohioans—and whether they should even try. But for the moment let us simply wander across Tappan Square, twirl once on the Oberlin O, which is a plaque where the diagonal walks merge in the center, and make a wish: wishing that Presti's had not evolved into a most elegant restaurant but had remained as in days of yore, a wonderful and full-bodied drinking hole that each Saturday afternoon smelled of stale beer, pig farmers, and the faint scent of a certain blonde's perfume. We'll have one last beer and bid fond farewell—as the poets say—to village, campus, and student body, the last caring little because they will be too busy kissing, reading Chaucer, and playing the French horn, the more adept doing all simultaneously. Some of the people who attended Oberlin? Well, there was Alan D. Schulz, Nancy Johnson, William Summers, and someone else, but he drank a lot. Anyway, Oberlin being academically sounder than most, all is well that ends well. Because of Oberlin and Antioch, we have Ohio State and Miami Universities; and, wheels within wheels, because of Ohio State and Miami Universities, we have need of Oberlin and Antioch—more than ever. Better that children should play at being grownups than grownups play at being children.

Now let's admire Wellington. The Penn Central roars through this village of about 4000. Here you'll find a collection of genteel homes, fresh cut from the gardens of yesterday, many with wrap-around and ornate porches and some with widow's walks up there on the roof. One, though, is a funeral home—the penalty of progress. The Wellington town hall, as noted, is the nicest anywhere this side of Disneyland. Wellington's business district is "Early American rural," and the village has industry about, as well as some sections that are less than charming. But Wellington is all right. Anyway, where else can you find an old-fashioned church with a wildly ornamented steeple?

Pittsfield, which almost blew away, may have. It is little more than a crossroads. La Grange, another small farming village, has a water tower, graveyard, a few farm buildings, a town square with a statue in it, and—well, that's it. Also in the area are Amherst and South Amherst; South Amherst has 3000 people and quarries.

Up the road from Oberlin is Elyria, which about 150 years ago was nothing but wilderness, a log cabin, a dam, and a water-powered mill on the Black River. Heman Ely founded the place in 1817. Now Elyria has more than 50,000 people, an industrial complex of more than 100 manufacturing establishments, and Cascade Park, a dab of green and waterfall within a parking ticket of the business district. Elyria—nearly 17 square miles of industry and 15,000 homes—is halfway between Chicago and New York on the turnpike and is the only Ohio city that claims [or cares to claim] the honor of being smack dab on the gadget. In Elyria you'll find the world's largest chrome-plating plant, producer of golf balls, manufacturer of man-made crystals, and producer of automotive brakes. Downtown, though, is a rather sorry and gray shopworn area that has beautiful shops but needs, as an area, a little beautification.

At first glance *all* of Elyria seems the dreary same: middle-class and lower-income housing bunched together and painted with grime. But look again—out along the Black River, for instance—and you'll see homes that have price tags of $60,000 to $100,000. And south of the turnpike on the west bank, homes sell for $50,000 to $75,000. Lest you feel that Elyria is a combination of the well-heeled and the poor, lest again. South and west of the Eastern Heights Recreation field homes peddle for $20,000 to $50,000. And in the University Heights neighborhood homes list as $25,000 to $35,000. If apartments excite you, Elyria has them, too. Point of these numbers being that Elyria is no junk heap.

Nor is the city filled with slobs. Culture exists there, too. There is the Elyria Little Symphony, a group of local musicians in about every age bracket beyond puberty. This group, which began as a string ensemble and then something happened, presents one concert during the Christmas season and another when spring comes. There is the Black River Playhouse—supposed to be the first community group in the United States to present that group-therapy theatrical called *Who's Afraid of Virginia Woolf?* The playhouse does about a half-dozen different productions each season.

How did Elyria start? In 1817, as noted, Heman Ely established a settlement on 12,500 acres of Western Reserve land where Elyria is today, locating at this point because of the water power from the Black River, which forks at this juncture into its east and west branches. He built a log cabin and a dam at the site, employing the water power to operate his saw-, grist-, and logging mills. In 1824 Elyria became the Lorain County seat, in 1833 was incorporated as a village, in 1852 the New York Central Railroad chugged through, and in 1892 Elyria became a full-fledged city. It was the first city in Ohio to draw water from Lake Erie. So today in Elyria are four municipal parking lots and many private ones, adding up to 4000 parking spaces, or—if women are driving—2374 parking spaces. Says the Elyria chamber, "Elyria has more than 400 retail outlets and $100,000,000 a year in basic buying income in a retail trading area that numbers 175,000 people."

179

The largest employer is Ternstedt Division of General Motors. The second largest is the Air Brake Division of Bendix-Westinghouse Automotive Brake Company.

Along Lake Erie between Sandusky and Cleveland is commercial, tourism, and loneliness—and always out there, unless Elyria drinks a lot, is Lake Erie. In the winter this is melancholy landscape. The whitecaps on the lake seem dark and mean, even when no storm is blackening the wide and empty sky. The chilly boatyards and the ice-cold inlets stand deserted when winter winds blow. This stretch is a wet and sloshy ghostland empty of summer people and empty of summer warmth. While it is possible to travel from Sandusky to Cleveland swiftly by expressways, let us travel the lake road. The first town east of Sandusky is Huron, home of yesteryear's steamboat builders, and today a gathering of substantial houses that are genteel and beautiful. Also, here and there: trailer camps. To us, Huron is about the most beautiful town on this whole stretch—and that means from Toledo to Ashtabula and Conneaut. But Huron has industry, much of it. Here you'll see freighters being loaded. Here is one marina after another, each more beautiful than the one before. Here are old-fashioned homes like New England used to make. What sort of place is Huron? Other than completely charming, it has—tucked away somewhere out of sight—2700 acres available for industry. Six miles thataway is the Ohio turnpike. Huron is served by the Norfolk & Western Railway as well as the Penn Central. A bunch of freight lines are on tap, too. One of Huron's industries is Agway Incorporated, an outfit owned and managed by farmers, the corporation being the result of a merger in 1964 of the Eastern States Farmers Exchange and the Grange League Federation. Employing around 170, Agway's principal product is animal and poultry feed. The Cleveland Stevedore Company leases the ore and coal docking facilities in Huron. Coal, iron ore, and stone have been handled through here since 1912. Waste carbon dioxide is obtained from the Dupont plant, where it is purified and turned into both liquid carbon dioxide and dry ice at the Cardox Division of Chemetron Corporation. That is in Huron—plus a bunch of other industries, making Huron sound like a sorry little town with a funny-smelling sky, but such is not the case. Huron is beautiful. In its Nickel Plate Park you'll find a bathing beach they call one of Lake Erie's finest—as, in this area, all beaches are listed. During the summer months Huron is headquarters for boaters, having docking facilities for 1800, with more docks being added each season. The town covers over five square miles and averages 231 sunny days a year. The county gets an average of 28 inches of snow each season compared with 42 inches in Cleveland and Toledo. A community of approximately 7000 people midway between Cleveland and Toledo, Huron is as they say, "in the heart of Lake Erie's vacationland." The town has about 2000 homes, of which 1999 are delightful.

In that long stretch between Huron and Vermilion—which is something else again—is a scattering of villages, billboards, and—since the advent of expressways emptiness. At Beulah Beach between the highway and the lake is the Christian Missionary Alliance, which has the appearance of a company town filled with the religious. Little Mitiwanga seems to be only a convention of motels, each out-bidding the other in everything but elegance. And scattered along the highway and Lake Erie are inlets and filling stations. Near Vermilion is Volunteer Bay, which, though it looks residential, can be driven through in two minutes with your eyes shut. But civilization along the lake road refuses to peter out. From the air at night a string of lights—houses, businesses, industries—link Cleveland with Toledo. There are occasional farms, farming occasionals and other things, but always on the lake side of the road you are within reach of a motel, an arm's-length reach. Some are beauties, some have seen better days, and for a few there were no better days. Dealer's choice. Then, before you know it, you're in Vermilion.

Vermilion calls itself the city with a million opportunities, a few of which it has missed. The first known permanent settler was William Heddy, who built his home on the west bank of the mouth of the Vermilion River. In 1850 Captain William Austin built the first sailing boat to leave Vermilion—that being the only way to exit. The timber along the banks of the river supplied the planks for its hull. And, says the Vermilion chamber, chips from the old shipyards of those bygone days are still found on the river's west bank. In 1841 things began to happen to Vermilion. The federal government began to look after the Vermilion harbor, the river was dredged, piers were built, and Vermilion was off with one of its million opportunities. First, it became a busy Great Lakes port, furnishing sailors faster than any other lake town. Also, Vermilion claims to have the lake's largest fishing fleet. Because the iron industry thought it might locate in Vermilion, railroads became interested in the town. So in 1842 one of the first six railroads in Ohio received a $44,000 grant to build a line that would connect Vermilion to Ashland. But something happened. The line was never completed —and out the window went one of Vermilion's one million opportunities. However, in 1853 the Lakeshore and Michigan Southern Railroad tooted through town. It didn't exactly toot the first time through. Its first locomotive was brought by boat across the lake from Buffalo and to get it from the docks to the tracks, teams of oxen pulled it. Since lumbering became one of Vermilion's industries, lumber sailing vessels and barges came to load and unload at the Fischer Lumber Company docks. As late as 1900 some of these boats were still moored at Vermilion in the winter, both sides of the river being lined with them, sailing and steamboats alike. William Austin opened the first Vermilion hotel, his clients being travelers and sailors. Other hotels were built: the Maudelton, Lakeside Inn,

Wagner House, Bassett (where the schoolteachers stayed), and the Stagecoach Inn. Many of these fine old structures are still there, but usually as something else.

The town says it has the largest small boat harbor on the Great Lakes. The area around Vermilion is mainly flat, with a few rolling hills, but where the Vermilion River valley is, the geography gets a little rowdy. The town was named Vermilion by the Indians because of the color of the soil. Vermilion today has nearly 9000 residents, two swimming pools, a bunch of private beaches, fourteen public parks, two outdoor skating rinks, and a putt-putt golf course. And in the summer, Vermilion has lots and lots of tourists. Its major ambition these days is to turn itself backward in time and make itself into what it calls "Harbourtown 1837" by having the businesses redecorate in old-time styles. They even have a flag: an all-white schooner on a background of nautical blue. Harbour Square is the brand-new old name given the block along Liberty Avenue between Main and Grand Streets. This is going to be the "trial" block in the antiquing of the town. A barbershop will be done over into yesterday and renamed The Captain's Chair. The outside of the coffee shop will be changed and the place given a new name: The Ship's Galley. Another shop being remodeled will end up an old sailing loft, a switch from the coin-op laundry it is. Say the city fathers, "When it all started we (realized) our city could go three ways. It could slide into decay, it could undergo urban renewal, or it could be preserved historically."

And so Vermilion launches into another one of its million opportunities, and we'll soon see what happens. Actually Vermilion right now has charm, some of which should not be tinkered with, but the city fathers are right: much of the place needs work. When you approach Vermilion from either side of the lake, you are greeted by a litter of advertising signs and so many commercial establishments that you have the uneasy feeling it will take Vermilion years to antique the whole shooting match. At the moment, its downtown section seems resortland quaint, but there's hope. One of the streets is called Happiness Street. Only in Vermilion, then, can you find happiness. We wish Vermilion well; or at least, we wish it something.

Between Vermilion and Lorain—still following the lake road which is U.S. 6—there is a constant stream of trailer camps, suburbia, and advertising signs. Here and there you'll see a huge plant. Around Vermilion, for instance, the whopping Ford plant. As you get nearer Lorain, you see smudges in the sky, and so the city announces itself. But if you look upon Lorain as strictly a steel-mill town, look again, and be surprised. Lorain—plunked down on the northern edge of Ohio—is one of the nation's more international cities. First things first, though.

When Lorain was platted in 1834 as the result of a survey, it was established at the mouth of the Black River. The plat, signed by surveyor Edward Durand and with its simple fifty-word description, has been called "Lorain's birth certificate," the filing of which was the city's first step to development. Three years later the place was called Charleston. It wasn't called Lorain until 1872 when the railroad came. Then the post office refused to call the town Charleston because the state already had one. So Lorain became Lorain. But it wasn't always the friendly place it is today. When the first white man attempted to settle there, he was told to move on—to Sandusky. He was David Ziesberger who came in 1787 with his Christian Moravian Indians to pick wild potatoes, eat wild plums, and catch wild fish. His group lingered only three days before getting walking papers. One of the first settlers—who stayed—was Azariah Beebe and another was Nathan Perry, Jr., who came from Vermont to Lorain when Lorain was nothing but plums, trees, lake, and mud. Perry opened a store to trade with the Indians. Three years later his uncle arrived with a bunch of other settlers, one being John Reid whose cabin served as tavern, post office, and justice office. By the time the Germans arrived in 1833, a lot of trees had been chopped down and the wilderness had been shoved to the village limits. First, Lorain was a shipbuilding center. Here in 1837 the first steamboat was launched, *The Bunker Hill*, named for a New England tourist attraction. In the middle of the 1800s, though, the Toledo-Cleveland railroad bypassed Lorain, going instead through Elyria. Much gloom. For the next fifteen years, Elyria got the business that might have been Lorain's. Many people left Lorain then. But good times again: there was the first passenger train chugging through, connecting Lorain with Cleveland and Wheeling. By having the railroad connect the port of Lorain with the Ohio River, Lorain became the transshipment center connecting the mills of Pennsylvania with the mines of the northern peninsula.

But it was the twentieth century—the period and not the train—that made Lorain come of age. Gloom had again come to the town. Cleveland—and not Lorain—was growing fast. Then the brass works which had been Lorain's chief industry shut down. But every cloud has a silver lining or at least a grimy one. When the officials of Johnson Steel Company said listen if you guys will improve your river channel, we might just move our steel mill up there—and Lorain did, Johnson Steel did, thus in 1895 the first "blow" of steel took place in Lorain, introducing the city to a brand-new destiny. About 1200 men were employed. The Lorain Works is now a part of United States Steel Corporation, its Lorain plant being the largest pipe mill in the block, and hiring about 8000 men. Right about the time the steel mill started, the Lorain horsecars were replaced by electric trolleys which, passing the mill and clanging bells at it, went as far as Elyria.

Illustrious citizens? Lorain offers you Admiral Ernest J. King, who in 1944 held the highest office in the Navy, that of Admiral of the Fleet, a position only equaled by chief petty officers.

Lorain calls itself the international city—and with good reason. This port serves interlake ships as well as those ocean freighters that come from places like pretty far away. In Lorain itself are more than fifty nationalities and ethnic groups. The 1960 census showed that 21,332 of the city's 68,932 residents were either foreign-born or foreign by mixed parents. The first major group of immigrants to settle in Lorain were from the coal fields of England, Wales, and Scotland—and from the shipping districts of Norway and Sweden. The steel works attracted bunches—and by 1900 people from Poland, Hungary, Yugoslavia, and Italy began fighting over seats in the trolley cars. Foreign nationalities having the largest representation in Lorain based on the 1960 census were the Polish, 3197; Hungarians, 2882; and the Czechs, 2219. Since the census was taken Puerto Ricans have come to Lorain, their number estimated in 1967 at 6000. The 1967 population figures give Lorain 81,400 residents.

The big event in Lorain is the International Celebration held each summer. All nationalities turn out. All kinds of eating exists. Just some of the booths and people and moods: German, Greek, Hungarian, Irish, Italian, Lebanese, Macedonian, Mexican, Negro-American, Polish, Portuguese, Puerto Rican, Rumanian, Russian, Serbian, Slovak, Slovenian, Syrian, Ukrainian, and one other. Lorain has its own United Nations and, at times, the one in Lorain seems more effective.

Lorain, of course, sometimes has a skyful of smog because that is the way steel mills are. Around 28th Street and Grove is a particularly disenchanting section. Here, as far as you care to look, are the great plants all decorated with safety slogans. Streets are lined with row after row of sad little houses. But on the west side of Lorain—away from the smokestacks—Lorain is okay. Here, bunched together and well-tended, are the homes one finds in an industrial dormitory filled with responsible people who care. So give Lorain A for effort. Or is that an E?

Let us proceed eastward. We pass through an area of lake, sky, sky smudges, and greenhouses. Avon is around here—a lower-middle-class sort of community, or so it seems, strung out at times one street wide forever. Then, there is Avon Lake.

Then there is Cleveland.

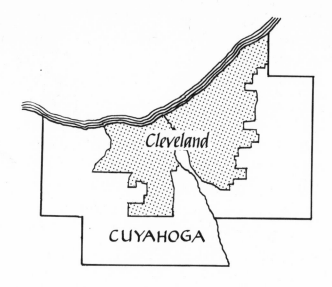

10

To put Cleveland and the county it dominates into one oversimplified pigeonhole is foolishness we'll not attempt. Cleveland with its many satellite communities—many of which are themselves separate and distinct corporate entities—is many things. Although Cleveland can be said to be the Cleveland Tower that looks out over all that it can handle, Cleveland is more than can be seen from there; it is a lot beyond: seen, unseen, on top, underneath, here, there, and everywhere. Because, you see, Cleveland is Ohio's largest city. It is Ohio's most metropolitan city. It is Ohio's most cosmopolitan city. But Cleveland was not always this. To be honest, it wasn't always here.

Cleveland was first surveyed in 1796 by General Moses Cleaveland, his premise being the location looked like a good place for a trading post. It wasn't until 1846 that coal trundled to Cleveland by oxcart from Pennsylvania. The coal merged with copper and iron ore floated across the lake from Minnesota. Thus a match was made to turn Cleveland into the industrial giant that is present-day. Cleveland, home of Don Martello's wonderful clan as well as of actress Ruth Saada, quickly became capital of the Great Lake iron ore industry. And for forty years Cleveland was oil capital of the nation. Cleveland evolved so much muscle that after the Civil War it was the second largest city in Ohio and by 1900, the largest. This is where the automobile industry began. This is where the aviation industry began. This is where, even in times of slack, a city booms. This is where the wind blows cold and, upon occasion, the Cleveland Browns play hot.

Cleveland—cosmopolitan, metropolitan!

When the first settlers came from New England and New York, the land was wilderness: trees had to be chopped to clear space for farming and Higbee had yet to hire its first floor walker. Cleveland grew fast from trading post to transportation hub. Irish came to dig the Ohio canal and tell Pat-and-Mike jokes. Italians came to lay the railroad tracks linking Cleveland with the east and west. Germans came to operate the machine tools and to work in textile mills. Welsh came to work in steel plants. From Central Europe came Bohemians, Lithuanians, Serbs, Poles, Bavarians, Austrians, and Prussians. From sixty-three different nations they came—some with hope and most lonely, each with his old-world language, customs, and religion to this place called Cleveland, where—almost overnight— the steeples of New England and Mormon churches were joined by spires of the Byzantine Orthodox Cathedral, all shouting twilight prayers up to where God is. At one moment three out of every four people in Cleveland were either foreign- born or of foreign-born parents. More than one half of everyone in Cleveland was under thirty. Cleveland was a young city, full of verve and vinegar, and beginning with youthful citizens, Cleveland has yet to get over its youth.

Forgive us Dayton, Columbus, and especially Cincinnati (where we were foisted off upon all of you), because if we seem pleased with the idea of Cleveland, we suggest only that our pleasure is reasonable, that we have a native pride in Ohio things, and that if Ohio is to have value, then Cleveland must have value, which, viewed as a stranger or as a friend, it has. In 1842 the brigantine *Columbia* crossed the gray and flat waters of Lake Erie with the first shipment of the aforemen- tioned Minnesota mine's iron ore—142 tons—to launch in Ohio our greatest city. During World Wars One and Two Cleveland muscle supplied the plates to build the ships our country needed.

Cleveland, technically, is a divided city. In the middle is the industrial and business district. On both sides exist vast acreage of tenements, old neighbor- hoods, and suburbia. Although the area in the Cuyahoga River Valley has been traditionally the iron and steel section, growing pains and need for elbow room are expanding this complex. But here's where you'll find Republic Steel, Jones & Laughlin, and so many others. And up there on the streets, a bridge crossing away, are the city's boutiques, beautiful restaurants, great department stores— plus wild and wonderful markets filled with clangor and produce.

After the oil strike at Titusville in Pennsylvania, the oil was first brought to Cleveland through the wilderness by creaking horse-drawn wagons. Now in Cleveland millions of gallons of gasoline are consumed at a gulp. Sixteen thousand people are employed in its chemical industry. And the things Cleveland doesn't make, it makes the parts for. Cleveland supplies the bits and pieces and hardware for both automobiles and airplanes. The first auto built for sale was built in

187

A city of bridges. Cleveland.

Ethnic festivals everywhere. Cleveland.

Beautiful people with broken English. Cleveland.

Cleveland—and here, too, the first auto was sold. It was an ice-cooled one-cylinder job, asking price $2000. Thomas White and his sons made trucks here. Here were made the Peerless, Jordan, Chandler, Sterns, Winton, Baker, and Rauch-Lang. Over the years as many as eighty different brands of automobiles were born here.

Cleveland certainly is more than a steel mill or a trolley to catch home. Greater Cleveland—and that means whatever you'd like it to mean—has over 17,000 retail establishments. Forty per cent of the people in Cleveland's Standard Metropolitan Area—another measurement you can picture however you choose—are employed in manufacturing. Services like barbers, auto mechanics, cab drivers, secretaries, porters, plumbers, et al., require a 56,000-person task force. Greater Cleveland produces three fourths of all the hothouse tomatoes in the world and has earned the title "Greenhouse Capital of America." Greenhouses dot the landscape south and southwest of Cleveland. From here come 64,000,000 pounds of tomatoes each year, from 4000 acres—all under glass. In Cleveland's construction business 28,000 people work. Nine hundred million gallons of water are pumped each day from Lake Erie (no wonder Lake Erie is the shallowest of the Great Lakes) and via nearly 4000 miles of water mains is distributed to those in Cleveland who care for the stuff. Cleveland, by the way, has on tap 30 per cent of the world's fresh water supply. This is the land where the cash register rings to the tune of whopper numbers because over 200,000 households have more than $10,000 to spend each year. Here is also the Federal Reserve Bank with branches in Cincinnati and Pittsburgh.

And Cleveland is more than industrial muscle and a guy going broke on $10,000 a year. Cleveland is a research center. One laboratory says that it alone during every working day of the year improves an old product or creates a new one. Consider Cleveland's University Circle Research Center, a non-profit corporation formed by the Case Institute of Technology, Western Reserve University, and the University Circle Development Foundation. When finished, the circle will contain 3,000,000 square feet of floor space in which you'll find 7000 research workers shouting new math at each other. This center will give commercial researchers access to the brain power of those professors and graduate students not on picket lines or signing petitions. Cleveland is also out of this world, being selected as a site for NASA engine laboratories after NASA gave sixty-one other cities the once-over. The NASA Lewis Center here does things with advance propulsion and space power generation.

The University Circle, by the way, has been called the "modern Athens," being the largest accumulation of education and cultural facilities in the world—or, should anyone quarrel with that, in Cuyahoga County. In its two-and-a-half-mile

191

area are buildings and galleries devoted to music, education, and the cultural interests of men if such cultural interests are above the reading of earthy paperbacks. As for Cleveland's culture, consider for a moment the Cleveland Art Museum, which has everything from Persian pottery to "pop" and "op" by local artists. Here you'll hear gallery talks and see art movies not shown at the less esoteric adults-only houses. Here are music festivals. And here each Saturday morning 1500 children descend like locusts to play at being Rembrandt. During the art museum's May Show thousands of Clevelanders get the chance to gape, look on in bewilderment or pleasure, and buy the works of regional artists. The Metropolitan Opera, sponsored by the Northeastern Opera Association, appears for a week each year in Cleveland Public Auditorium where famous opera stars sing operas at you. The Lake Erie Opera Theatre also has a three-week season at Severance Hall and sponsors, in addition, a Youth Opera Week to interest the area children and George Condon in same. The Cleveland Ballet Guild has a season, also, at Severance Hall, usually on tippy-toes. As for drama, there's a Don Martello homecoming plus the Cleveland Playhouse, which operates three theaters on a permanent basis with professional actors and professional theater technicians. Plays and Broadway musicals are the usual fares. Each year the Children Theater trains 400 smallfry. The Shakespeare Festival for Children plays each season to 2500 students. And the Caramu House, which started as an interracial community center in 1950 has become a showcase for dramatic, music, and choreographic events.

If you like to sniff flowers, consider the Cultural Gardens: that unbroken, heavily sniffed chain of nineteen gardens along the fringe of Rockefeller Park. Dedicated in 1939, each park is supposed to represent a nationality group which contributed to cosmopolitan Cleveland. The descendants of these various ethnic sets have been encouraged to put up art objects, statues, and flowers reminiscent of their homeland culture. The city of Cleveland itself, though, goes around and cuts the grass. There's the garden for the blind, a beautiful thought, the latest and most unusual addition to the park system. The garden is designed so it abounds with flowers of many different fragrances. Here, too, are signs in Braille and tape-recorded messages the blind can hear. Who said we never promised you a rose garden?

On the other hand, if you're allergic to greenery, books might turn you on. Cleveland leads all cities per capita in the circulation of books. Each year the Cleveland library system circulates more than 7,000,000 volumes—many of them by Faith Baldwin. Downtown its main facility is the architectural marriage of two separate buildings. Also, the system has three dozen branches as well as 40 libraries in schools and 1100 in classrooms. Two bookmobiles add to the rush-hour traffic, delivering joy. One of the nation's three Union Catalogue Systems is at the Western Reserve University. This system has more than two dozen contributing academic libraries—and is said to be the largest in the nation. It catalogues books and journals and other materials not usually on tap. This free service is available to business and research people.

Musically, there's Severance Hall again, where the concerts are played. And between seasons there's Blossom Center between Cleveland and Akron, where the Cleveland Symphony does its summer thing. Other than the Cleveland Symphony, there's the Philharmonic Orchestra, the Society for Strings, the Suburban Symphony, the Cleveland Chamber Music Society, the Cleveland Women's Orchestra, and the Chamber Players. Concerts and recitals are held, in addition, at the Cleveland Art Museum, the public library, and the Institute of Music.

For conventions, consider Cleveland's Convention Center—a $17,000,000 complex that has nearly 500,000 square feet of space inside. Here is where everything happens from flower to boat shows. The Convention Center is within walking distance of the downtown hotels (on wintery windy days, within running distance) and overlooks a concrete mall which is a spacious thing of fountains, gardens, landscaping, and a great pool that winter causes to steam. Underneath all this is a 500-car garage.

While involved in cultural items, let us look at the Rumanian Folk Museum to be found in St. Mary's Rumanian Church in the Cultural Building on west side's Warren Avenue. This is the only Rumanian folk art museum this side of Rumania—unless, that is, you peer into flat buildings that contain Rumanian grandmothers—here being found a bunch of peasant costumes, 500 pieces of embroidery, ikons, weaving, rugs, ceramics, Easter eggs, as well as a typical Rumanian peasant room lifted bodily from the old world and plunked down in Cleveland.

If you are interested in eating, either nationally or internationally, Cleveland is the town for you. Check the shops. You can find strudel dough that is stretched so thin it hangs over the side of a kitchen table. Yes, the Cleveland bakeries have everything. So do the markets, both the Central and West Side markets. And anyone with imagination—or a friendly cab driver and Cleveland has plenty of those—can discover small ethnic restaurants as well as good eating at church bazaars and food fairs. Try the bakeries along the west end of Bolivar Street for baklava. Another bakery on Lorain Avenue sells honey-rich dough that lets you make your own. A Buckeye Road bakery sells Hungarian nut rolls. Man can not live by bread alone, but on the other hand, if he wants to try, we suggest the Cleveland bakeries for variety. Many of the bakers were trained in the old country methods. In butcher shops scattered about the city you'll get sausages and meats —cooked to national specifications. Each ethnic group has its own soul foods. If chiterlings and tripe turn your taste buds on, Cleveland has those too. And where else can you get peanut butter—ground while you wait? Much of these goodies you'll find at places like the Central Market, East Fourth and Huron, or the West Side Market, 25th and Lorain. These markets are rowdy, noisy affairs with row upon row of stall after stall, each containing an Italian angrily shouting his wares. Although only the lower class seem to battle this horn of plenty, look carefully, and you'll see the stingy rich tasting melons, too. A visit to the Central Market is one long, loud harangue of non-stop stalls, pushy people, and bright-colored foods. In the winter you can catch a gourmet meal there—or pneumonia. Whatever your hankerings—from fish to fruit to meats—the Central Market has it. The atmosphere is festive, inexpensive, damp, and wonderful. Outside the great structure, a traffic jam is the entertainment. Inside is another. But everyone— vendor and shopper alike—seems to get along with everyone else and, we presume, they all go home in the evening, exhausted, hoarse, and happy.

Other than food of that sort, Cleveland manufactures a lot of other kinds: frozen prepared foods, frozen fish products, bread, pretzels, potato chips, food for restaurants, and—as mentioned before—all those tomatoes, plus water cress. If you want to pass the salt, Cleveland has its own salt mine. In restaurants you can eat anything you like: German, Chinese, Hungarian, French, Greek, Italian, Jewish, Mexican, Polish, Serbian, and one other style that has not proved too popular this time of the year.

Or, as they say in the Navy, if you can't shape up, you can ship out, Cleveland being an international seaport. Cleveland, largest city on Lake Erie, is also Lake Erie's largest overseas general cargo port as well as the best equipped. It has the largest heavy-lift crane of any lake port, the crane being able to lift 150 tons without batting an eye it doesn't have—and swing the load around with a 65-foot radius. For most ships coming into the lakes from overseas, Cleveland is the first port of call, being the shortest transit time to mid-America. Also, Cleveland is the last stop for overseas jobs going back home before leaving the lakes, still being the shortest transit home the other direction, which is actually the same direction only reversed, but you get the idea. By sea and the St. Lawrence Seaway, Cleveland is up to 300 miles closer to many European ports than are our east-coast cities of New York, Philadelphia, and Baltimore.

Sixteen steamships agents do their agenting in Cleveland. They represent forty different steamship lines. Cleveland welcomes all of them, because Cleveland has twenty overseas vessel berths plus more dockside and transit sheds than dreamed of in Vermilion's wildest dreams. The Cleveland harbor is twenty-seven feet deep

Central Market, wild and wonderful. Cleveland.

B'   est port on Lake Erie. Cleveland.

out there, as well as in here where the docks are. But the only thing Cleveland—and the rest of the lake ports—lacks is a twelve-month season for overseas shipping. However, says the chamber, the advantages of Cleveland for eight months are substantial and attractive. And, backing off a bit, says the chamber, although Cleveland is closer to some European ports than New York is, shorter by those 300 miles, almost always the freighters going home stop at Montreal for a cup of coffee and to top off their cargoes for the greater load limits permitted on the open seas and in the deep-draft European harbors. This cuts into the 300 miles' sailing time. But ships from New York also stop at Philadelphia to see the Mike Douglas Show or load up or both, so things even out. Thus, counting the coffee breaks, Cleveland still comes out ahead on transit time. But not as a year-round port. Navigation on the St. Lawrence Seaway is generally eight months out of the year, usually from the first or second week in April until the first week in December. The opening of navigation each year is a hit-or-miss proposition. The opening depends on the disappearance of the lake ice, the condition of the locks, and on which side of bed Cleveland got up that morning.

Other forms of transportation in Cleveland are hitchhiking and railroading. Cleveland has five major railroads. Two of these have national headquarters in town. Three others have regional offices. Three of the largest international railroad brotherhoods—in other words, unions—call Cleveland home. The Penn Central has in Cleveland the world's largest railroad research center to study ways of keeping railroading ahead of the times and—we presume—to shove the passengers off the train at the next flag stop. Three piggy-back facilities—for railroads, that is—have been built in Cleveland. And, in addition to the railroads themselves, over 200 manufacturers in the area turn out bits and pieces of this and that, such as railroad car frames and components for diesel engines. In Cleveland you can also purchase HO stuff.

Trucks? Cleveland has trucking the way barns have mice. More than 140 common carriers help make the Cleveland traffic interesting, Cleveland being one of the largest truck terminuses in Ohio.

For those who fly, there is the Cleveland Hopkins International Airport which has more than 380 landings a day to handle the more than 10,000 passengers who hope none of its ten airlines are taking an unexpected trip to Cuba. The airport is owned by Cleveland. Here, years ago, the early greats of aviation used to fly, sometimes with planes. Connecting the airport with downtown Cleveland is the rapid transit which, within twenty minutes, gets you one way or the other, depending upon where you started from. An airport even closer in, five minutes from the Public Square saloons, is the Burke Lakefront Airport. On the east side of town is the Cuyahoga County Airport. The last year measured, these three fields said hello and good-by to more than 150,000 people. Note, also, sometimes the people stayed home and their things went. Cleveland has, in addition to the passenger lines, three all-freight air-lines.

Expressways now ring Cleveland, but still many workers ride the buses which have replaced the trolleys. More than 116,000 Clevelanders go back and forth each day, many using the transit system buses, the rapid transit trains, and the Shaker trolley—that beautiful trolley line which, though operating in the grand old manner of the beloved trolley cars, is a recollection and a service, but as a service you can't beat it. Also, Cleveland has some commuter trains. Not enough to write home about, though. The rapid transit system is fairly new for Cleveland, but being fairly new, still makes it the best—and only—rapid transit system Ohio has. Cincinnati got ambitious once and started to build a subway, but the subway never got off the ground (you know what we mean) so now the Cleveland Rapid Transit gets the bows while the bus line in Cincinnati gets the bum's rush. The Shaker Rapid Transit which operates the trolleys is owned and operated by the city of Shaker Heights. Fifty beautiful streetcars operate over the line's two branches, carrying an average of 20,000 of the luckiest people in Ohio each day because where else can you ride a trolley? In reality, this is the last trolley line in Ohio. Oh, you can perhaps ride a trolley at the museum in Worthington, but however charming the adventure, the result is not the same. The Shaker trolleys are the last God ever created: the PCC models, or the President Conference Cars. While they lack much of the beauty of antique trolley cars, nonetheless they themselves as the result of too many years, are beginning to acquire a special antiquated charm as they screech around curves and glare—with one angry headlight—at freight trains in the railroad yards of the Cleveland bottoms. Beautiful, beautiful.

In 1847 the first telegraph pole erected in Cleveland connected the city—via dots and dashes—with the east and west. In 1842 the Cleveland *Plain Dealer* began, now called the world's largest morning paper. It employs nearly 2000 people. In 1878, starting as a penny press, the Cleveland *Press* was born. Now it is called the largest afternoon paper in the country. It employs 16,000. The *Wall Street Journal* has offices, printing facilities, and distributing facilities in Cleveland, which also has eighteen foreign-language newspapers and so many suburban dailies and weeklies that wrapping fish is the least of Cleveland's problems. Here, too, you'll find trade papers and magazines printed. And Cleveland—bless you— is the country's largest manufacturer of Bibles, so says Edwin Kuhn, Jr., of the World Publishing Company.

In 1817 Cleveland had only one school; now it has 174, employing 6200 teachers. In addition, out in the county are 31 suburban school districts which

Rapid transit—and the trolley. Cleveland.

employ 7000 teachers. Parochial and independent schools employ another 3200. Of the 15 colleges and universities scattered about here, some are Western Reserve University, Case Institute of Technology, John Carroll University, Baldwin-Wallace College, and the Cleveland State University; these offering graduate courses. The Cuyahoga Community College began in 1963. In 1965 the Cleveland State University acquired the physical plant of Fenn College and it is doing its business there. When recess comes, the students have all kinds of places to play. And so do the grownups.

Cleveland's park system has 63 baseball diamonds, 70 tennis courts, 18 picnic areas, 13 playgrounds, three skating rinks, two artificial skating rinks, 15 football and soccer fields, four boat-launching ramps, bushes to hide behind and kiss, and two 36-hole golf courses, plus a bunch of what are called "in city" parks, where trees are. The metropolitan park district has more than 17,000 acres of what they call an "emerald necklace," the necklace having started in 1915. Here you'll find mile upon mile of bridle paths, numerous playgrounds, softball diamonds, candy wrappers, barbecue pits, woods to explore, trees to climb, streams to fall in, and poison ivy to get. Along the lake shore, everywhere you look, unless you look in the wrong places, are yacht clubs and boat docks. The Cleveland Zoo, started in 1882, now covers 100 acres and has 400 different kinds of animals and things. The Children's Farm there has domestic animals as well as those native to Ohio. Four miniature trains toot from one sight to another, giving the giraffes a change of scenery as each new trainload of disbelievers goes by. If you like to wet your line and no one is looking, try sneak fishing at the Cleveland Aquarium where fishing is frowned upon and where fluorescent sea animals, blink fish, and more than 100 species of marine life are just waiting to go for the bait. Or, second thought, don't fish there. The people who visit after you will have nothing to see —but you being hauled off by the cops.

Cleveland is a town of sports. Here you'll find curling and judo as well as all kinds of horse racing, usually with horses running, trotting, and things like that. In Cleveland people play tennis, skate, ski, and swim. Here the Cleveland Open Pro Classic is held. Here the Davis Cup Champions compete. Cleveland has an American League soccer team. It has a National League football team. It has an American League baseball team. And it has an American League hockey team. Also, Cleveland has 27,000 hardy lads playing in the industrial and softball leagues. With a little luck, you can manage to avoid all of this.

Structurally, Cleveland has a mayor-council form of government. Its 33 councilmen each represent a particular ward. The mayor appoints nine directors to his cabinet to keep an eye on things and help out around the place. In Cuyahoga County, out there beyond the Cleveland city limits, there are about 1,700,000

Ohio's last operating trolley line. Cleveland.

Every city has its zoo.

people governed via 35 cities, 22 villages, and 4 townships. Three of these cities —Bedford, East Cleveland, and Cleveland Heights—have council-manager forms of government, the rest do as Cleveland does. Most of these suburban entities keep control of their own police force, speed traps, school and housekeeping functions. But they leave the matter of welfare, the judicial, and tax collecting to the county government. So there sits Cleveland and the Cleveland Tower, trying its best to be a megalopolis, and out there, smiling blandly, are all those mayors.

The Cleveland Tower, by the way, is the world's eighth tallest building, soon the ninth when that big job in Chicago gets topped. Union Station is located in the underground area of the tower, the station site embracing about 35 acres under the public square whose music shell has the appearance of an overturned Dixie cup. A viaduct three fourths of a mile long connects trains on the western approach over the river valley. The train platforms are used (sparingly these days) by the Penn Central, Norfolk & Western, Erie Lackawanna, Baltimore & Ohio, as well as local transit systems, including the Shaker trolley. The tower goes up 708 feet above the concourse and from the observation deck on a clear day you can see forever and on a foggy day not even the federal courthouse on the square. Look down on a bright, sunny day and you'll see some colorful dots sloshing about, these dots being well-dressed and colorful ladies, Cleveland having a large supply. Says Hyacinth—fashion editor of the *Plain Dealer*—Cleveland "has more fashion shows, more visiting couture designers, more trunk showings, more well-known label fashions than other cities in the United States with the exception of New York and perhaps Chicago, Beverly Hills, San Francisco, Miami, and Philadelphia." Which, when you think about it, doesn't quite put Cleveland at the top of the heap, but no matter. She concludes amiably by suggesting there is nothing new under the sun that Cleveland hasn't heard of or isn't able to get. Says she, "Cleveland has a Fashion Group, part of an international organization composed of women whose lives are dedicated to working in fashion. These are women who annually present a millinery show in the early part of February to let Clevelanders know what is in for the season. Cleveland probably has more fashion shows than any other city its size. To name a few of the larger ones, there are those presented annually by the Junior League, the Great Lake Shakespeare Society, the Council of Jewish Women. . . . "

But none of this tells us what Cleveland really is. We'll try another way. Cleveland, founded in 1796, largest Ohio city, eighth largest city in the country, has an estimated 1967 population of over 800,000 within its city limits and more than 2,000,000 out there fighting crab grass beyond in Cuyahoga, Geauga, Lake, and Medina counties. Metropolitan Cleveland covers some 1521 square miles, reaching about 50 miles along Lake Erie, and dipping inland as far as 20 miles. The east

203

and west sides, as noted, are divided by the heavy industry of the Cuyahoga River Valley, which lies down there practically at lake level, while up there on either side—60 to 80 feet up—the business district is. In more distant suburbia, the subdivisions are as much as 200 to 600 feet above lake level. Downtown is the Public Square from which the city's main streets radiate out and up—east and south and west—to wherever they seem to be going. The county's original network of highways was a network of Indian trails that linked one camp with another so the Indians could say hello or whatever it is they say. Some of these Indian trails became thoroughfares: Lake Road, Center Ridge Road, Turney Road, Aurora Road, Samuelson Pike, and Euclid Avenue. The first street in Cleveland was Superior Avenue.

Once western-style stagecoaches bounced through the dense forests which the bulldozer has cleared for suburbia. The coaches bounced all the way from Buffalo, Pittsburgh, Columbus, and Detroit. But in winter, the roads were silent, snowed in, and closed. In 1827 the Ohio Canal opened. The trip to Cleveland from Portsmouth took only 80 hours. Then came the steam railroads. Then the expressways. The first highway out there in the Cleveland boondocks was a plank road opened in Chagrin Falls in 1849, built by a private company who charged admission to drag on it. Soon plank roads were everywhere: to Willoughby, Twinsburg, and so on. The trolley car—bless it!—tooted along through the woods, too. Those were the Gay Nineties. Soon, interurban trolleys were going everywhere—along Lakeshore Boulevarde, Euclid Avenue, Mayfield Road, Kinsman Road, Goldflies Pike, Lorain Road, and Westlake Road. By riding the magnificent Toonerville trolleys one could live in the country and work in the city. But soon, alongside each trolley and trying to blast it from the highway via its Klaxon horn, the tin lizzie brayed, honking the trolleys to their deaths. In that lonesome period between 1925 and 1938 the Cleveland area kissed trolleys good-by. All except the Shaker line which we caution you, guard it with your lives. Railroad commuter trains vanished, too. Buses and cars were everywhere, but mostly in front of you. And so there sits Cleveland, wondering what happened.

And around it, the hodge podge of smaller communities. For instance, Parma Heights where the first settlers settled in 1818. Before that Parma Heights was only forest. But in the spring of 1818 along came Conrad Countryman—yes, that's what they said—who built a log cabin. That was the start of Parma. At the present, murmurs Parma Heights, most of its population is 80 per cent American-born but notes that the predominate nationality of some of its foreign-born are German, Polish, and Hungarian. Or consider North Olmstead. Aaron Olmstead who was a soldier in the Revolutionary War and a tea captain in the China trade gave the town its name, his heirs receiving the deed to the township. In 1807 Captain David

Elija Stearns with his two sons, all on horseback because the trolley wasn't running, began the town. In October 1964, North Olmstead led the state in building permits issued. Does that tell you anything? Add Rocky River to the collection of communities. It's on the lake on Cleveland's west side. Rocky River is nearly five square miles of suburbia, most of its 8000 homes being single-unit affairs. Rocky River has just about run out of land to build on. Add Berea, fifteen miles from the Cleveland Tower, in the southwest part of the county. Ninety-four per cent of its homes are occupant-owned. As for business, Berea is mostly a place of small specialty shops. But here, too, you'll find Baldwin-Wallace College, a church-centered liberal-arts college with more than 1500 undergraduates and an evening college with 1000 more. Berea was once described as "nothing but wilderness inhabited by wolves and bears." A lot of sandstone has been found around here—and John Baldwin, in 1830, found most of it, starting Berea's first major industry: the manufacture of grindstones. From that he managed to start Berea Institute with $200,000. The institute and four others combined to become Baldwin-Wallace. The city's name, by the way, was chosen with a toss of a coin. That was in 1836. Berea won. Tabor lost. Berea does manufacture things: bolts, corrugated boxes, knives, nylon stuff, and college grinds, as well as chemical compounds.

Over in the southeastern part of this complex is Solon which calls itself—and rightly so—an industrial suburb of Cleveland. It hinges its future on expressways as well as a bunch of railroads. Whereas some of the suburbia about is filled to brimming, three out of every four parcels of real estate in Solon are available. Some of the business the community has already attracted: Kroger, Container Corporation, Western Electric, and Warner and Swasey. Solon began in 1960 as a city, then with 6000, and now says it has 9000 people. Of the 22.4 square miles which is incorporated Solon, more than 2000 acres are zoned industrial, with 700 acres already industrially developed. Solon at last count had 2500 homes and 74 different kinds of industry plus a bandstand. Planning, says Solon, is the key. The city also proclaims that dirt, grime, smoke, and fumes usually associated with an industrial city are absent in Solon. So give it A for effort. Scattered about Solon are many amiable residential areas.

Chagrin Falls was amiable to begin with and still is. According to the post office Chagrin Falls is the only place anywhere named Chagrin Falls, a fact in which Bob Robbins takes considerable pride. Between 1820 and 1825 Chagrin Falls was settled by such people as Cerenus Burnet, Caleb Alson, and James Fisher. By 1840 industry was there: paper products, flour sacks, woolens, ironware, and woodenware—all getting power from the dams that tried to harness the Chagrin River. Before we get too deep into the innards of Chagrin Falls, let us look thoughtfully at the Chagrin River, a rebellious little stream which drains an area about 260 square miles. The river starts southeast of Chardon, where a small creek flows nonchalantly into Bass Lake, the origin being some 40 miles from where the river finally dumps out into Lake Erie north of Willoughby. Since the river starts 762 feet above the level of Lake Erie, the stream has a lot of downhill running to do before it gets to its mouth. The average drop is nearly 16 feet per mile, more than twice the fall of the Cuyahoga River. During the spring run-off, after a heavy rain, or when anyone upstream spits, the Chagrin River is not the best place to wade. Over 200,000,000 gallons of water a day pour out of the river into the lake. At Chagrin Falls more than 6,000,000 gallons of water go by every twenty-four hours, ten times the amount that the Chagrin Falls water system needs, since Bob Robbins doesn't touch the stuff. Plans for harnessing this power are always being dreamed up. A favorable rate of fall made possible, though, the early industry along there. Now only one mill is left that has need of the stream: the Chase Bag Company which uses only the water and not the power the water can create. And that's the Chagrin River.

The question now stands: how did Chagrin Falls, the city, get its name? Well, it was named for *Shaquin* which means *clear water*. *Shaquin* became *Shagrin* and *Shagrin* became *Chagrin*, and there you are. The town started because of the water power Noah Graves discovered. He had great plans to turn Chagrin Falls into an industrial empire, water power abounding, but his plans went sloshing down the stream to Lake Erie and were never realized. Thus, Chagrin Falls exists today as a serene residential community located, as they say, in the heart of northeastern Ohio's most beautiful residential area. The falls are still there, right on the main drag. Pretty things, too. Add charm to the place. Although residential, Chagrin Falls does have industry, the aforementioned bag company being the oldest and largest in town. Each month it manufactures 2000 tons of paper. Basically Chagrin Falls is a cordial setting of hills, steeples, and school towers. It has four barber-shops, two of which don't have telephones. It has a harness shop, a pair of funeral homes, a dozen beauty shops, eight real estate offices, five taverns and restaurants—some named cute, and a place that sells tombstones.

There is a clutch of other communities in the vicinity, for instance: Moreland Hills, which was organized in 1929, when the world was coming apart at the seams. It has eight square miles of what it says is "scenic rural" as well as golf and polo clubs. The homes are renovated farm homes or better. Add: Orange Township, where James A. Garfield was born. Bentleyville has the distinction of having the smallest population of any city in Cuyahoga County, being two and a half square miles of scenic stuff; the Cleveland Metropolitan Park District waters the grass in 540 acres of the village. Add, too, the Russells: Russell and South

Russell. Russell, a Cleveland suburb, used to be hayseed land, but farms have disappeared. South Russell, on the other hand, dates back to 1849. It occupies a patch of the world one mile wide and four and a half miles long. Anyone for Gates Mills? The village started in 1826, when Halsey Gates built a dam across the Chagrin River, the better to power his sawmill. Here you'll find the Chagrin Valley Hunt Club, said to be one of the most beautiful private clubs anywhere. Gates Mills itself is semi-rural quaint, where polo players talk polo things and if you should ever lose a fox, you'll find a club here that gets its jollies hunting them. The village, located in both Cuyahoga and Geauga Counties, is crisscrossed with riding trails. A section of the village known as Daisy Hill is where the Van Sweringen brothers lived. They built the Cleveland Tower.

If you like villages with interesting names, there's Pepper Pike, which saw the light of day in 1924. Thirteen miles east of the Cleveland Tower, Pepper Pike has two golf clubs: one for family fun and one labeled men only. Woodmere village, which began in 1946, occupies less than one square mile but gets its fame by being the gateway to Chagrin Valley as well as entrance to the outer belt freeway. Bainbridge used to be called Bissell's Corner and Kent's Town. What is there now is rolling suburbia. Plus woods and lakes. Also, consider Auburn, not the wonderful car of yore, but the place. It began in 1815 as forest and farmers, maple syrup being its preoccupation. Then there's—but do you mind if we sit a spell? The area has too many towns: good, bad, and indifferent. We could go on forever sorting out the particles that corporately make up what is, in essence, Cleveland. The towns would fill a book, but not this one.

Cleveland, as we mumbled at the beginning, is too many things. It is the ethnic family trapped in a flat and going to the dogs; and it is the dogs that bay in pursuit of the disenchanted fox. It is neighborhood after neighborhood after neighborhood. It is more suburbia than a bulldozer could love. Cleveland is industry: huge complexes that create steel and a Central Avenue stall that creates shouts. Cleveland is young, old, middle-aged, and everything else. Cleveland is Lake Erie and those who, from one year to the next, never see the lake at all. Cleveland is the Catholic nun, the train station bum, a thousand housewives, and on that corner the man dressed as a woman. Cleveland is Euclid Avenue, a neighbor named Krtchmareck, and the Shaker trolley. Cleveland is expressways and narrow alleys. Cleveland is all the people you'd ever want to meet—and then, five more, waiting to say hello. Cleveland is everything, Cleveland is nothing, Cleveland is —and only is—in the heart.

One last try to capsule this awful wonderful noisy thing: enter Cleveland from the east. Travel Euclid Avenue from where air is fresh and clean through the many neighborhoods till you reach downtown. Maybe somewhere along the way you'll find what Cleveland is. Come with us. Gently. As we come from the east Euclid Avenue—way out there where fresh air is—is U.S. 20. Here, also, is Euclid, the community. Here Charles F. Brush was born. He developed the electric dynamo (who these days has read Eugene O'Neill's spiritual play based on that gadget?) and the arc lamp. Brush gave Cleveland in 1879 its first street lights, Cleveland being the first to have them. Around here and most of the way into town Euclid Avenue will be a wide thoroughfare. Here in Euclid, it is lined with apartment buildings on one side, neat industry on the other. TRW is one of the big antiseptic-looking plants that seems to go on forever. Now we pass 228th Street: a neighborhood of well-built two-story barracks we moderns call apartment buildings. One can feel each family inside its unit, a locked door for a moat, watching color television, and seeing the world through scanning lines. More apartment buildings, more industry. The Fisher Body Division of General Motors, a yellow brick building that goes as the TRW building did—and on and on and on. At 196th Street: the Rosemary Treatment Center for Handicapped Children (fallen sparrows housed in brick). Suburbia apartment buildings overwhelm. There are not this many people in the world. Captives of color television and brick. But the mood of the street begins a subtle change. Still wide, still apartment-littered, a few hills, but gradually, a difference. Though the apartment buildings are well-maintained as are the people walking in and out of them, the neighborhood seems older. Suddenly, passing Arabella Street, we sense the city itself. Too many plants that are too old move in. The feeling we had farther out— that combination residential-industrial—is lost. Here, industry is winning. Thus, Euclid Avenue, filled with this dread feeling, goes on, seeking the Cleveland Tower. Side streets that now cut off from it are lined with acres of two-story one-family homes. Closer in, the buildings get grimier—not from soot but from age. A rapid-transit station appears. The neighborhood has not changed but the faces of the people have: from white to black. The avenue is still six lanes wide, but with cars parked on the curb lanes, the street seems narrower. This is the area of East Cleveland. Here are huge old homes, once magnificent. Now time has crowded them together, making them rub tired shoulders. The side streets? More exhausted housing. We pass a graveyard and another rapid-transit station. We are at 117th Street, surrounded by a sea of factories. There's the Commodore Hotel. The Western Reserve University is here. Or is it? Powerful antique buildings plucked from Grade B movies dominate us. We enter a lonesome little business district of lonesome little shops where buildings—seven stories high— make the street a dark canyon. But here, too, is the setting for wild and beautiful churches, each constructed with stone, mighty as the hand of an angry angel. Now the street is lined with old old homes, many churches, and there—well, that's

A city waiting to happen. Cleveland.

"Who'll buy my balloons?" Cleveland.

the 77th Street Theater in what appears to be a discarded temple. Around here the presence of the blacks is felt. Waiting. Hordes of blacks waiting. The road is wide but the road is lonely. So much waiting. Too much waiting. When will Cleveland happen to them?

If the neighborhoods that lined Euclid Avenue were lonesome before, the loneliness increases, baby. But here, too, is a Holiday Inn. And far off we can see the Cleveland Tower—mecca?—calling. As we cross 36th Street—an area of motels—we see hippies. So what? More of them are at 30th. By the time you read this they will have moved from that corner to another or, via time and troublings, evaporated into thin air. Near Cleveland State University we meet expressways. At 17th Street, movie houses take over. And so do tall buildings. And there's the triangle at 14th—and we are downtown. Yet, back there, as we write this, Euclid Avenue still exists, thousands of people suspended in time in brick buildings called apartments. Cleveland, we offer you apologies. These things are you but none of these things are you.

Yet somewhere in this—between the Cleveland Tower and the melancholy neighborhoods and the pleasant suburbs decked out in early American Formica and the factories and all the people these items feast upon—exists the dream, the beauty, and the anger that is Cleveland. Because Cleveland is much more than an empty terminal lobby, where, on days the wind blows cold, old men assemble, waiting to die. Cleveland is not waiting to die. Cleveland is a child dashing from the school door, running down the street (steel mills in one hand, a million people in the other) racing hell-bent down Euclid Avenue, upsetting yesterdays, racing straight into tomorrow.

11

In the southwest—or lower left-hand—quarter of Ohio, you'll find cities with diverse personalities and moods: Dayton, Xenia, Cincinnati, Circleville, Portsmouth, Hamilton, and Cuba, which Ohio has and to which few planes are hijacked. Geographically this southwest quarter has not one but several personalities. Part of this section is flat-out farmland, with the hills being only an occasional suggestion. Another part is forest wilderness, a place of deep ravines and hills that are the angry foothills of angrier mountains to the east. Here, too, is rolling farmland. Here, scattered about, you'll find cities, villages, pig farms, and coeds. This part of Ohio has some villages that are exhausted and some cities that are exhausting.

Twenty-five miles south of Marzetti's Restaurant in Columbus is Pickaway County where Circleville is. This is the county the Scioto River sloshes through in search of the Ohio River. Agriculture is in the county via 1360 farms each averaging 225 acres, but see one farm, and you've seen 'em all, so let us look instead at Circleville which is parked on 3.28 square miles of land and where, with luck, you'll visit when the Pumpkin Festival is at its height. Circleville is famous for many things, one being Ted Lewis ("Is *everybody* happy?"), a local after whom the city named a park that contains ten acres of tennis courts, ball diamonds, shelter houses, mosquitoes, and picnic areas. So much for the fine arts.

They say that Circleville is one of the few—in fact, there aren't any others—cities to be built to conform to a circular prehistoric earthwork. But you can't tell by looking at it. The earthwork is partly a square enclosure 900 feet across—and connected to a round 100 feet in diameter. No scientific study was ever made of the historic heapings for several reasons. The city fathers kept tinkering with it. First they dug at pieces of it so the canal could get through. And about 1838 they started pecking away at it to square up the streets. So now, thanks to those early American tinkerers, the town's historic asset is no more, but they write about it a lot. Some archaeologists say the earthworks were the result of the Adena Culture. Others say the earthworks were the fault of the Hopewell Tribes. No matter. When digging for the canal, way back then, the diggers came across many interesting items: prehistoric bones, artifacts, and—some say—a few candy wrappers.

To be realistic, except for the different shapes, one Indian mound or earthwork is the same as the other. They each have the stylized differences that separate one Holiday Inn menu from another.

When Pickaway County was formed in 1810, it had no settlement to be the county seat, so Daniel Dresbach started from scratch and laid out the new town. Building it first around the now obliterated circular heap, he designed its streets going every which way from the center like spokes from a wheel. One nickname for the place is Old Roundtown, but there it sits, becalmed and modern and squared. It even has a five-story building. Other than Ted Lewis, listed as one of the top citizens, there's Caleb Atwater who has been called the father of the Ohio public school system. He lived in Circleville for a while, where he wrote the first history of Ohio. Another volume to come from Circleville came forth in the 1880s: a folio called *Bird Nests and Eggs of Ohio*. Benjamin Hanby also lived in Circleville. As all the teen-agers know, he wrote "My Darling Nellie Gray." And that is Circleville, only city of Pickaway County. Its population is about 13,000.

All the other major cities in Pickaway County are pleasant little villages. New Holland, for instance, has a water tower, traffic light, a tired little business district, and about 700 most pleasant people. Williamsport, on the other hand, has nearly 950 equally pleasant people, houses, and water tower with its name on it, too.

Down the Scioto River from Circleville is Chillicothe, in Ross County, which is 40 miles south of Columbus. The county has only one city: Chillicothe, which has nearly 8500 people, plus a few others who are in the Chillicothe Correctional Institute, a clink sponsored by the state to house several of its malcontents. Chillicothe was the first capital of Ohio. In Chillicothe the 1802 Constitutional Convention was held, from which the state of Ohio hatched. A year later a Chillicothe man named William Creighton, Ohio's first secretary of state, designed the state seal of Ohio, an antique and rosy rendering of the hills and valleys as seen from Adena. On the seal—which is as American as blueberry pie and hasenpfeffer— arrows indicate Ohio's sequence into the union, a field of grain stands for the state's fertility, and the rising sun in the background indicates either that Ohio was the first state west of the mountains or that we somehow had a hand in the bombing of Pearl Harbor. Chillicothe, by the way, is Indian small talk for *town*. Nathaniel Massie started the place in 1796 (we'll meet his brother in Portsmouth later) and Edward Tiffin was the state's first governor there. When the canal came through in 1832, Chillicothe was a prospering port. The Mead Corporation started to make paper in Chillicothe in 1892—and hasn't stopped since. Now the Chillicothe Mill for Mead represents one of the world's largest paper complexes and employs nearly 4000 people. Here, too, you'll find the corporate offices for Wear-Ever Aluminum as well as the United States Shoe Corporation, which makes United States Shoes. Present-day Chillicothe is architecturally mixed: Greek Revival, workingman bland, and suburbia decked out in early American Formica.

During World War One more than 50,000 recruits descended upon Chillicothe for training, one of them being Harold Jobes from Greenville. To build the 2000 buildings the Army needed and to lay out the 20 miles of street that Camp Sherman required, more than 18,000 workers assembled. Chillicothe, as is suggested, was a boom town back then. At the end of the war, however, the military post was transformed into a federal industrial reformatory and a veterans hospital, the latter still being there.

The first dental college—open the book wider, please—this country had, started in a small town named Bainbridge, now a town of 1100 people. Also, four miles north of Chillicothe the Hopewell Indians created another one of their many mounds. Thirty-six miles southwest of Chillicothe is the Serpent Mound State Memorial, said to be the largest and most famous earth effigy in the country, or, if not that, years ago before Ohio was settled, the state was populated with rather large moles. So we take fond leave of earthworks . . .

The rest of the county where Chillicothe is, is farming: to be exact, 1333 farms. The leading source of income is from cattle and hogs. Corn comes in third. Ross County ranks first in Ohio with the number of farms that have 400 or more acres, the county having at least 13 of the king-size ones. The county also ranks first in the number of beef cattle, having over 1200 head—as well as the rest of the animal. Elsewhere about the county are only villages like Lyndon which is a train siding, general store, and one unpainted frame structure wondering what happened. Lattaville has a dozen or so houses scattered on the side of a pretty hill. And Slate Mills

215

is a few houses plus highway signs touting the traveler on Chillicothe. Kingston, on the other hand, has over 1200 people, is several blocks wide, and contains many simple but pleasant frame houses, some of which have wonderful porches on which to rock away the summer afternoons. Kingston's downtown business district, if you could call it that, shouldn't be called that.

West of Chillicothe is Washington Court House in Fayette County, the county being second in the state for the sale of hogs and third for the production of same which, via new math, means the county sells more hogs than it raises. Seventy miles northeast of Izzy Kadetz's Kosher Restaurant in Cincinnati, 38 miles southwest of the Jai Lai in Columbus, and 49 miles southeast of Erma Bombeck in Dayton, Washington Court House takes up 4.26 square miles of the county's overall 406 square miles. If you like history, visit Morris Sharp's home in Washington Court House. It is now the Fayette County Historical Society. When he built the huge place he is supposed to have said he wanted to build "the show place of Washington Court House" and whether or not he succeeded is anybody's guess. Here, in the museum, you'll find iron slag supposedly from an Ohio furnace operated by the Vikings long before Columbus got here. Captain A. H. Mallery, who wrote *Lost America* suggests the iron exhibited is the first iron made in North America. The building itself, which can catch you by surprise and make you look twice, is a thing of wonder: a huge and massive and mid-Victorian that goes up five stories, decorated with cathedral-type windows and on the roof an iron fence. Ten years after Mr. Sharp built this place a tornado hit town, did $500,000 damage elsewhere, but his heap survived unscathed.

Washington Court House, population about 14,000, county seat, and only city in Fayette County, started on 150 acres of land donated by Colonel Benjamin Temple in 1811, the colonel and his officers and men having been given land there for their efforts in the Revolutionary War. The colonel said he would like to have the town named after his commanding officer, George Washington. The "Court House" was added to the name to follow the Virginia custom of naming its county seats. The first railroad arrived in 1852, another in 1875, another in 1879, and another in 1884. Originally the land where the city is was swampy, lonely, and vacant. The nearest Indian trail was three miles thataway through the woods. The town grew. Three years after its first log cabin was finished in 1807, the town had enough people standing around and wanting to buy things that Joseph Raunck decided to open a store.

Today Washington Court House is a collection of workingmen's homes, fashionable neighborhoods on the hills, and a business district that isn't quite Fifth Avenue. A good place, however, to park your industry because, as locals are proud to point out, labor strife is either nonexistent or is few and far between. Governor

Museum—with fence on top. Washington Court House.

James Rhodes has called Washington Court House Blue Ribbon U.S.A. because in one three-year period its good people transformed ninety-five acres of farm land into a modern industrial park. Some of the industries that have taken root: the Farm Bureau Cooperative, the Kenskill Trailer Corporation, the Mead Corporation, the Sugarcreek Packing Company, and the Washington Aluminum Casting Company. The park being industrial has no swings but it does have railroad spurs from both the Penn Central and the Baltimore & Ohio Railroads.

West of Washington Court House and 40 miles northeast of Jake Held in Cincinnati is Wilmington. Although the Baptists built the first church in Wilmington, most of the community's early settlers were Quaker. Wilmington is the county seat of Clinton County—and, as with so many counties about here, the only city the county has. Says the Wilmington Chamber of Commerce in a way that charms you, "If you're looking for a city of skyscrapers and a sprawling industrial complex, its streets teeming with shoulder-to-shoulder humanity and bumper-to-bumper traffic, Wilmington is not for you . . ." Well said, fellows. And to that we add that if you seek a county courthouse architecturally different than most that Ohio has, Wilmington again is not for you. On the plus side, in Wilmington is Wilmington College. On the minus side, certain approaches to the city are guarded by a lot of places that sell cars and tractors and hot dogs. Also, Wilmington seems to have more body shops than it has bodies in need of handling. But once inside the city, Wilmington is serene and beautiful. One setting: the four-story brick Denver House where you can rent a room or buy a martini or a meal is one of the most attractive buildings Ohio has—and Ohio has a lot. The Wilmington business district is cramped but clean and shiny. Wilmington has, beyond the Children's Home out there, a swine research center and out there, also, Wilmington College has a dairy farm. Wilmington College, founded in 1870 by the Religious Society of Friends (Quakers), is an architecturally and academically sound four-year liberal-arts college. Its student body is comprised of 900 parts assembled from Ohio, 21 other states, and 13 foreign countries. Here is one of Ohio's better small colleges.

Clinton County, where Wilmington is, is mostly farmland: 90 per cent of the land the farmers tinker with. The county is second in the number of hogs produced in Ohio—and third largest in the whole United States. Near all the pig farms is the Clinton County Air Force Base (does Clinton County *really* have its own air force?), and all around are good highways, railroads, and some industry. Cincinnati Milling Machine has a plant in Wilmington. So does the Champion Bridge Company. So does the H & H Aluminum Casting Company and the National Gear Company. And others. Many villages are in the county. Clarksville with nearly 625 people is one of them: a small and exhausted town. Outside of

Clarksville which is surrounded by flatland stretches of fields and sky is mini-suburbia: a couple of new homes. Then, as mentioned, there's Cuba. It has fewer than a dozen houses strung carelessly along the highway. Although this land in these parts is basically flat, with only an occasional rise, you can sense the presence of hills to the east, and beyond them, the dark presence of mountains and empty forests. And always the villages where township roads meet. New Vienna with 950 people is, however, a town that has a water tower, two church steeples, and a handful of older homes that look pleasant, plus the New Vienna fire department, which houses its equipment in the building that once showed the flicks. But a drive through Clinton County is a melancholy journey. The roads go on forever, farm-houses are few, and except for sudden villages, not a soul is to be seen anywhere. But all around is farmed land. Nothing wild and untouched. Just outside of Wilmington, Lumbertown sits becalmed: a few houses and a huge auto graveyard and that's all—not even a highway sign to slow you down. That might account for the auto graveyard. Oakland is no bigger: a few houses, a gasoline pump, and an entrance to Camp Kirkwood, the Ohio Baptist Convention. Harveysburg is a few more houses, another gasoline pump, and a church in need of paint.

South of Wilmington is Hillsboro in Highland County, the county being 40 miles east of Cincinnati. In Hillsboro was born the Women's Christian Temperance Union. The teetotalers organized in 1873, chief instigator being Eliza Jane Thompson. Her ladies used to go from saloon to saloon, praying a lot in each, and within a month after they started, 100 saloons in 250 Ohio towns bit the dust. Hillsboro, unlike Cincinnati, which some say is but isn't, is built on seven hills. And if you don't drink to that, at least drink to Eliza Jane Thompson.

Highland County, being part of the Virginia Military District, was settled by soldiers from the Revolutionary War. In 1803 Ohio became a state. Two years after that Highland became a county. The county has 594 square miles carved up into 17 townships, its first county seat being New Market which was a village few could reach. So the county seat was moved to Hillsboro. Originally land cost fifty cents an acre in Hillsboro, or at least that's what the hilltop area's 200 acres were purchased for. Located 66 miles southwest of Columbus, 56 miles east of Cincinnati, and 55 miles southeast of Dayton, there sits Hillsboro, a scant 35 miles from the Ohio River which means the river valley hills are closer. Industry in Hillsboro includes the Acro Manufacturing Company which makes snap-action electrical switches and relays; the Gross-Feibel Company, which makes safety deposit boxes and bank vaults; and the Hercules Trouser Company, which makes what you suppose it does. Plus other industries including one that is unique: the C. S. Bell Company, a century-old company that makes—of course—bells. Its steel alloy bells are created from a mixture which, says the company, only it knows how to mix.

219

Says the bell company, "While other firms claim knowledge of secret processes of manufacture unknown to this company, we simply state: that we have engaged in the manufacture of steel alloy bells for a longer period of time than anyone now in the business, and are now making more bells each year than all others combined; that there are no secrets in the trade that we are not fully advised of; and that we have originated more improvements in design and materials peculiar to this class of bells than any other maker. If the hundreds of foundries that have at one time or another engaged in making bells, nearly all have given up for want of success." Other than giving a cold shoulder to fly-by-night dingalings, the company makes farm, patio, and a lot of navy bells—one such navy bell being the "invasion bell" used on landing craft for World War Two's cross-Channel invasion. The company manufactures ship bells for the United States, Great Britain, and—by default— North Korea as the result of the *Pueblo* affair.

Hillsboro, with nearly 6500 people, is the county seat and largest city Highland County has. But at least Highland County has another city: Greenfield, with nearly 6000 people and a high school named after the Greenfield local who invented the horse collar and pad, thereby making a mint. His name was Edward Lee McClain. Greenfield is an amiable community of older homes and some new suburbia. The older homes, if not lavish, are clean and charming. The Greenfield business district, if Greenfield were the county seat which it isn't, could be called "county seat antique." Other towns: Leesburg, population about 1000, is primarily a residential splatter in a slightly rolling terrain—and it has a Friends Church, plus one house that is Spanish stucco and out of place, but nice. Monroe is a smaller version of Leesburg, minus the stucco. It contains a handful of houses, a grocery store, a gasoline pump, and—well, that's it. And all around are dark hints of mountains.

Just up from Portsmouth on the Ohio River is the village of Waverly, population 5000, and the county seat and largest village in landlocked Pike County which has only two other villages. Beaver with 400 is one; Piketon with 1400 is the other. Here and there, though, are crossroad settlements that have names, houses, sadness, and a buzzard circling slowly high overhead, which should give you an idea of the county but doesn't. This is hill and hollow woodland terrain, a lot of the county is the national forest, and most of the county looks lonely and disenchanted. Only 2200 people occupy the county's 444 square miles—and the county has only 770 farms. But here is where you'll find Ohio's billion-dollar atomic energy plant. The place employs about 1400. Located seven miles southeast of Waverly this vast plant gobbles 1,800,000 kilowatts to keep its gaseous diffusion gadgets gaseously diffused. But the big plant doesn't help the county's mood too much. Color the mood one of longing and loss. Ringing the silent forests that seem to go on forever are ramshackle little sawmills. The small mountains here make the cramped valleys dark except at noon. One little settlement called Givens—a wide spot in the road, a railroad crossing—seems to have collected all the junked and rusting campers the nation has. Fields are littered with them. And all around the hills are angry and uncivilized. Now and then a wide valley—flat and farmed—catches you by surprise. But not often enough.

This county's first settlers came from Virginia and Pennsylvania. From 1815 when the county was organized until 1861, the county seat was Piketon. But when the Ohio and Erie Canal came through, everyone said, "Hey, Waverly is going to be a real great big city," so the county seat was moved there, where nothing happened either. Well, something *did* happen in the county. History tells us that Pike was the first county and Waverly was the first county seat ever to have air mail service. But even that was a fluke. On July 4, 1835, Richard Clayton, English balloonist-turned-Cincinnati jeweler, started for New York by balloon, his balloon carrying a mailbag of newspapers plus mail. Unfortunately he never quite reached New York. His balloon got caught in a Pike County tree where he spent the night. Next morning, farmers got him down, he took the mail to the Waverly post office, and so there we are: the first air mail service. Near Waverly, by the way, is the cave where William Hewitt lived as a hermit after he had a fight with his family. He was a Virginia aristocrat-turned-hermit.

Also in this empty and beautiful county is "Bristol Village" which lists itself as a non-profit retirement village that now has nearly 400 homes. Its purpose: to bring together all the active senior citizens from every corner of the United States.

Right below Pike County is Scioto County, where the Scioto River empties into the Ohio River. Portsmouth is here. And, frankly, if it were not for Portsmouth's enthusiasm, Portsmouth could be called Hardluck City, U.S.A. At first glance, it appears to be a grimy industrial town. At second glance, it still is. Portsmouth, which now has about 33,000 residents, once had 42,000. River floods and labor problems caused the reduction. It was not until 1951 that Portsmouth shook off its gloom and began to start over again. Portsmouth, where iron and steel marry coal and ore, covers twelve square miles, most of the coverage needing work. Right next door is its look-alike twin: New Boston with 5000 people, industry, smokestacks, and grime. Actually, these two communities are the drab counterparts of Ironton and Steubenville upstream.

Around the county are narrow ridges, deep valleys, and steep slopes. Here are cramped little valleys and, upon occasion, a flatland plain. The county, 500 feet above sea level at Portsmouth, rises with fits and starts to 1200 feet above sea level in its northwest part. The eastern section, known as California Valley, is occupied by the Scioto River a lot, and occasionally by broad farmland.

Portsmouth was laid out in 1803 by Henry Massie, who came to the territory

221

with his brother Nathaniel. His brother, you may recall, started Chillicothe and Manchester. Nathaniel first located his settlement in Alexandria, floods came, the settlement went, so he tried again on the higher ground where Portsmouth is now. By 1820, five hundred people lived in Portsmouth. By 1817, Portsmouth had become such a city that an ordinance was passed to prevent pigs running loose in the street. The county—and city—were settled by the English, plus a few disgruntled French. Says one Portsmouth historian, "An organization of rogues operating in Paris . . ." and—well, maybe we'd better tell it. French con artists conned the French with the idea that the Ohio Valley was civilized and that they— the con artists—owned land which they'd peddle cheap. The French bought, came, were bewildered, some went home, some stayed, and so, as we said, French are in the vicinity too. In addition to Portsmouth and New Boston, the county has a scattering of villages. Otwa (sic) enters the list with 242 kind souls; South Webster has nearly 850; and there's Rarden with 250—later to change its name a little and come to Oxford to practice medicine on student bodies.

When the steamboat came through in 1810, Portsmouth got going. When the canal was completed in 1832, that helped Portsmouth keep going. One could travel, via slow-motion canal, from Portsmouth to Columbus in twenty-four hours. In 1846 the shipload of shelled corn which left Portsmouth for Ireland was said to be the first such shipment to cross the Atlantic.

Today Portsmouth leans heavily toward steel—because everything is handy for making same. The first blast furnaces were built in 1818. By 1830, within ten miles of Portsmouth there were nearly a dozen such furnaces, plus ten forges. Soon the land was dotted with the gadgets, all manufacturing smog. But until 1832 no one thought to mold the pig iron into a manufactured item. Rather, the stuff was hauled to the Ohio River, put on barges, and shipped elsewhere. In 1832, however, Gaylord's Rolling Mill started the production of iron bars and nails. From the coke furnaces came foundry pig, malleable pig, Bessemer pig, basic pig, ferrosilicon pig, and other kinds of non-kosher iron. When was the first actual iron and steel factory built in Portsmouth? In 1872. The Burgess Steel and Iron Company built it. And, until labor strife and the 1937 flood, Portsmouth was going places.

Also Portsmouth is a shoe-making town. In 1869 the R. Bell & Company started to make shoes on the top floor of their warehouse, producing 200 pairs a day by machinery that operated by foot-power. Now the Williams Manufacturing Company employs 2000 to produce several million pairs of shoes for milady each year.

You who seek the finer things, note that Roy Rogers was born in Portsmouth— and left.

The one event that gets Portsmouth excited it its River Days Festival. Started only in 1960, this week-long affair offers the North American Championship Boat

River Days. Portsmouth.

Races in which the national champions make hash of Ohio River's serenity by sloshing about at top speed in both hydroplanes and runabouts. These races are sanctioned by the National Outboard Association and are sponsored by the Ohio Valley Boating Association as well as the Scioto Valley Festival Association, so don't get the idea this is a dinky small-town event of little consequence but a lot of noise. Anyway, if you *like* noise, here is where you'll head the piercing wail of unmuffled outboard engines screaming things at one another as they each try to outrev the other. The dramatic moment, say racing buffs, is when the drivers whip their crafts about for best starting position. With one eye on the clock, one eye on the starting line, and one eye on the competition—if we have not lost count somewhere—the drivers play for keeps. Up goes the second hand, there starts the race, and zip! zip! zap! go the boats by the judges' stand. The drivers zoom lickety-split— if you wish to be technical—into the critical first turn from which several don't come out of. The first turn is where the spills and splashes are. The boats go sixty miles an hour and sometimes in the water.

For culture less dampening, Portsmouth offers its Little Theater group which dishes out a smorgasbord of good productions from slapstick to high drama. Also, Ohio University has a branch in Portsmouth, sponsoring many art, music, and literature exhibits. Because Scioto County contains the state's largest forest— Shawnee Forest—the area is sometimes called the "little Smokies of Ohio." The county also has prehistoric earthworks—and a lot of tired buildings which are the latterday peopleworks.

But you just wait. Portsmouth is a city on the move—and it could end up a gem. Or something.

Shall we leave quietly and head west along the river? Next to Scioto is a lonely little river county that goes back a far piece into lonely hills and valleys. Although the county has no cities at all, West Union with about 2000 people is the county seat because, listen, every county seat has to be somewhere. West Union once had the dubious honor of bragging that it was the only county seat without a railroad. Once steamboats and stagecoaches stopped at Manchester (population 2400) but lately none have appeared. Manchester also once was the county seat, but something interesting happened which used to happen a lot there, but not so much any more. About the only thing the county brags about these days is the giant serpent-shaped Indian mound that has the appearance of a snake swallowing an egg. The thing stretches out 1254 feet. Historians accuse the Hopewell Indians of creating it.

About the only thing exciting that happened in Adams County, happened somewhere else. One river bend west of Manchester is Straight Creek Bar on the Kentucky shore near Maysville, Kentucky. Here was fought the duel between William

T. Casto, onetime Maysville mayor, and Colonel Leonidas (sic) Metcalfe. They dueled because one had caused the other to be put in the clink. They stood sixty yards apart, pointed some kind of guns at each other, the silence of the lonely river valley was broken with a pair of bangs, and—as Fred Way, Jr., in Log, *Cincinnati to Pittsburgh* wrote—"Casto was shot just below the heart and died in a few moments." That happened in 1862. Captain Way goes on to say gently that, "many other persons have shot one another along the Ohio shores since, but devoid of such pomp and circumstance . . ."

Says Betty Blake Simcox of Captain Way, "I've always been in love with (him) even before I read the first line of his book or knew him personally. I've always been in love with someone like him. He is a master story teller who brings you into his story and with his gentle humorous words gives you his river. He spent his early years as a steamboat pilot and master. He's the kind of writer who puts two *l*'s in *marvellous* because one isn't plenty. And he consistently spells *replentish* with a *t* . . ." Thus with a nod to Mrs. Simcox, of the *Delta Queen*, the last of the overnight river packets, we dip further into Log, *Cincinnati to Pittsburgh* so that we might better pass along to you the mood of this stretch of river. Captain Way writes that around Adams County "there are mocking birds . . . Mistletoe is a parasite on trees all the way from Cincinnati to the Kanawha River. Turkey buzzards wing their slow heavy flight all the way to Pittsburgh, although above Wheeling, they prefer the West Virginia hills and seldom cross the river." Way notes that the eleventh President, James K. Polk, may have steamboated on the Ohio River to Pittsburgh but none of the rivermen cared because Polk, as President, vetoed an appropriation for snag removal—and thereafter rivermen called the infernal snags "Polk stalks." This stretch of the Ohio River—between Louisville and Pittsburgh, for that matter—is like a stepladder compared to the river south to New Orleans. In the upper Ohio River, boats must climb 270.77 feet—straight up, for 470.2 river miles. Way says that the last stretch, the 90 miles from Wheeling to Pittsburgh, is the worst: the river rises one foot per mile. But dams, of course, create a series of lakes—and there go the boats, locking through, up and down the wet stepladder.

Next to the west is Brown County. By this point, we are getting close to Cincinnati which is only 30 miles more to the west. Along the river there are hills, of course, but back upland, the hills give way to rolling farmland and to one of the most beautiful pieces of real estate Ohio possesses. Some of it, being so close to Cincinnati, is beginning to be suburbia. Sorry about that. Along the river is Ripley, a cheerful river town of about 2500 people and a few tobacco warehouses. Here you can see John Rankin's House, the first established station on the Underground Railroad. In this house Harriet Beecher met Calvin Stowe; they hit it off

225

pretty good and later got married. In this house, with its anti-slavery moods, Miss Beecher is supposed to have got a few ideas for *Uncle Tom's Cabin*. Also, Ripley before the Civil War was second only to Cincinnati in the packing of pork.

In Georgetown is a school where Ulysses S. Grant studied. Georgetown, the county seat, maintains the school as kind of a memorial. The other villages in the county, Brown County having no cities, are: Aberdeen with around 950 people, Fayetteville with 500, Hamersville with 560, Higginsport with 434, Mount Orab with 1250, Russellville with 420, Saint Martin with about 160, and Sardinia with around 900.

And, creeping over the horizon, the bulldozers announce the approach of Cincinnati suburbia.

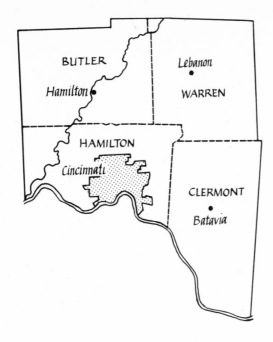

12

Cincinnati, which began as a clearing on the banks of the Ohio River—thousands of bullfrogs glumping love songs at one another—is Ohio's counterbalance for Cleveland: Cincinnati being in the southwest corner of the state and Cleveland being in the northeast corner. Although everyone likes to say that Cincinnati is the city of seven hills, it has many more hills than seven, and more going for it than hills. And though Cincinnati is called "the Queen City" no one agrees who first called it that. Some suggest that Henry W. Longfellow did when he sat up where Eden Park is now, looked out over the valley below, and dashed off a pre-Hallmark bit of verse that crooned:

> ". . . And this song of wine,
> This greeting of mine,
> The winds and birds shall deliver
> To the Queen of the West,
> In her garland dress
> On the banks of the beautiful river."

On the other hand, long before Longfellow got his valentine to scan, Benjamin Drake in 1838 published a book called *Tales and Sketches of the Queen City*. But along comes Alvin F. Harlow, who says via his book *The Serene Cincinnatians* that C. D. Arfwedson in still another book published before Drake's never once mentioned Cincinnati without adding such surnames as "the wonderful" or "the western queen." How the name Queen City got applied to Cincinnati is exhausting us—and anyway, none of that says what Cincinnati is today.

Incorporated Cincinnati—the political and municipal entity—covers 77.62 square miles of hills and valleys in Hamilton County. Cincinnati is the county seat. 227

Old German homes on a hillside. Cincinnati.

Cincinnati is a bunch of things: the aforementioned hills and valleys, old neighborhoods, fresh new suburbia, vast industrial districts, expressways, and glittering new business sections that are replacing more pooped commercial swaths. Unlike Cleveland where the preponderance of the foreign-born came from the polka-dancing and fiddle-playing innards of Europe, Cincinnati's foreign element—past and present—is German, Irish, and—lately—Italian. Cincinnati has ants in its pants: it is practically tearing its downtown section apart and starting fresh. Gone is the grime. Glitter is the key. New buildings rear high in the sky, changing the skyline forever; and old buildings, like dirty old men, have been bulldozed into eternity. Overhead walkways allow you to travel entire city blocks without once trafficking with street-level traffic. Thus, Cincinnati is old, new, and just about everything else in between that is good, bad, and bewildering.

Here is the sales center of the United States for bituminous coal—but where's the soot? The air, allowing for smog, blows clean and free in and out of city. Yet, Cincinnati handles more than 600,000 coal cars annually with a tonnage of 32,000,000 tons. On the river another 3,000,000 tons are shipped, making Cincinnati the largest inland coal port. But ask most Cincinnatians about this coal, they look at you becalmed. Coal? Coal? What does Cincinnati have to do with coal? And Cincinnati used to be a hog center. It was once nicknamed Porkopolis. Wild hogs used to root the garbage in the gutters as the city's first garbage men. But those days are gone forever, too. And so is most of the hog business.

But just as Cleveland is divided into two distinct sections by the Cayuhoga River Valley's industry, so Cincinnati is divided by the Mill Creek Valley which extends in a most casual and smelly manner north from the edge of downtown. Out in this wide valley, guarded by plateau-shaped hills, is the heart of Greater Cincinnati's industry—*Greater* Cincinnati because much lies outside the city limits. Also, not only in this valley, but everywhere, industry is scattered. Cincinnati is the machine tool capital of the world. Cincinnati is where most playing cards are made. Cincinnati is where if you think soap, you think Procter & Gamble—or have your neighbor down on your neck. Cincinnati is also a front-running city in building materials, tin cans, chemicals, coffins, anchovy pizzas, jet engines, mattresses, pianos, shoes, valves, and a bunch of other things, one of which is not important this time of the year. The Greater Cincinnati area has 2000 industrial plants which employ altogether 50,000 people, paying them $1,000,000,000 each year. The county where Cincinnati is has 10,000 retail establishments and more than 2000 wholesale places. And, because Ohioans are homebodies and/or because no liquor is sold on Sundays, the streets of Cincinnati, Cleveland, and the rest on Sunday evenings are deader than a mackerel.

But let's look at Cincinnati in a logical manner. As we suggested in *Vas You*

Brand-new glitter. Cincinnati.

Ever in Zinzinnati?, Cincinnati is unlike any other city. It hasn't the hurry of New York, the anger of Chicago, or the buttoned-down sophistication that San Francisco affects. We suggest that what Cincinnati has is innocence. It is the innocence of Fountain Square. It is the innocence of old ladies lugging shopping bags. It is the innocence of typists preening themselves in store window reflections. It is an innocence expressed by nuns hurrying along Fifth Street and by hordes of teen-age girls in Catholic school uniforms. Cincinnati's innocence has a voice. Its voice is Kentucky drawls, Hoosier twangs, here and there a German guttural, Negro laughter, and the newsboy's garbled cry.

Where Cincinnati's tallest building, the Carew Tower, is now, Madame Tournaire's Circus used to be. But that was before the Civil War. Delegates to the 1856 Democratic Convention in Cincinnati were hard-pressed to stick to business; they were more fascinated by a balloon ascension originating at the circus. They did stop gaping long enough, however, to nominate James Buchanan. The 48-story Carew Tower was built in 1930 during the heart of the depression. It stands 574 feet above Fifth and Vine streets, the intersection considered "the heart of Cincinnati." From the tower's observation deck you can not see the Cleveland Tower but you can see Cincinnati spread before you like a smoky map. Anyway, the Carew Tower wasn't always there, which brings us to history.

When Ben Stites arrived in Cincinnati in November 1788, Cincinnati wasn't here, either. He and his group had floated down the wilderness of the Ohio River to get the place going. When they got here, they waded ashore, knocked the rafts apart, and built quick shelters. They named the settlement Columbia. Three days after Christmas of that year, Israel Ludlow who was a surveyor landed at the foot of Sycamore Street, now the vicinity of the stadium, and together with his twenty-three companions started another town called Losantiville, which was the original Cincinnati, Columbia upstream a little being one of its suburban areas. Why Losantiville? Well, *L* is for the Licking River across from which was where the men were; *os* means *mouth* in Latin; and *anti* means *opposite*. Put them all together, add *ville* which means what you think it means, and that's how the town got its name. Later John Cleves Symmes drifted by Columbia and Losantiville to head ashore at North Bend. His plans: to start the biggest city ever. You have only to look at North Bend today to see that something went wrong. What went wrong was, an army lieutenant who had come along to look for a fort site started messing around with the wife of one of the North Bend settlers. The settler got fed up, took his wife to Losantiville, the soldier followed, surveyed the fort site there— and our regrets forthwith to North Bend, a pleasant enough village today, but sitting around with the feeling it missed the boat.

The three settlements began to settle down, Losantiville settling down the most.

231

Two taverns opened. A ferry service was started across the Ohio River. The town had its first crime wave: someone got caught stealing cucumbers and for his efforts received thirty lashes. How do we get from *Losantiville* to *Cincinnati?* Well, when Governor Arthur St. Clair dropped by for a cup of coffee and some Indians to shoot, he is supposed to have said, "Losantiville? Say, listen a minute, you guys, is that really a very good name? Like, what I mean is, why don't we call this place Cincinnati?" Or words to that effect. St. Clair later proved no better at Indian fighting than at tact. He led 1400 soldiers north through the Ohio woodland emptiness so they could shoot at Indians, the Indians shot first, and things looked dark for Ohio because it was, then, defenseless. About 40 Cincinnati families moved across the river to the safety of relatively civilized Kentucky. Ringing the struggling village of Cincinnati were outpost stations of farmers and a soldier or two, in stockades, watching out for Indians. But along came General Mad Anthony Wayne, a no-nonsense Indian fighter. He went north, met the Indians at Fallen Timbers, shot a bunch of them, they surrendered, and that—compressed—is the way the West was won, this then being the West. Cincinnati, reasonably safe from Indians, could go about the business of becoming a city.

The first steamboat wouldn't come down the Ohio River, though, until 1811. Meanwhile traffic was via raft and keelboat, the keelboats made famous by Mike Fink whom Walt Disney cleansed for home consumption. About 150 keelboats operated between Cincinnati and Pittsburgh. They floated downstream when the river had enough water in it but going east had to pole the cargo boats along. A round trip took two months and sweat. By this time, the beginnings of the 1800s, Dr. Daniel Drake who had come to Cincinnati to study medicine became a one-man chamber of commerce attracting industry and settlers to his adopted hometown. Later on he also helped start the University of Cincinnati. Among the other newcomers of this period was Nicholas Longworth who arrived when he was twenty-one, read law, dabbled in real estate, and by the time he was forty-six he had dabbled so well, he gave up law to concentrate on his holdings. In 1811, as noted, the first steamboat appeared. Built in Pittsburgh, it was a Tinker Toy side-wheeler named *Orleans.* It had the speed of eight miles per hour.

The canals which brought life to many Ohio cities worked the same commercial magic for Cincinnati. Around 1827 the Miami-Erie canal connected Cincinnati with Middletown. A year later, one had a choice of traveling arrangements: canal, train, or bumpity-bumping along in a stagecoach over washboard roads. Cincinnati then had 20,000 citizens, fifty-four foundries, four steam engine factories, a powder mill, hogs roaming the street, two paper mills, a sugar refinery, nine printing plants, and a steamboat docking at the landing, one of its passengers being Mrs. Anthony Trollope, mother of the writer. She was the one who toured America

Serene parkways. Cincinnati.

and made fun of its manners. In Cincinnati she started a department store to peddle culture for bucks—and lost her shirt. When she first looked at Cincinnati, she said, "What an uninteresting mass of buildings!"

Around 1850 Cincinnati was booming—at least around the public landing which was as organized as a Chinese fire drill. Five thousand steamboats put in there that year. Day and night the landing was at full cry. Negro roustabouts wrestled bales and barrels between ship and shore. And amid the confusion of the cobblestone landing, horse-drawn carriages and drays clattered. The center of town—that particular moment—was Third Street. Later it would move up to Fourth Street and higher ground. Now goodness knows where it is. Around 1850 Cincinnati was happily infested with the Irish. They had started to arrive as early as 1840 because the potato famine back home made life a sticky wicket. By the mid-century mark, so many Pat and Mikes were on tap that factories and stores put up signs that read NO IRISH WANTED. The Irish made up 12 per cent of Cincinnati's population. The Germans accounted for 28 per cent. The English numbered a scant 4 per cent and blacks only 2 per cent. The rest? Native-born— or from the eastern states: Virginia, New Jersey, and Maryland.

Charles Dickens had visited Cincinnati during this period of happy fermentation. He arrived by river boat, for which he had little affection. He felt the gadget would at any moment blow sky high—and he had every reason to feel this way, because some did. Dickens wrote of these early steamboats that "to see the great body of fire exposed, raging and roaring beneath that frail frame of painted wood, the wonder is that *any* journey can be safely made. These western vessels are foreign to all the ideas we are accustomed to entertain about boats. They have no mast, cordage, rigging or any other boat-like gear; nor have they anything in their shape calculated to remind anyone of a boat's head, side, or keel. Except that they are in the water and display a couple of paddle wheels, they might have been intended to perform some unknown service, high and dry upon a mountain top . . . "

If you think Zanesville had trouble with its Y-bridge falling down, consider the problem Cincinnati had bridging Mill Creek. Cincinnati's first bridge was a foot bridge across Duck Creek, built in 1800. But in 1806 the first bridge across Mill Creek was constructed of yellow pines that grew at the mouth of the creek. It was a fine bridge, everyone was properly pleased with it, but along came high water. A boat tied beneath the bridge raised when the creek did, ripping the bridge from its moorings, and when last seen the seven-hundred-dollar bridge was floating down the Ohio River. Five years later, Cincinnati tried again. Another bridge was thrown across Mill Creek. High water nailed that one, too. A third bridge, however, lasted ten years until the flood of 1832. After the river crested

Where the elite gather. Cincinnati.

at 64.2 feet, Cincinnati discovered that its third Mill Creek bridge was resting on an island a few miles upstream from Louisville. Fed up with the nonsense, the bridge builders towed the bridge back to Cincinnati and installed it again where it had been.

Bad times, other than bridge troubles, came upon the Ohio Valley and the rest of Ohio in the mid 1800s. Cholera. But Cincinnati's public landing was busy as ever. Barrels and bales and bundles were heaped everywhere, roustabouts sang, pigs squealed, boats tooted—business as usual. But from the city's churches came the day-long and nightlong tolling of bells. And the songs the roustabouts sang were songs of fear and voodoo. In 1849, voodoo made as much sense as any preventive Cincinnati offered. And it satisfied the frightened blacks. Negroes even began to practice almost-forgotten African rites in the semi-secrecy of their hovels. Later as the deadly summer and cholera wore on, the rites were hardly a secret: the noise was too loud. Lacking drums the blacks beat sticks upon sticks and chanted. At times the Cincinnati landing resembled an African coast, crowded with blacks who chanted and swayed and prayed to ten thousand gods.

As we wrote in *Vas You Ever in Zinzinnati?*: "It was impossible to keep account of deaths in the summer of 1849. Some doctors guessed that in July alone, 103 people died every day. But there was no official tally. It was a torrid and feverish summer, that year of '49. Now and then a thunder storm would bring relief, but even then the violence of the lightning bursts seemed to enflame the cholera even more. On most days, the dry air suffocated. When the sun got hot at noon, the rivulets where the garbage flowed seemed to turn to steam . . . "

As for Cincinnati during the Civil War, Charles R. Wilson in *Cincinnati's Reputation During the Civil War* wrote that "Cincinnati was really neither pro southern nor pro northern. Whatever sectionalism she revealed was western, but as a matter of fact, she tended to discount even this in the interest of the Union. She was Unionist to the core." Said Dr. Lewis Leonard Tucker, onetime director of the Cincinnati Historical Society, that when word of Fort Sumter reached Cincinnati, "If there had been any doubt about Cincinnati's loyalty to the north, it was quickly dispelled. One persistant cry rang through the streets: 'Union, Union, Union!' "

In one way or the other, generally a little of each, Cincinnati got through the Civil War.

The last part of Cincinnati's nineteenth century was filled with runaway horses and industries giving birth. During this last quarter of the century, Cincinnati invented Ivory Soap, put the finishing touches on the Mount Adams Incline, built Music Hall, and started the Hebrew Union College. Also after the Civil War Cincinnati completed the Suspension Bridge across the Ohio River, the bridge being the older twin of the Brooklyn Bridge, both designed by the same man. But who needed a bridge to cross the river? For fourteen days in February 1893, the river was frozen solid; people could walk across. The same thing happened in 1899. And don't forget 1877: from December 1876 to January 1877, the river was gorged solid with ice for thirty-one days.

Horsecar lines—each a separate company—were expanding over the face of Cincinnati to connect the valley business district by the river to outlying and heretofore isolated communities. Anyone could start a horsecar line in those sweet days. All he needed was $150 for a horse, a horsecar that could hold twenty passengers, and a franchise. To get a franchise he had only to suggest a route the city engineers favored and only had to agree not to charge too much. His track, though, had to be the proper gauge: five feet, two inches wide. But it was a case of horsecar line eat horsecar line. Thus, by 1873, most of the lines joined together, calling their collection of hayburners the Cincinnati Consolidated Street Railway Company. Also, to get up the steep hills that had horses hollering uncle, Cincinnati built inclines. Now all are gone. The age of inclines almost ended earlier than necessary when, in 1889, the clutch at the top of the Main Street incline failed, and down plummeted the car, crashing at the bottom, killing all but one passenger.

Procter & Gamble, making 200,000 cakes of soap a day, introduced Ivory the last part of the nineteenth century, as noted. Ivory Soap was actually an accident. The workman who ran the blending machine went to lunch, forgetting to shut the machine off. The mixture blended itself silly, and the result: hard soap that could float. Customers who got the soap liked it and wanted more. To Harley Procter, though, the soap was a cut above the P & G White Soap; it was a whole new world of soap, so he wanted a new name for it. One morning in church he read Psalm 45:8: "All thy garments smell of myrrh and aloes and cassia, out of the ivory palaces, whereby they have made thee glad." And so Ivory Soap got its name.

The start of the twentieth century in Greater Cincinnati saw the start of the Kemper Thomas Company making calendars and the Heekin Can Company making cans. In 1902 the Cincinnati Gas Light & Coke Company changed its name to the Cincinnati Gas & Electric Company. And on a quick trip along saloon-laden Vine Street, Carry Nation refused to lift her ax once, noting, "I would have dropped from exhaustion before I had gone a block." In 1903 Alice Lee Roosevelt married Nicholas Longworth II, the Cincinnati Country Club was established, Mary Wood entered burlesque as an exotic, and the cable cars stopped running.

The biggest man—"in size and bulk," some are too quick to point out—who entered the White House was William Howard Taft who accepted his nomination from the front porch of his Cincinnati home which is now a serene and charming

237

museum. In 1909, when Taft went to Washington, the Cincinnati Milling Machine built its plant in Oakley and in Norwood the American Laundry Machine Company started.

Cincinnati got through the first World War reasonably well. At its conclusion, of course, Fountain Square was a mob scene of merriment. Automobiles tooted through the pedestrian Emery Arcade, where the Carew Tower now stands, lots of ladies got kissed, church bells clanged, and from the upper floors of the business district, confetti poured in fluttering celebration. But soon another event fought for newspaper space: Prohibition. The headline in the May 25, 1919 *Commercial Tribune* read:

QUEEN CITY BIDS GOODBYE TO SALOONS
IN GREAT RUSH OF LIQUOR PURCHASING;
FIVE THOUSAND OHIO DRINKING PLACES CLOSE

And so with that, many of Cincinnati's fine old German restaurants were shuttered—and a wet and beautiful tradition bit the dust. This was the same year the Cincinnati Reds won the pennant and the World Series, after which they, too, went into a twilight. For a long time Cincinnatians wondered if they had a baseball team at all. This was also the year Proctor & Gamble introduced Ivory Soap Flakes. In 1920 the canal which once had connected Cincinnati with Toledo was drained, ending another era. But good riddance. The canal in its old age had become a smelly eyesore.

In 1929 Cincinnatians were taking another look at the Ohio River—and with good reason. President Herbert Hoover had dedicated that granite obelisk in Eden Park that overlooks the stream, the President declaring that the river was about to embark on a new and exciting career. It had been completely canalized, as they say riverwise, and was ready for action actionwise. Before this moment—before the dams and locks had been installed—the river flowed mostly by whim. It used to get so low in the autumn that at times to wade from one shore to the other was a lark. To illustrate its erratic behavior of yesteryear, note that on October 6, 1908, the day Jack Samuelson made his first parachute jump, the Ohio River at Cincinnati was less than 3 feet deep; that April it had been more than 55 feet deep! The river usually averaged lows of three to four feet, but the lowest it ever got was in September, 1881: less than 2 feet deep. After the river was canalized and the dams were functioning, the new average low was 9 to 10 feet. Now, with even greater dams harnessing the river, the normal pool stage for Cincinnati is 25.4 feet deep, which makes the river one long wet highway that can handle deeper-draft tonnage. The highest the river ever reached was in January 1937, but its official flood stage at Cincinnati has varied. Until 1888, flood stage was 45 feet, was changed then to 50 feet, and in 1922 was changed again to its present 52 feet.

Anderson Ferry. Cincinnati.

The subway that never happened. Cincinnati.

After World War Two, Cincinnati burst at the seams with the return of its veterans all who wanted homes, blueberry pie, a wife, and babies—in that order. Farmlands in the once tranquil countryside became subdivisions. The developers built as far out as they could because land was cheap and the building restrictions less restricting. Postwar families followed the Pied Piping developers, and thus, the older and closer-in neighborhoods went down a few notches. One neighborhood after another was emptied by all who could afford a down payment. Shopping centers in the hinterlands were at first only Tinker Toy afterthoughts but have since become magnificent emporiums in their own right. Perhaps a few numbers can show the trend of that period. In 1958 Cincinnati had 98 apparel stores downtown and only 38 in the suburbs. Five years later, downtown had only 80 such stores while the suburbs had 51. Sales in men's apparel, for instance, in downtown stores dropped from $12,500,000 in 1958 to $10,200,000 in 1963. Sales in suburban stores, in this same category and in this same period, increased from $2,600,000 to $5,400,000. Add more numbers to the pot: in 1952 Cincinnati could boast of 345 doctors downtown; 140 have since moved to the suburbs. So that was the trend of Cincinnati as a city. There went thousands beyond the city limit, never to come back, even to shop. And there downtown Cincinnati sat, ringed by neighborhoods that decayed. Let matters alone and Cincinnati would have rolled over and played dead. But however old-fashioned Cincinnati might seem, or slow-poke staid, Cincinnati got its dander up—and as of now, the scene has changed dramatically. A new downtown Cincinnati is abuilding. Real glamour. As they say in vaudeville, "You wouldn't recognize the old place now!"

Entire neighborhoods have now vanished via the bulldozer's touch. The old West End, which at first was a thing of beauty then a thing of decay, has given away to an industrial-commercial complex that is low-lying, clean, and energetic. And on the edge of downtown is the $10,000,000 Cincinnati Convention Exhibition Hall. Massive, dramatic, alive. Where it is now, an old neighborhood used to be, but toward the last, the old neighborhood had little charm. The Cincinnati *Post* was published in a grimy two-story brick building. Its workers once help set the mood of the old neighborhood—and so did the flophouses (another mood) and around the corner so did the Sixth Street Market (still another mood). Great place that Sixth Street Market of yore. But these moods have been replaced by a newer and fresher one: the mood of a city on the move.

In *Raymond and Me That Summer* we visited the old market place and the old West End itself when we wrote that "buying the week's groceries was a day-long walking adventure that took us all over the West End. At one place we'd buy day-old bread. At another we bought canned foods. We bought our

241

Expressways replaced old neighborhoods. Cincinnati.

meat in a dirty butcher shop from a butcher who had dirty hands. But his prices were low. Most of his customers were Negroes. They bought chitlings, hog jowls, and pig ears. The butcher said they'd fry the pig ears with greens and serve both, greasy and sizzling, as a dish they'd call 'hot listeners.' After hearing that, we almost stopped buying meat from him, but we didn't. He was the cheapest butcher on the cheapest street in the cheapest part of town. In the West End itself, while shopping, we passed block after block of falling-down tenements. They were decorated with wrought-iron long since gone to rust. We read each chalked note that said who was in love with whom. We gaped at Negroes and they gaped back at us. We were strangers wandering in a strange land. Every window was open, the heat was awful, curtains—tattering and grey—waved in the warm breeze. Stench and decay were everywhere. Thousands of Negroes leaned from windows, sat on curbs, and leaned against walls. We watched tired Negroes push tired pushcarts that wobbled with loads of junk; destination: the junk yard and a dime. Radios blared. And always there was laughter. It was a sad and happy neighborhood all at once.

"Finally we arrived at the Sixth Street Market. There was no sadness there, only happiness and noise. Where Sixth Street (once) widened between Elm and Central, the market stood: two red brick market houses from some far-off German village. The first was wet and cold inside. It smelled of meat and milk. Slabs of beef hung from hooks and dripped blood. The second market house—its twin—contained only stalls that sold flowers. It was a gloomy greenhouse, a noisy funeral home, a blur of scents and colors and fat women. Outside these market houses, lining the streets, were stalls they had to take down each night when the market was closed. It was as noisy there as it was inside. These makeshift stalls sat side by side until they went out of sight. Shoppers pushed and shoved and shouted—but vendors shouted the most. They screamed their wares in each person's ear. The smells were wonderful: sauerkraut, tripe, melons, and cheese. There were cherries, strawberries, red bananas, beans, and mint. Ignoring the din, mothers poked this melon, prodded that one, frowned at both with suspicion, and grunted with disfavor at the price.

"Raymond and I headed to the market house which sold meat. Raymond liked that place best and so did I. I liked to sniff the sausages that dangled in a row. Another butcher sold pickled pigs' feet but we avoided his stall; pickled pigs' feet were sad. I kept thinking about the pig that couldn't run any more—or was that him, that dead ham on the butcher's hook? Raymond didn't care to sniff sausages. He went to the stall that sold poultry. He could stand for hours and watch the butcher chop off the heads of chickens.

" 'Some of them put up a fight,' he said. 'That's more than sausages do.'

243

" 'Sausages don't splatter blood,' I said.

" 'They don't make any noise either,' he said. 'What fun are they?' "

Well, now the Sixth Street Market is no more. The Convention Center and parking lots take its place. A city growing up can't stand still, can it? But where did the blacks vanish? To a hilltop neighborhood called Avondale. This is where the riots were and loneliness is. The prices and kinds of housing offered in Avondale tell the melancholy tale of that community's twilight. Avondale streets are lined with stunning and great homes that used to be single-family dwellings, but now that is not generally the case. When the West End was gutted—for civic improvement—the displaced blacks did not, as some hoped, vanish. Most of them came to Avondale, and through no fault of their own, brought the ghetto with them. To paraphrase the poets, each city is its own heaven and hell.

Cincinnati has many interesting old neighborhoods—and one of them is Clifton. Here, atop one of the hills, is the University of Cincinnati. Some of the streets around this section have homes that leave you spellbound. Turn a corner, stroll a few blocks, and you'll find the spell broken. The same kind of home has been whittled into multi-family dwellings and is declining fast. Clifton is filled with surprises. Some are happy ones. Others can break your heart. A hilly community shaded by ancient trees, it is crisscrossed with streets and byways (some actually gaslit) that take aimless turns and occasionally end up nowhere. In this neighborhood are great old homes that have, now and then, a "modern" one for a next-door neighbor, but these modern jobs are as out of place on some Clifton streets as "pop" art is at a Rembrandt festival. French doors, verandas, turrets, wrought-iron grills, porticoes, fluted stone columns, floors of hammered and dressed stone, carved marble fireplaces, and hand-carved mantels—these are the delicacies that Clifton mansions have feasted upon. Serenity is the password to many streets in Clifton. The password to others is despair.

Immediately north of the revitalized downtown business district used to be the German section called "Over the Rhine," the Rhine being the canal which is now a parkway under which is a subway the city forgot to finish. At one time this "Over the Rhine" section was a workingman's place of beauty, but that is long passed. "The Over-the-Rhine district has become a shabby neighborhood," we wrote in *The Roundhouse, Paradise, and Mr. Pickering.* "In the long-ago world of our grandfathers, the district had been a happy area, good natured and filled with malty joys. There had been signs that said: 'Free Weinerwurst with every drink.' Vine Street had been a noisy and respectable thoroughfare lined with beer gardens, concert halls, shooting galleries, and bowling alleys. Between 12th and 13th Street had been 23 saloons. (This) had been a Teutonic world of German music and German cooking. There had been beer halls with singing waiters;

244

and 21 steins of beer cost a dollar. Bars had sawdust on the floor and tanbark. The food: steamed dumplings, hausenpfeffer, potato pancakes, ham noodles, kidney soup, beef goulash, sauerbraten, and ham hocks with corn meal dumplings. On side streets each morning, old world housewives had gotten down on their knees and scrubbed each door sill clean. The district struggled back to life after prohibition ended, but it couldn't recapture its yesterdays. The Germans, no longer laborers, have moved to the suburbs. Time chipped away at the German restaurants until only Grammer's in the district remains. Grammers finds itself a novelty on a street where it had once been one of many. German bands oompahed their final oompah and were replaced by a Tennessee tune. Vine Street dwindled into a dreary thoroughfare of second-hand stores and tired little bars. Door sills are no longer scrubbed. German is no longer the language; hillbilly is. Twilight is Vine Street's saddest hour. People lean from third floor windows and watch the action of the street. Children screech at sidewalk games. The noise of cars and trucks and buses is constant. The music of the juke box blends with the noise of trucks, and there is no quiet. The smell of bacon frying hangs in the summer night air and so does the smell of sweat, beer, and the disinfectant the bars use. Vine Street has become a honky tonk world of honky tonk people. Darkness makes the street a little better. All you see is neon. All you hear is noise, juke boxes, children, and trucks. Night makes everything above the street level disappear. Across the street from the chili parlor comes the smell of onions, chili beans, coffee, and grease. This smell is hurled by a powerful fan into the street to mingle with a thousand other smells . . . "

But what of Cincinnati *today?* It has its brighter side. A look at a Cincinnati map shows you that geographically Cincinnati is bounded on the south by the Ohio River and bounded just about everywhere else—east, north, west—by separate corporate communities which restrict Cincinnati itself from getting annexation happy. Just as Cleveland's mayor is surrounded by dozens of mayors, so is the Cincinnati mayor. But Cincinnati per se is the county seat, if that cheers you, and Cincinnati has much culture and much industry, which thought should cheer the chamber. A look at some of Cincinnati's industry would be in order here. But this means we shall look at Greater Cincinnati because a lot of it is elsewhere. Consider the industrial tours available. Out in Blue Ash, for instance, the Fred Pagel Storage Company will show you the latest method of packing and storing and other heartwarming adventures of that nature. If antiques and glassware get you glassy-eyed, try the A. B. Closson Jr. Company on Race Street—and tour there one of Ohio's oldest galleries. If you'd like to see a piano or organ put together, visit the Baldwin Piano & Organ Company, but don't make jokes like, "Gee, Dad, it's a Wurlitzer," or we'll not be responsible for the consequences.

245

Old restaurants, like rare wine, linger. Cincinnati.

Some old neighborhoods stay. Cincinnati.

Go sixteen miles upstream to the Cincinnati Gas & Electric Company's Walter Beckjord Station—and watch electricity being made. This plant, by the way, has no rail service; all coal is brought in by the Ohio River. Want to see how a bank works? The Fifth Trust Union Trust Company has a tour. No samples, though. Or, visit behind the scenes at southern Ohio's largest department store—Shillito's —and you'll see everything but Georgia Glynn do her famous tap dance on Dollar Days. If show business intrigues you, tour WLW-Television where many live network shows originate. Want to see wood preserved? Visit Permawood, Incorporated. Their lumber, as the rest of us are, is treated under pressure. Smart cookies visit the United Biscuit Company of America's Strietmann Supreme Bakery on Wooster Pike to see cookies comes to life, crackers made, things like that. And, of course, there's always Procter & Gamble. A tour of their manufacturing and packaging operation is available. You can see, in nearby Sharonville, the Ford Company make automatic transmissions on an automated transfer line that is 485 feet long. For those who favor the finer things, our Meier's Wine Celler on Plainfield Pike. Here is Ohio's largest winery that produces—it says of itself—quality wines. We'll drink to that. And for a tour you'll not forget, take the five hour tour of Izzy Kadetz's Kosher Restaurant any time but during Lent.

Cincinnati, as we have said, is the machine tool capital of the world. Here in 1850 a fellow named John Steptoe fashioned a wood planer in his foundry— and that was the start of everything. What is commonly known around Cincinnati as the Mill means the Cincinnati Milling Machine Company, the granddaddy of the tool industry, but Cincinnati has, besides the Mill, many others—and they all have value. More than 12,000 people work for more than sixteen different machine tool companies, producing each year $237,000,000 in machine tools, and taking home each year $6,000,000 in pay envelopes—plus side benefits. Some of the companies are the Cincinnati Milling Machine Company, Cincinnati Lathe and Tool, Cincinnati Shaper Company, American Tool Works Company, Avey Machine Tool Company (a division of Motch & Merryweather), the Carlton Machine Tool Company, Cincinnati Gilbert Machine Tool Company, G. A. Gray Company, R. K. LeBlond Machine Tool Company, Lodge and Shipley Company and we could go on forever, but we'd rather not. You get the idea. This is machine tool land.

This is also culture land. Here is the Cincinnati Symphony, Summer Opera, May Festival, and any number of museums including the Art Museum, the Taft Museum, and the Museum of Natural History. The public library [its bright new building downtown next to the burlesque] has 39 branches, 4 bookmobiles, 44 school stations, 5 hospital stations, and to service these: 2,344,166 books. More than 300,000 people in Greater Cincinnati have library cards. If each card holder

Mill Creek's industry. Cincinnati.

Coney Island. Cincinnati.

took out eight books, the library would be—temporarily—out of business. As for parks, the city of Cincinnati has 84 areas covering more than 3000 acres, plus 60 playgrounds. Academically there's the University of Cincinnati, Xavier University, The Atheneum, The Hebrew Union College, and more colleges operated by Roman Catholic nuns for the girls than you ever saw. As for sports, Cincinnati has the Cincinnati Reds who play baseball, the Bengals who play football, the Royals who play basketball, and Leo Underhill who doesn't play as much as he used to because of a sick headache. For drama, see the new stadium. Sports drama, that is. For real drama, there's Playhouse-in-the-Park; the Shubert downtown with Lenny Goorian; and every community, ready or not, seems to have its own community theater.

Cincinnati itself has around 500,000 residents; there are that many again just beyond the city limits, both in Ohio and Indiana, as well as across the river in the dormitory counties of northern Kentucky. In Hamilton County, of which Cincinnati is the county seat, are 16 other cities. Also crowded in are 20 villages. Plus about 4000 people out there in the county somewhere not attached to city or village. That makes the county sound like standing-room only, but it's not that crowded. Somewhere out there also are over 600 farms. And all of this is contained on 415 square miles of Hamilton County. The villages and cities that ring Cincinnati are diverse. Some are separate and quite distinct entities. When you're in some others, you can't tell where Cincinnati stops and they start. The villages range from grimy nothings to posh somethings. We would like to mention them all. We won't.

The three Ohio counties that keep Hamilton County locked into the lower lefthand corner of the state are Butler, Warren, and Clermont Counties. Clermont is the county directly east of Cincinnati. It is a place of suburbia, farther out there are farms, and throughout are hills, pleasant valleys, twisty roads, and along the river there's the river. At Point Pleasant, a small river village that sleeps so sweetly, Ulysses S. Grant was born. Also in Clermont County was Utopia, established in 1844 as a communist society, but the spiritualists took over. Because Greater Cincinnati is heading east as fast as babies and furniture can be delivered, Clermont County expects its population to increase 50 per cent. In five years! Thus what once were pleasant rural communities will become hardly more than acres of suburbia, crab grass, and creeks that everyone will want to put into underground pipework. Newtonville, a town of about 400, almost got blown away in a tornado in the mid-1960s, but it's still there, strung casually along a country road. And although Loveland is the only city in the county (it has about 2000), the county seat is Batavia.

Northeast of Cincinnati is Warren County. Lebanon, which has around 8000

251

The oldest inn. Lebanon.

people and the county seat, also has Ohio's oldest hotel: the Golden Lamb, in operation since 1803, the year Ohio was admitted to the Union. Its present building dates back to 1850. This is where Charles Dickens stayed. The hotel is decked out as old English, whatever that means, but the effect is pleasant. Here and there are odds and ends of the Shaker period of the county. Every guest room in the hotel has a fancy name, the names being for some of the more famous guests, including the Harriet Beecher Stowe Room. If you're tired of Holiday Inn sameness but still seek quality digs, the Golden Lamb is for you. And so is Lebanon: a serene industrial-pleasant town in the winding hills. On some of Lebanon's side streets you get the feeling of antiquity. On others, though, you feel nothing.

Nearby Union Village, which is now Otterbein, was a Shaker settlement in 1805. Although many of the old buildings are still waiting around, the Shakers aren't. The original members of the community were members of the United Society of Believers in Christ's Second Appearing—or, for short, Shakers. They had walked clear from Lebanon, New York, to set up church in Ohio. The men and women lived together as brothers and sisters which accounts in part for their having no children to carry on the religion. In 1913 the last Shaker left. The building now is the Otterbein Home, a center for orphans and the aged, operated by the United Brethren Church. Over to the east of Lebanon is Fort Ancient, high on a bluff. Here's where the Hopewell tribe built another one of their mounds. The hilltop enclose which is divided into three sections looks like a whopperjawed putting green. Also around Lebanon—because that's where everything seems to be—is a marble statue dedicated to a Poland China Hog which is supposed to be about one of the best hogs this country has. Franklin, up the road a piece, is a city in its own right with Dayton fifteen miles one way and Cincinnati thirty-five miles the other. Most of Franklin is bland and ordinary, although sections of town are less than that.

Directly north of Cincinnati is Butler County. While sections of it might be considered dormitory for the city of Cincinnati, other sections are entities—good and bad—to themselves. This is hilly and flat territory, part pig farming, part industrial, and part parks. Butler County has parks the way some barns have mice. Parts of the canal is now a park. An old Indian burial ground (Indian Creek) is now a park. Butler County covers 471 square miles. It has more than 1300 farms, including one owned by Bob Douglass, and it has many college students, most of them at Oxford's Miami University or, if not there, staring into a pitcher of beer at Oxford's Purity—ice cream parlor-turned-saloon. Three cities exist in Butler County: Hamilton with about 80,000 people; Fairfield with about 15,000; and Middletown with about 50,000; none of the three would win prizes

253

from any garden club; but, in fairness, let us look at them from another point of view, starting with Hamilton, which is the county seat.

Hamilton began when General St. Clair built a fort there. A few years later, the town really got started. When the canal came through, the town got started again. Hamilton is primarily an industrial city that contains nearly seventy different manufacturing and fabricating industries which make everything from blankets to steel. Some plants hire as many as 3200 workers; others hire as few as a dozen. As a place to live, Hamilton is confusing. It has much ticky-tacky suburbia, shabby areas, and several streets that would—historically—take your breath away: they are that charming. Hamilton, insofar as culture goes, is as a Thurber cartoon character described a wine: "It's a naïve domestic burgundy without any breeding, but I think you'll be amused by its presumption." Culture in Hamilton is the Hamilton Civic Theater, its productions on the play-it-safe side. Also, there is a thing called the Rotary Club Revels, produced annually, and Hamilton says it is equal to the professional of a Broadway musical or—if you have seen a Broadway musical— equal to a bunch of nice guys getting together and wearing lampshades. Hamilton also has a symphony orchestra, the Palette Club which plays around with painting and sculpting, and there's the Hamilton Choral Society which sings a lot. Once a year all these groups get together to put on a free-of-charge fine arts festival well worth the price of admission. Downtown Hamilton is presently undergoing a facelifting. Entire city blocks are being redone. When finished, Hamilton will have every reason to be proud of itself. Miami University (in Oxford) has a Hamilton branch. The oldest citizen of Hamilton is James Newton.

Since Hamilton is prettying itself up, Middletown is a horse of a different color, the color being gray. Middletown began with good intentions as a log cabin built in 1791 on the east bank of the Miami River. Today the town covers nearly twenty square miles, usually with smoke, and most of its land is occupied with industry, many bland homes, and a few streets that contain some beautiful ones. Thirty-eight manufacturing companies make up industrial Middletown but outsiders can usually name only one: Armco which is the Armco Steel Corporation and Middletown's muscle. Pioneer Daniel Doty started the town via the aforementioned log cabin which floods washed away. Then he opened a hand mill— Middletown's first industry—grinding corn for his neighbors and himself. After that came a water-powered gristmill which in 1800 ground both corn and wheat. The mill was located on Elk Creek, and for black history buffs, we'll note it was built by Negro Bambo Harris described as a talented Negro mechanic. In 1815 Middletown's brickyard opened. In 1826 the first canal lock was opened at nearby Excello, the first lock tender's house being built at Amanda. In 1851 Middletown was connected to Cincinnati by railroad. And in 1852 the Middletown Hydrolic

Industrial muscle. Hamilton.

Company built an industrial canal to supply power that would turn the water wheels that would put Middletown on the map. Thus the forerunner of the Sorg Paper Company was built there. By 1900 the Armco Steel Corporation was started by George M. Verity, soon to develop the continuous steel rolling process which a John B. Titus thought up. In 1929 the Middletown canal closed, Wall Street laid an egg, and the rest is history. But, to be fair, Middletown is more than a smudge in the sky. Here you'll find bits and pieces of culture. The Middletown Symphony Orchestra, for example, dates back to 1936. Eugene Goldflies, father of this book's photographer, was the symphony's very first conductor. He helped organize the group, too. When the orchestra plays, around a dozen members of the Cincinnati Symphony Orchestra sit in to help out. Which sums up Middletown.

Fairfield, the third city in Butler County can be, for better or for worse, listed as for better or for worst. Here is a huge industrial-suburban spread that draws, or seems to, all reason for being from elsewhere. The city covers twenty square miles, a lot of which is still open country. But with population explosion, Fairfield will soon be full up. But to be realistic, compared with other Ohio cities, towns, or villages it did not start out from a central business district or a settler's cabin. It is an after-the fact sort of community. After draining whatever sustenance it could from Hamilton and Cincinnati, it started out on its own. It has no major business district. It is nothing but factories and homes and shopping centers. It is, insofar as Hamilton and Cincinnati go, a city that might be called Lucky Pierre. But nice people live there and nice industry locates there. Thus Fairfield is a place of 3500 homes, 92 per cent owner-occupied. It has 5000 automobiles, handy for getting elsewhere to shop, to culture, or to anything. Its biggest industry is the Fisher Body Division of the General Motors Corporation, making auto bodies there. Fairfield looks as if it is a Hamilton subdivision.

Rounding out Butler County we have the village of College Corner which straddles the Ohio-Indiana line. There is Millville which has the Rainbow Dinner House which has the best steaks you'll ever find. And there is Seven Mile which has over 700 people and is so named because Seven Mile Creek sloshes through the village which one would gather is seven miles north of Hamilton. Add industrial Trenton with its 5000 good people trapped under the Middletown smog, one or two other villages, and with the exception of Oxford, we've covered the county.

Oxford, of course, is where we are typing this and where Miami University is and where—just across the road out of the village limits—Western College for Women is. Oxford's business district is clean as a whistle, charming, and antique. Brick streets. More advertising signs that anyone in his right mind could read.

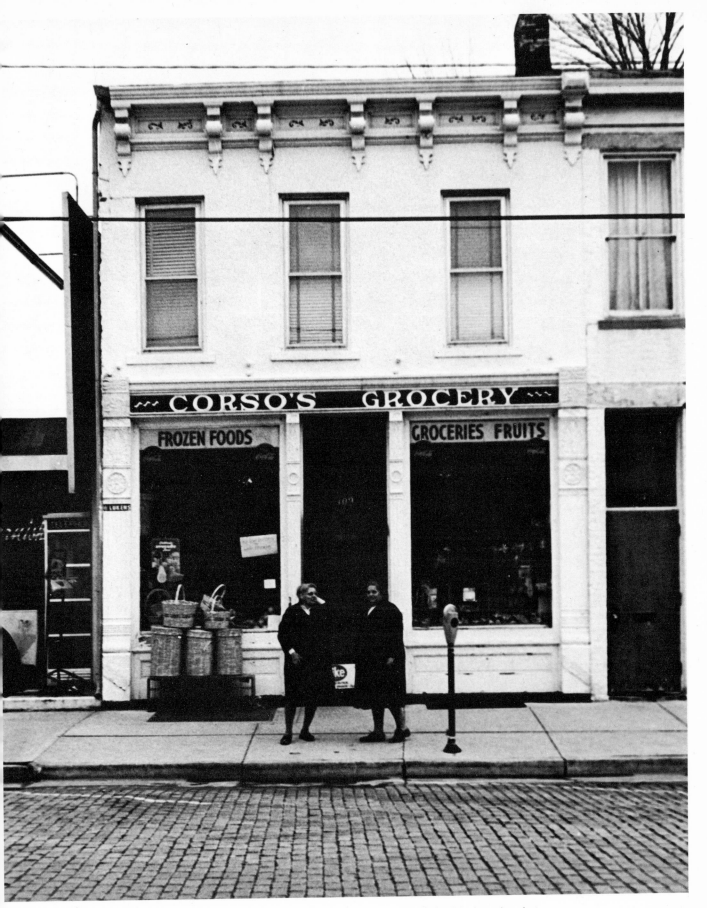

All Oxford isn't university!

Education is the basic industry. Lately, other industry has shown interest in the place. The Oxford village police department is about the best ever assembled and about the most underpaid. Miami University is a good school if teaching is what you want to do. They turn out good teachers here. The other departments? Well, judge for yourself, but an Oberlin? Miami is not. A Harvard Business School? Miami is not. A place to learn theater, broadcasting, brain surgery, or basket weaving? Miami is not. But it has a nice campus. The university covers over 14,000 acres with brick, students, faculty, and a preoccupation with all kinds of architecture just so it's Georgian. Here is where Jack Samuelson once did a very unusual thing. And here, too, is about the only place you'll find a plaque commemorating Lottie Moon, Confederate spy. Across the way is Western College for Women. Its buildings are architecturally mixed and its teaching is academically sound. It has about 500 students—and doesn't want any more. But a state-supported place such as Miami University can't play that kind of game. It must be everything to everybody—and so there it sits, happy and bland, the mother of fraternities (Beta Theta Pi, Phi Delta Theta, Sigma Chi), only no one ever says who the father is.

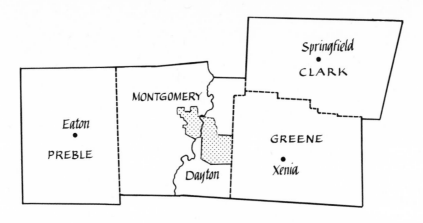

13

A few pig farms, Lilliputian valleys, and minuscule mountains north of Cincinnati is Preble County. Although Preble County is too far north of Cincinnati to be considered Cincinnati's suburbia, it is twenty miles west of Dayton and, by a stretch of the imagination or a fast trot, the eastern section of the county might be claimed as Dayton's suburbia. Here in Preble County, as in Butler County, is our old friend College Corner, the village in both counties being one and the same. College Corner not only straddles the Ohio-Indiana line to exist in two states, on the Ohio side it straddles two county lines to exist in two Ohio counties. Calling a cop in College Corner can—to be frank—confuse all: the caller, the cop, and the crook. For that reason most crimes are committed elsewhere. The College Corner school building itself is in both states but as far as the students are concerned going from one grade to another or the bathroom is no interstate contretemp; they look upon the building as a unit.

So many streams wiggle and slosh through Preble County that the county is riddled with ravines and gulleys. Also there exist great swaths of hilltop and valley flatland acreage that makes for beautiful—and productive—farming. The chief industry of Eaton, its county seat, is therefore catering to the needs of the rural. Eaton with about 6000 people has, of course, the typical Ohio county courthouse and its residents have the benefit of nine television channels—all originated somewhere else. Indiana is ten miles one way from Eaton. Interstate 70 is five miles another. Although basically a farming kind of county seat, Eaton does have its share of industry, manufacturing items like hydraulic hose and tube fit-

259

Double-barreled covered bridge. Eaton.

tings, industrial uniforms, restaurant equipment, paperboard shipping containers, and surgical gloves. In 1805 Eaton began when William Bruce came from Kentucky to look for a place to park his mill. Even before Mr. Bruce started his mill, General James Wilkinson built Fort St. Clair there, the fort being a penny-ante afterthought used to guard the supply route from Cincinnati to Fallen Timbers, where Wayne wanted to say hello to a bunch of Indians. The only attack the Eaton fort endured was in November 1792. Indians attacked—and stole all the pack horses. Exactly what *kind* of fort Eaton had is not known. Only by digging around could people find where the fort had been. Its four corners are now marked by stone markers. Three miles south of Eaton—on a country back road— is the Roberts Bridge. Built in 1829 it is said to be the oldest in captivity, but is maintained, and stands painted a cheerful red. Also it is the only two-lane (double-barreled) covered bridge in the state and one of seven in the United States.

Time was when you traveled north from Cincinnati via U.S. 127 after you left Hamilton you zigged and zagged through a wide valley that contained an assortment of farms, a single-track railroad (when double tracks were the rage), and Seven Mile Creek, the last of which you crossed back and forth over so many times you tended to lose all sense of direction. Now, high on a hill overlooking the valley, the new U.S. 127 travels, rendering a handful of bypassed villages into Rip Van Winkle communities. One of them, bypassed Camden, with nearly 1500 people and a train station nobody loves, dozes fitfully, its main street silent, many of its stores vacant, and its traffic light directing traffic which, for the most part, is now elsewhere. Yet, even in the silence, these villages have life and so do their residents. The coin-op laundry—on Saturday—is the sudsy town meeting. Life, in spite of new highways, goes on.

Travel east from Camden and you plunge into an area of wild hills and discontented gorges, plus a road that twists and turns every chance it gets. This is a land where, if farming is done at all, a block-and-tackle is required to work the plow. Dirt roads—with fresh tire tracks—mysteriously leave the black top road you're on and vanish quickly into the scrub wilderness. Suddenly, there is Gratis. Great village. With nearly 600 people, most of whom seem to be forever inside, Gratis is, as we noted in the first chapter, the village that from one season to the next keeps its streets (there are several) decorated for Christmas. Climb a hill, turn a corner, Gratis and the ragged hill county is behind you; flatland farming and only a few hills are about. That's the way Preble County with its 36,000 people and its 428 square miles is. Head east from Eaton, there's West Alexandria. And soon, there's Dayton.

Dayton located itself smack dab where the Miami, Mad, and Stillwater Rivers plus Wolf Creek all meet. It located there despite Indian mutterings of floods.

261

Forsaken train station. Camden.

Where veterans sleep. Dayton.

Dayton should have listened. In 1913 the city was practically wiped out by a $100,000,000 flood. The result, though, was the start of flood prevention in the valley, set up by this country's first comprehensive flood control project: the Miami Conservancy District. This effort was financed without state or federal aid, a thought that today strikes most people as obscene. Let us look upon dried-off Dayton and see whither it goest.

This is the only Ohio city in which you'll see trolley buses; it is where in a bicycle shop the Wright brothers played hob with gravity; it was the scene of Barney Oldfield racing his "Old 999" racing car; and here was where lived one of the nation's more recognized poets, Paul Lawrence Dunbar, who happened—by chance—to be black. Dayton is a city of awfully wide streets, some awfully old buildings, many glittering new structures—and a feeling that all around you are cash registers because, insofar as making change goes, the National Cash Register Company founded by John H. Patterson put Dayton on the map. But the wonder is that present-day Dayton—a most dramatic city—ever got off the ground. In 1823 carriage-maker Joseph Voorhees refused to set up shop in Dayton (he chose Centerville) because he said that Dayton, then a swampy little town where frogs glumped, would never amount to a hill of beans. Now occupying 36.5 square miles of valuable real estate and with about 280,000 residents standing around on same, Dayton chooses to call itself the heart of *Mega-City 70–75*, the nation's tenth largest service market. *Mega-City 70–75* includes twenty-six other counties around Dayton; twenty-one counties in Ohio, four in Indiana, and two in Kentucky. The combined population of this chamber of commerce gerrymandering is 4,000,000 people. But, a few mutter, isn't this the same as New York City including Philadelphia, which might not want to play? Solve the problem as your heart dictates. The Dayton metropolitan area—a four-county proposition—is impressive enough for most: 1000 plants and 121,000 workers are in the area. Thirty-seven per cent work in manufacturing industries. Nearly 15 per cent work for Uncle Sam at Wright-Patterson Air Force Base, the Defense Electronic Supply Center, the Veterans Administration Center, and other federal service units. Fifteen per cent are employed by retail and wholesale firms. The area's seven firms that each employ more than 2000 are the Air Temp Division of Chrysler Corporation; Delco Moraine Division of General Motors Corporation; Delco Products Division of G. M.; Frigidaire Division of G.M.; the Inland Manufacturing Division of G.M.; and, not affiliated with General Motors at all, the National Cash Register Company and the McCall Corporation.

Poetry and airplanes are Dayton's products. The Wright brothers—Wilbur and Orville—who traveled the route from selling bikes to manufacturing them to tinkering with aviation put Dayton on the map aerodynamically. On December

Wide streets, dramatic buildings. Dayton.

17, 1903, the bike merchants were the first in history, so says Dayton, to make a powered and sustained and controlled flight in an airplane, the first hop lasting fifty-nine seconds and covering a half-mile in the air. Three years later, after they had tinkered more with their gadget, the Wright brothers made the second in their series of powered flights, this series including turns and circles, the longest flight being more than five minutes. Then, later, they made flights of thirty minutes, and from that point, we assume, they hired Grandma Moses as a stewardess, and went into business for real. Was Dayton impressed? Not really. In 1903 the Dayton *Journal* carried news of the Kitty Hawk flight on the back page.

As for Dayton's poetry, we offer Negro poet Paul Lawrence Dunbar who lived —and died—at 219 North Summit Street, now a state memorial. Elevator-operator-turned-muse (he once ran the lift in the Callahan Building) in the last five years of his life he published two novels, two volumes of short stories, and six volumes of poetry, one being *Lyrics of Lonely Life*. His early poems appeared in magazines while he was still operating the elevator, causing him to suggest, "I am often despondent, for it is hard to sing in the dark." The only black student at Dayton's old Central High School, he was first named to the Philomathean Literary Society and then made its president; and in his senior year in high school, he edited the *Times*. From his parents, both former slaves, he came to feel "the pangs which Thou didst feel, when slavery crushed Thee with its heel." He called his study on North Summit Street his "loafing holt."

There is much to see in the Dayton area, for instance, Carillon Park. Located behind Deeds Carillon, one of Dayton's better-known landmarks, and tucked among the sycamores, is a series of museum buildings. The whole thing covers 61 acres which had been swampy land. But Mrs. Edward A. Deeds wanted to put up a carillon there. And her husband wanted to build a museum there which would compliment the bells. So everyone got together with the Miami Conservancy District, the pot was privately sweetened, and thus we have the parkland museum. Here you can see an antique tavern—gristmill and all. Also for gaping at is a "grasshopper" locomotive, said to be the sort that once tooted through the lonely midwestern forests in search of villages. Here, too, is an actual section of the Miami-Erie canal, complete with locks. If you hanker to look at a covered wagon, one is here. So is a 1912 Cadillac, the first type of auto to be equipped with the self-starter that Kettering thought up to change motoring from a nuisance to a pleasure. We'll hear more of him on our visit to Kettering (the place not the man). Suffice to say here that Deeds who put up the park was one of the fellows who, along with Kettering, founded the Dayton Engineering Laboratories Company to produce the self-starter. The company became known as Delco and is now a division of General Motors. Deeds was called colonel because in the first World War that's what he was.

And Dayton, as every schoolboy knows, is called the birthplace of aviation (listen, everything has to be born *somewhere*) which seems to be why Dayton is now considered the country's aeronautical research center. But Dayton is more than flyboys. Dayton is the Dayton Art Institute. It is the Dayton and Montgomery County Public Library, whose headquarters is on East Third Street and which has nineteen branches, three bookmobiles, and over a half million books, a lot of them on scientific, technical, and business things because that's the way Dayton is. Dayton is also the Dayton Museum of Natural History. If you want to go for a canoe ride, Dayton is Island Park—and you don't even have to supply the canoe; you can rent one there. Dayton is the planetarium, part of the Dayton Museum of Natural History. And, says Ralph Vines, who has made a study of same, Dayton has many show bars where a man can wet his whistle and oggle an exotic. For drama, Dayton is the Trotwood Circle Theater. For music, Dayton is music under the stars at the Island Park bandshell, the music ranging from municipal band, Philharmonic Summer orchestra, to barbershop singing and jazz concerts.

If show-and-tell tickles your fancy, many Dayton companies will be glad to show you their things and tell all about them. The Dayton *Daily News* and the Dayton *Journal* will let you tour their facilities. The Dayton Power and Light Company, which supplies power for twenty-four counties, will give you a tour of its museum, customer-service communications, maintenance facilities, and customer accounting—so you can see why your light bill was what it was. To see automobile tires made, no need to go to Akron. In this part of the state the Dayton Tire and Rubber Company will give you a tour. Or visit the world's largest and most misspelled manufacturer of fire-fighting equipment: the Fyr-Fyter Company. Or look in at Frigidaire and see how ice cubes are done to a turn. The General Motors Delco Products Division has tours which show the birth of appliance and industrial motors as well as generators and shock absorbers. The National Cash Register Company—entering the area as the world's largest manufacturer of retail record processing equipment and a leading producer of computers, accounting machines, and adding machines—has a tour that lets you see all this happen. For a department store tour, try Rike-Kulmer and get behind-the-scenes glimpse of what makes a department store tick, if the store is ticking at the time.

Or, all you have to do is lean against a building and watch the yellow trolley buses hum silently by. This is more than you can do in any other Ohio city.

Wright-Patterson AFB research of all sorts. Dayton.

Tours—but not here. Dayton.

But will Dayton keep its trolley buses? "Well, yes," says the transit company, "because we have lived though the building of expressways and the rerouting of streets and our overhead lines are still in good shape. We'll keep the trolleys until someone invents something that has their advantages without the disadvantages of diesel fumes and noise . . . " Dayton at one time had six different streetcar companies, ending with only one, the last streetcar running through downtown Dayton in 1947. But it still has trolley buses. And, in an ambivalent kind of way, that is worth the price of admission.

Does Dayton have a personality? You bet. Though many of its downtown streets are lined with buildings which look exhausted, the city of Dayton—and the people dashing about it—seem young and full of energy. Some cities seem old and mature. Dayton doesn't. The wind that whistles along its wide thoroughfares on cold winter days only seems to make the typical Daytonian that much more eager to make something of himself and his city. Dayton lacks the European touch that Cleveland has. Dayton is what might be termed "midwest open and friendly." Dayton lacks the touches of the heritage that Cincinnati has. In this sense, Dayton—the kid sister of the cities—is of a new generation. For how can a city be old when up there, leaving vapor trails in the sky, are the things that make Dayton and the twentieth century the go-getter that it is? Much of Dayton, of course, is the corporation man, properly uniformed, and properly dedicated. But when he comes home, the person he used to be rises to the surface and thus, each and every evening, Dayton enjoys a wild and wonderful—and most satisfying —rebirth. You bet Dayton has a personality. It has more personality than it knows what to do with.

To be fair, not all that is Dayton is Dayton, or shall we have another go at that? What we mean is, Dayton is tight up against other cities, separate corporate municipal entities which either have a reasonable dependence upon Dayton or have such self-sufficiency they have no need of Third and High. One of these places is Centerville; so named because it was laid out in 1803 to be equidistant from Springboro, Ridgeville, Miamisburg, and Dayton. Centerville is farmland turned suburbia, or as the Centerville locals are quick to suggest, "Cornfield to cosmopolis." Before it was cornfield, it was swampy lowland. Located about ten miles south of Dayton, Centerville began when three Kentucky brothers-in-law— Aaron Nutt, Benjamin Archer, and Benjamin Robbins—surveyed the place in 1796. All had come this way on the strength of Daniel Boone's bragging about how beautiful everything was. They marked off land and Aaron Nutt returned to Kentucky to get his family. Upon his return the Archer and Robbins families said for the Nutt clan to stay with them till Aaron Nutt could build a cabin, but Nutt was strong-willed. He said he wasn't about to unpack until he could stow his

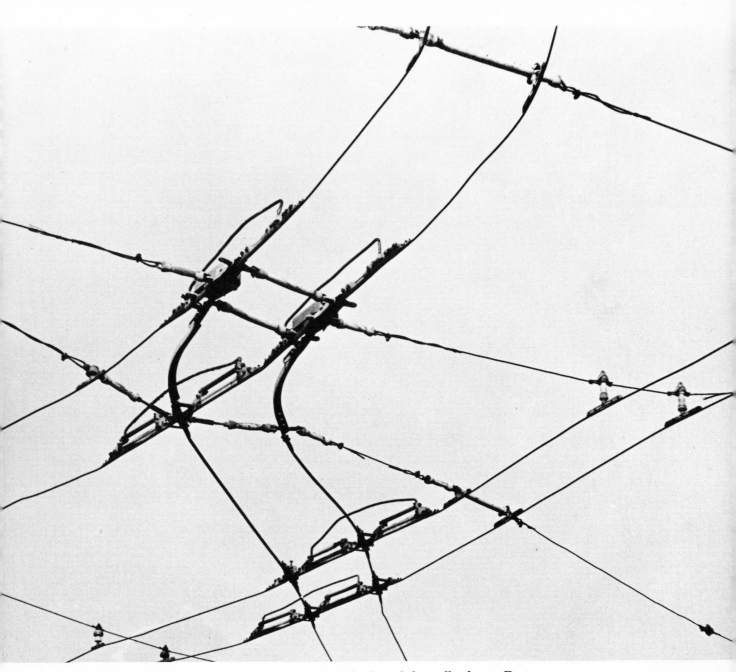

The last of the trolley buses. Dayton.

Gone but not forgotten. Dayton.

belongings under his own roof. Having said that, he strolled nine miles to Franklin to find help, easy for him to find because he oiled the enthusiasm of his helpers with Kentucky moonshine. He oiled his helpers so well they slapped up his cabin in just one day. How long it stood, no one says. Anyway, back then Centerville was beset with problems undreamed of in Erma Bombeck's philosophy: one day on his property, Ben Robbins killed 400 rattlesnakes. But Mrs. Bombeck can relax. There hasn't been a black bear killed in Centerville since 1826, which means there are none left—or a lot roaming free. Centerville's first doctor—Dr. John Hole—had so little medicine to practice that he started a pair of sawmills. By 1875 Centerville had a dry-goods store, two groceries, a butcher, a blacksmith, two wagon shops, a shoe shop, an undertaker, a hotel, a post office, two doctors, several taverns, three churches, and a bunch of schools. After the second World War the township lost its rural airs and became another suburbia. Here now thousands lived who once lived in Dayton—and each year thousands more are on the way. From its present population—township, 20,000; of which 6500 live in Centerville—the township expects by 1976 to have 40,000; and by 1990 to have 100,000, all of them being people.

Between Centerville and Dayton is Kettering, which brags that it is the youngest of four cities of the world to have that name. The oldest Kettering is in England, dating back to the Roman Empire. Another Kettering is in Tasmania, named by an English immigrant from the English one. There is also a Kettering in Jamaica. Kettering would have still been there if there had not been a Charles F. Kettering but he did help put the city on the map. In 1909 he started, as suggested earlier, the Dayton Engineering Laboratories Company, now Delco Products Division of General Motors. Kettering has been called the "pliers and screwdriver scientist." Together with Edward Deeds and William Chryst, he tackled the problem of the auto. He came up with the first self-starter, doing away with cranks. He also improved the early auto's lighting and ignition systems. From this tinkering, Kettering became a General Motors vice president in charge of research and Kettering—the place—became a city. When the first settlers arrived around 1796 they were not bothered by auto headlights and ignition for several reasons. Also they were more interested in the stone they found. Kettering's first industry was quarrying. In 1939 the town had 5000 residents and a year later, 6000. Nine years later, 1949, when Kettering found it had 22,000 residents it decided to look into the matter of incorporating. In 1952 it became a village. In 1955 it became a city. And hasn't stopped growing since.

North of Dayton where the airport is, is Vandalia. Vandalia seems to have come of age as the result of everyone's urge to go somewhere else, not from Vandalia, that is, but via Vandalia. When stagecoaches rattled along the dusty

National Road (old U.S. 40) Vandalia sweetened the travelers' journey by opening two saloons. When the Dayton and Troy trolley clanged through Vandalia about the turn of the century, Vandalia became a rustic commuter point. When the Dixie Highway became the main north-south artery, it passed through Vandalia—and once again Vandalia was crowded with travelers, some of whom stayed to raise babies and things of that nature. Yet, unlike many cities, only 5 per cent of Vandalia is old, which means it lacks the Gothic business districts that plague so many Ohio towns. Located ten miles north of Dayton, Vandalia occupies nearly five square miles of land. Each year the Grand American Trap Shooting Association gathers in Vandalia to shoot a lot of trap.

Northeast of Dayton is the Air Force Museum, world's largest military aviation museum. Displayed are nearly 100 aircraft and missiles, plus a bunch of airplane stuff that dates from Kitty Hawk to the day before yesterday. A tour of the place is always in order. The Wright-Patterson Air Force Base with its 7098 acres in both Greene and Montgomery counties is the keystone of what has been termed the scientific community. Around here are all the basic, applied, and—if you like fancy words—developmental research projects that apply to aerospace technology. The activity at this base covers almost every phase of the air force including systems engineering, systems procurement, aerospace medical research, refilling the Coke machine, foreign technology, education, logistic support, and strategic operations. The complex also includes the Air Force Logistics Command Headquarters of the Aeronautical Systems Divisions. Dayton, by the way, is one of only five switching centers for Autodin, the automatic digital network; this network is about the biggest thing ever to come down the pike to handle digital data, the sort of information upon which computers feast. The network, electronically outdistancing Hallmark by a country mile, can transmit 12,000,000 messages each day.

Other cities and villages are near Dayton. There's Germantown with its 4000 residents, well-tended lawns, suburbia, and some huge old homes with wraparound porches. The Germantown business district is that rural-suburban concoction that is antiseptic, Disneyland, and pleasant. The old brick store fronts are painted antique white. Fairborn, where the Air Force stuff is, on the other hand, is just what you'd expect: military plus suburbia plus a bunch of established —or quickie—businesses catering to the needs of all, including—for heaven's sake! —one called *The Gourmet Carryout*. And always in the sky, pigeons and planes. Surprisingly enough, in spite of this county having so much action, it has enough room left over for 1600 farms.

Up the road from Dayton and thirty miles west of Columbus is Clark County, where Springfield is. In Springfield the Mad River and Buck Creek meet, a fact which prompted James Demint in 1801 to say, "Well, isn't this a real nice place to build me a home." Or, at least, words to that effect. The convergence of the two streams also prompted Simon Kenton to put a gristmill and a sawmill where the International Harvester Plant is now. Mrs. Kenton looked at the streams, commented something womanish on same, and that is how Springfield got its name. In 1839 the National Road coming through livened up the town as did a year later the arrival of the first railroad train.

In the 1880s the Crowell-Collier Publishing Company got started as the result of P. P. Mast's publishing *Farm and Fireside*, more to advertise his wares than to peddle to the literary. In Springfield hybrid corn began and so, in 1902, the 4-H Clubs, founded by school teacher A. B. Graham. Today Springfield—an energetic city that contains few surprises, unpleasant or otherwise—occupies 15.7 square miles and has a population of about 85,000. More than 7000 are employed in the area's retail and wholesale businesses; around 3000 are at work in services; 1700 are in transportation and utilities; and 1500 are doing something in finance.

The leading industries are transportation equipment, electrical and non-electrical machinery, fabricated metals, food, printing, and publishing. Springfield makes trucks, diesel and gasoline engines, wire products, machine tools, road rollers, electric motors, radar equipment, and funny noises when you comment on the departure of its once-beautiful train station, which in the end became an eyesore. Springfield has two senior high schools (one is an ornate heap with a dome), six junior high schools, and twenty-three elementary schools.

In addition, the Seventh Day Adventists have a grade school and the Roman Catholics operate five grade schools plus a four-year high school. For higher education, there's Wittenberg University which was founded in 1845 and is affiliated with the Lutheran Church of America. Undergraduate enrollment is about 2300. The Wittenberg School of Music offers a Master's Degree in Sacred Music; and the Hamma School of Theology confers degrees of Master of Sacred Theology as well as Bachelor of Divinity. So you can see, if you look closer, that Springfield is a lot more than its cramped and busy downtown business district of narrow streets and middle-aged buildings. Springfield is also culture.

There's the Springfield Symphony Orchestra, eighty-four pieces that play everything from classics to show tunes. A Youth Symphony assembles each year, ready or not, to let elementary and junior high school students traffic with whatever musical muse they can nail down. The eighty-voice Symphony Chorale is a mixed chorus that sometimes sings with the symphony. And the Springfield Civic Opera offers each year light and grand operas, but no matter which they are, they're sung in English. The Civic Theater has drama and so does the Children's Theater. As added starters for Springfield culture, Wittenberg College has drama, musicals,

277

Yesterday's eyesore. Springfield.

and noted speakers on tap. The Springfield Art Center provides both local and traveling art shows. The Crabill Art Center, affiliated with Wittenberg University, has many noted artists. And the Warder Library has three branches and three bookmobiles. Wittenberg University is noted for its collection of religious writings and publications.

Question is: what KIND of city is Springfield? Well, a workingman's kind of place that seems to stretch out forever, this way and that. Frame houses, mostly bungalows, abound. And Pleasant Street isn't all that pleasant. But head out Limestone Street beyond Wittenberg University and you'll see side streets heaped with pleasant homes, none of which are elaborate, but they're not look-alike suburbia, either. Beyond the city limits in that direction suburbia takes roots and seems to be self-multiplying. In fact, suburbia is everywhere out that wide valley which follows the railroad to Northridge and the immense International Harvester complex: a great structure that covers more ground than some small farms. Its parking lot isn't filled with cars but with the trucks and stuff IH makes, this being the truck division. On the west side of Springfield, next-door neighbor to the massive Ohio Edison plant and smokestack, is the Ohio Masonic Home, from which a school bus, painted blue, toots the oldsters into town. On the eastern side of Springfield, around LaGonda Street, factories make the neighborhood what it is, but farther out, and up a hill, things improve.

Springfield is the county seat of Clark County, the only city the county has, the villages being Catawba with around 400, Clifton with 70, Donnelsville with 300, Enon with nearly 1800, Lawrenceville with 300, New Carisle with 6000, and several others who were not home that day. The county has 1062 farms. But Springfield? Basically it is a hodgepodge of just about everything but the kitchen sink: industrial, serene residential, grubby neighborhoods, wide boulevards, beauty, ugliness, and you name it—the same as most cities are. But Springfield exudes an old-world metropolitan mood that many midwestern cities can't emulate. Perhaps its business district, bustling and crowded and somewhat antique, evokes this mood, but the mood is there and the mood is good. Springfield is a self-contained, proud city. If you live there, you needn't shop elsewhere. In Springfield you can buy clothes you'd buy on Fifth Avenue—or Skid Row. If many of the downtown buildings look tired, don't be fooled. Via the cash register's ring, they brim with life.

Xenia is more of the same, only with less people. Xenia calls itself the City of Hospitality. It started in 1803 and its first business opened in 1804. In 1834 Xenia was incorporated into a city. Midway between Cincinnati and Columbus it has for railroads the Penn Central and the Baltimore and Ohio. Xenia is in Greene County, a place of gentle hills in the west and flatland farming in the

Not a subway car within miles. Springfield.

east. The county is rich in colleges: a half dozen are within its borders. There's Antioch at Yellow Springs. We'll talk about that place shortly. Near Xenia is Wilberforce University, one of the country's first permanent educational institutions for blacks. It was established at the refurbished Tawawa Springs Health Resort in 1856 and named for the English abolitionist, William Wilberforce. First financial problems and fires plagued the school, but the school hung on, and there it sits today: an academically sound plant. Nearby, also, is Central State College, which grew out of a Wilberforce reorganization. Cedarville College appears to be a trim collection of antique schoolhouses. It was established in 1890 by the Presbyterians, but the Baptists took over. Here also in this county is Wright State, which started as an extension of both Miami University in Oxford and Ohio University; it soon spun into orbit with an identity of its own. Add to these, Mount St. John Normal School, a Catholic institution, and there you are, ready for recess.

Although Xenia with around 26,000 people is the county seat, Fairborn with around 32,000 is the largest city but it is over there, a satellite of Dayton. The Ohio Soldiers and Sailors Orphans Home just on the outskirts of Xenia has a beautiful turn-of-the-century setting via its many brick dorms that contain 700 kids of all ages. This is along narrow Holm Avenue on the south side of Xenia. As you get closer into town itself—by a railroad freight station that has a sick headache—the town opens up into a street six lanes wide. But dominating the town at its main intersection is a nondescript heap of a building, six stories high, gloomy, frustrated, and in the moonlight: sinister. North of Xenia are beautiful homes and tranquillity. Xenia, also, contains many little neighborhoods on quiet streets. Not fancy. But shady and awfully nice. Xenia, headquarters for District Six of the Ohio Division of Wild Life, doesn't seem to have much of its own. Its public library has over 135,000 books, in the county 43,000 people have telephones, and in the area you'll find 240 retail establishments. Also, 1200 farms. Xenia has diverse industry, more than two dozen different kinds of industry, to be exact, employing 2000 people. Xenia says it is a good place for manufacturing and warehousing because it is the center of a triangle between Columbus, Cincinnati, and Dayton. Columbus is 55 miles distant, Cincinnati 54, but Dayton is only 15. On the other hand, there are triangles and there are triangles.

A scattering of villages exists in the pleasant countryside. Cedarville which has nearly 2000 is the birthplace of Senator James H. Kyle, who—as all school children know—was the father of Labor Day. Cedarville, site of the aforementioned Cedarville College, is tranquil with charming old homes and a few dreary ones. On the outskirts of town, next to a gravel pit, is what's called the Ohio Skindivers Headquarters, listing itself as a supplier of compressed air. Spring Valley, in another

281

A theatrical heap. Xenia.

direction, is in a theatrical valley, 700 people are there, and so is a railroad and a Friends Church. Bellbrook with 1500 is an idyllic village beyond which to the west are hills and beyond them, the clatter of Dayton suburbia. Clifton with only 200, none of whom seem to be there, is an interesting lived-in ghost town that has a mill still operating to grind things and gratify tourists. A few miles thataway is Yellow Springs and Antioch. Do we dare?

First let us see what Antioch College has—officially—to say of itself. This is only fair, because the place has been accused of just about everything, including letting the inmates run the asylum. Antioch College says that in addition to the usual college experiences, it offers its students three opportunities: to contribute to the world as an adult worker on jobs off campus, to take part in a democratic campus, and to study and work and live abroad for a year. This means, translated, that students can mill about overseas; have a voice in what goes on in the college more than, say, other students do at other colleges; and that students are divided into two groups, one studying on campus while an equal number is elsewhere working at real jobs. Half the students begin their studies in July, the other half in October. The July entrants begin their "off campus experience" at some job selected by Antioch College at the end of the summer quarter. This way students alternate study at college and work elsewhere, which—to us—seems better than containing a child for four straight years in a college or university, and hoping that when the urchin is dismissed he will have evolved, by magic powder and blue books, into a mature creature. The Antioch student spends only half his time on campus. He spends the other half in the wide, wide—and distasteful—grown-up world, where another kind of reality exists. In this fashion, the Antioch student, for better or for worse, leapfrogs academically toward either his liberal arts or science degree.

Founded in 1852 by the Christian Church, Antioch opened its doors a year later with Horace Mann as its first president. Later, with Unitarian support, Antioch was reorganized as an independent college. In 1920 Arthur E. Morgan introduced the co-operative program—or work-plus-study—which fourteen years before had originated with the University of Cincinnati and which, since, 114 other colleges and universities have latched on to as a reasonable operative premise. Although much noise is made for Horace Mann, Arthur E. Morgan should get more credit for Antioch's emergence because it was he, as the students say, who "turned Antioch on." All of which brings us to Antioch College today.

The place has been described as having the tone of Greenwich Village and a Quaker work camp. So said Arno Karlen in *Holiday* (June 1967) who went on to suggest of Antioch students that they were "all isolated on a small campus in a little country town, like passengers on a mad cruise. You fell in love, but you knew at the end of the period you'd go off on a job in San Francisco, she to one in Provincetown. It was an emotional hothouse, everything growing and dying at a jungle pace." According to Karlen, Antioch wasn't a college but a cult, a subculture that marked a person so permanently with its five unique and harrowing years that wives of survivors found they'd married into a minority that was clannish and obsessed with both its character and its past. Antioch College has—and rightly so—been called a daring and experimental place. Some disenchanted middle-agers, especially in Ohio, call it other things, too.

Hence, a word of caution. To those of you who have witnessed a bearded Antioch unwashed arrested by the cops for civil disobedience, Antioch College must seem that awful place in Yellow Springs. To those other of you so obsessed with the sight of intellectual youthlings creating cosmic Halloween mischief, Antioch College must be deified as rapidly as possible. May we suggest—here and now— that when the name Antioch College flashes on the magic screen, you forget your preconceived angers or delights? We suggest simply that Antioch College (and add Oberlin to the list) is a lot more than you've read about quickly in the newspapers. Scrape away the bulletinlike drama and scrape away the shenanigans of the students (actions as permanent as twilight mist, and with as much substance when parsed) and chances are you'll find yourself saying that Ohio should be proud of its Antiochs. Such places are few and far between. One is here, so is another, so we're doubly blessed. Or do you feel otherwise? To each his own. But if you feel that way, skip real fast to the next section of this book. Okay?

Students from other colleges and universities forever query their Antioch counterparts about such items as the football team (rah! rah!), the fraternities (swat!), the school colors (huh?), and a bunch of other Dear Old Siwash Essentials. Antioch students can answer only with bewilderment, because Antioch is the kind of college June Allyson never attended via the movies. On the other side of the coin, to attend Antioch does not endow you with super powers. As in any college, you can only take away—reasonably honed—that which you brought in the first place. Said Karlen of the Antioch students, "I know . . . that behind many of the bizarre outfits are bland souls. But there are also faces sharp with intelligence." And on both counts he is right. It takes all kinds of students to make a campus, they don't all end at Antioch or Oberlin, but the ones who do are generally the cream of the crop which—to be frank—doesn't mean that each is the second coming of Christ. Such students, testing their knowledge, disagree with most of us. But how can they agree with us when they can't even agree among themselves? Do *we* agree among ourselves? Says the college bulletin, "By the time (the students) are seniors, most of them have gained more personal

Part sweet, part wild. Antioch College.

autonomy; they are less authoritarian and more tolerant, flexible, and democratic; their outlook is more complex, they are oriented toward abstract ideas; and even though many of them come to Antioch with liberal attitudes, most of them gain in liberal attitudes while in college."

Not all is fun-and-games or pin-the-tail-on daddy. Antioch College, is, in these days of easy-does-it and don't-rock-the-boat, that rare academic vineyard where kids study over weekends instead of getting drunk, and where hard work—at the books—is not considered poor taste. The Antioch student, unlike his brother elsewhere, can't get by with a winning smile, by knowing the teacher's wife, or by sheer bluff or bull. Textbook answers don't win blue ribbons. Snap courses? There are none. That's the kind of cruise it is. Result: it's students against all assembled knowledge, testing that knowledge to see if it works. There's much sharing between the students: of problems, of dreams, of pains, of joys. They live —each a lonely soul—in a pressure-cooker world. There's no time off for good behavior. This is why Antioch College says its students have two sides. One, the student is polite, considerate, and thoughtful. Two, the student is demonstrative, assertive, rebellious, and freewheeling. Think about that a moment because that is, in other words, the average soul coming of age.

True, true. Some of you are murmuring—with either horror or fascination—about the supposed sexual freedom (everybody out! rally! bonfire!) which everyone believes is rampant at Antioch but which is no more rampant there than it is at Bobby-Socks High School. We admit that girls can, if they choose, visit the rooms of boys and the reverse is true also. We admit also that upon occasion several of these confrontations might be less than esoteric, but if people that age—and they are that age—are going to play house, they're going to play house— somewhere. Having tried to entice girls into dorms for similar purposes, we can only suggest that a warm dorm is better than the dewy grass upon which one can catch his death of cold. And the cost of motel rooms these days, as any college urchin will confess, has made free association an item that should be budgeted. In other words, who are we kidding? And in other words, people cart about with them the values they learned at home. Why blame that junk on the college? A fact of life is, there are girls who do and girls who don't; and you can find both at Antioch College as well as at the most restricted female campus. So much for Ohio recreation.

The village of Yellow Springs, where Antioch College is located is a neat and casual place of 5000 residents who either service the needs of the educational plant or the gastronomic needs of the students. Unlike Oxford (a delightful place) where the business district looks nineteenth-century Gothic—in neon— the Yellow Springs business district has the appearance of a papier-mâché Disney-

286

land. Antioch College's campus has 43 buildings which are an architectural mixture. The college itself has an enrollment of around 1900 students; 54 per cent are men, 44 per cent are ladies, and 2 per cent are still deciding. The college has 100 full-time faculty teachers as well as 200 research and administrative and part-time faculty teachers. The students come from just about every state in the Union and nearly twenty foreign countries. Most of them—nine out of ten, in fact—don't come from Ohio.

The Antioch students are unlike the ones we found on other campuses in Ohio. The Antioch student seems preoccupied unto himself. Stroll through the campus at Ohio State, for instance, and chances are one out of ten students will speak or at least smile. Not so at Antioch. Withdrawn. But we tested this lonely remoteness of the kids; we smiled and spoke to them first; and in each and every case got —in return—a slow, shy hello. Wonderful. Their iciness was only in our imagination. But the clothes they wear? Agreed that their uniforms are at times outlandish, but are they any more miserably styled than any college or high school child? The girls present something of a problem. Most seem to dress in such a way that beauty and charm go skittering. On the other hand when dressed for a junket into Dayton for the weekend the girls look like a million dollars: all stunning, all sensual, all alert, all interesting, and all exhausted.

Are we suggesting that only the small independent colleges—the Antiochs and the Oberlins—have value? No. The great universities of Ohio are great in more than size of physical plant or student enrollment. Each has value unique unto itself. At the University of Cincinnati, for example, the laser beam was played with, and discovered was a polio vaccine that practically eliminated polio. In this fashion each and every Ohio university, private or otherwise, can point with chamber of commerce pride at one or a series of accomplishments. So can, in proportion, the smaller colleges. But, as we have said before, big universities are big business—and big business, except around the water cooler, tends to be too impersonal. Too rigid. They operate on yesterday's premises. The same danger lies with Antioch and Oberlin. Seeds for the defeat of such small colleges come from within, not without. The rigidity that is a college's defense is also its death weapon. Antioch could, by ingrowth (students become teachers, hanging onto yesterday's status quo) die of its own imagination. The moment anyone or anything—be the structure a college, religion, civilization, labor union, board of directors, or marriage—becomes rigid it becomes ossified. A tree that lives bends with the storm's anger. A tree that is ossified falls down. The danger to structures is always from within. This is the danger to Antioch College if, say, it should insist on ferment for ferment's sake. This is the danger to state universities if, say, they should insist on status quo for status quo's sake.

Arno Karlen said of his years at Antioch (once in a discussion with latter-day Antioch students): "Antioch helped me outgrow my middleclass home and my background and then I had to outgrow Antioch, with its limits and cultic beliefs. I had come to believe that a soul strong enough to survive protest and a cold-water flat is strong enough to survive success and central heating. But if you go on thinking most of the world soulless, it's your loss, because it's the world that's dramatic, not one's own self-dramatizing. And that part of what you often call evil was only what you were afraid of . . . "

And later, to himself, he said: " . . . I lie smoking in the dark, realizing that besides telling what I think is the truth, I was taking revenge on myself for what I was like ten years ago. And I remind myself that it is a vain thing to mock your own past. I smile to think that next week, in New York, I will advise a bright young high school senior to go to Antioch; I would still suggest it first to any imaginative adventurous person choosing a college. Antioch did give me a rare education in honesty, idealism, and democracy. It put a truly high value on things most people and institutions serve only with words, not with their lives. To learn such values in a protected laboratory is better than not to have known them. If sometimes my years at Antioch seem to me a little like a distant love affair that went sour in places, it is because its very nature demanded that if I stayed, I must invest so much of myself in it, good and bad, that to hate it utterly I'd have to hate myself. I can think of no institution, no time of my life, toward which I have quite this odd blend of impatiences, and deep, good feeling."

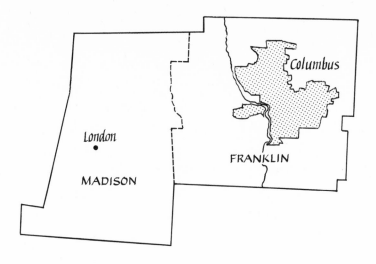

14

Before we visit Columbus and the Ohio State Fair to see which pretty young thing is this year's Miss Poland China Pig, let's stop off in London—London, Ohio, that is. London is in Madison County, the geographically monotonous but agricultural winner of a county twenty miles west of Columbus. In this flattened county are some of the state's largest farms, a few with 5000 acres, a lot more with a lot less. London, with around 7000 people and county seat as well as only city in the entire county, is where many of our friends are contained: in the state prison farm. The community—London, that is, not the clink—takes up less than four square miles. Stockyards brought it fame of sorts but one stockyard has since been remodeled into a lumber yard, illustrating how fleeting fame is. Much of London's business district is starting over. The First National Bank has torn down two old buildings to erect a bright, new banking facility, old landmarks once apartments are now modern offices, and that's London which has a quiet warm pride in itself and should have. For action, Greyhound buses toot in and out of town five times a day. And the Penn-Central—as the result of the Pennsylvania Railroad merging with the New York Central—finds itself in the awkward stance of crossing itself in the community. The villages out in the windblown county are Jefferson, with about 3500; Midway with 370; Plain City with about

1500; South Solon with 444; and Mount Sterling with around 1500 and six miles distant, the Southwestern Franklin County Airport that Columbus is building. Mount Sterling, by the way, in 1920 had 1103 people; 40 years later, it had 1338, so things are looking up. Which leaves us with one last place to cover in this book, the place being Franklin County, where Columbus is and where we have arbitrarily parked the center of the state, though it isn't the center at all.

Before we stroll the streets of Columbus and see what the governor is doing to earn his pay, let us first explore the rest of this county which contains the capital from which all legislative blessings—good, bad, and indifferent—flow. Consider, if you will, Worthington. Founded by Colonel James Kilbourne in 1804, Worthington—a most pleasant community—is nonetheless a place that starts colleges which get away. In 1808 the Worthington Academy opened, in 1819 became Worthington College, and in 1832 became the Reformed Medical College, taking off for Cincinnati and never being heard from again. The Female Seminary used to be in Worthington. Now it isn't. The Ohio Central Normal College used to be in Worthington. Now it isn't. On the other hand, in Worthington today is the Pontifical College Josephinum, a seminary for priests that, they say, is administered directly by the Pope himself although he has yet to show up to take attendance. Worthington also has the wonderful, wonderful Railway Museum. This place has trolleys and steam locomotives, all in working condition, and all adored. The place in summer is open to the public Saturday and Sunday afternoons from two to five. In winter, weather permitting, it is open the same days from around two to four in the afternoon. Here are assembled the most beautiful streetcars in the world. Worthington itself, other than having the charm of the trolleys, has much residential charm as well as about 14,000 residents. The city is, for the most part, a Columbus dormitory. Columbus is surrounded by such critters. One, though, Columbus itself surrounds: that being Bexley; Bexley's 15,000 people are entirely surrounded by incorporated Columbus. Bexley, as you can imagine, is residential—*good* residential—plus commercial lining several of its main streets. Gahanna, however, with 10,000 people is part rural, part suburbia, being out there where once only farmland was. Reynoldsburg has around 13,000 residents; old U.S. 40 slices right through the place and Interstate 70 makes passes at it. Mostly residential. Whitehall with 28,000 people is much the same. So is Obetz with 25,000. Grandview Heights has 10,000 and Marblecliff has 750 *and* the Scioto River. Upper Arlington with nearly 40,000 people has both the Scioto River *and* the Olentangy River. But these separate corporate entities, while they do have some personalities of their own, derive most of their characteristics from the proximity of Columbus which means we can stop beating around the bush and take a look at Columbus itself.

290

If you like valentines we suppose you'll like Columbus because Columbus—born on Valentine's Day 1812—has been called by some the valentine of Ohio. Also locals who get carried away with history and rhetoric like to say that Columbus as a capital city is unique because it did not become Ohio's capital, Ohio's capital became Columbus. Surrounded by such gems one can see why Columbus native James Thurber—described as a logical man at grips with an illogical world—went east to write humor. We suggest only that Columbus is better than its rhetoric. You see, when Ohio was a brand-new state, every Ohio town wanted to be the capital. One such place was Franklinton, founded by Lucas Sullivant, now a street, on the west bank of the Scioto River. He wanted the capital, too. But on the aforementioned Valentine's Day 1812, the legislators—sweethearts all!—put the capital on the Scioto River's east bank directly across from Franklinton.

As soon as the legislators decided to put the capital in Columbus, which, at the time, wasn't there, the absent village was quickly platted, a big public sale was held, and—because everyone wanted part of the action to be—buying was brisk. By the time Columbus was a year old, it had 300 residents. By the time it was four years old it had 700 residents—a few reluctantly contained in the prison that had just been erected. Columbus in those early days had a swamp in the middle of town, several sawmills, and, because it was the seat of government, several distilleries and breweries. By 1824 Columbus absorbed Franklinton across the Scioto River. By 1833 when the National Pike potted through town, stage-coaches rattled in from as far away as Washington, D.C., and St. Louis. Three years before that, the first canal boat had arrived on the Ohio-Erie Canal. With all this going on, Columbus was a boom town. In 1850 the first train (Columbus & Xenia Railroad) whistled at the capital. During the Civil War many military establishments were settled in the area and some are still there. If you wish to call Columbus a horse-and-buggy town, no one will get upset, because when buggies were the rage, Columbus manufactured them for every state there was, turning out as many as 20,000 of the gadgets. When the first auto came through, something happened to the carriage trade which, in Columbus and elsewhere, hasn't been the same since.

Columbus, as state capital, may seem preoccupied with government and education—Ohio State University is there—but the surprise is that fewer than 12 per cent of its people are on government payrolls. And, although its chief industry seems to be telling Woody Hayes how to run the Ohio State football team, around 25 per cent of the Columbus area workers are involved in manufacturing, 6 per cent in construction, nearly 18 per cent in service industries, 7 per cent in transportation, 8 per cent in finance, and more than 25 per cent in wholesale and

Born on Valentine's Day. Columbus.

retail. Franklin County workers are employed by firms that make transportation equipment, electrical machinery, fabricated metals, food stuffs, printing, publishing, stone and clay and glass products, and instruments. Plus other items. About three dozen different insurance companies—of about every size and persuasion— have home offices in Columbus, including Motorists Mutual Insurance Company, Nationwide Insurance Company, and The Order of The United Commercial Travelers of America. Who is the largest employer in Columbus? The North American Rockwell Corporation employs 7500. A close second is Western Electric Company, Incorporated, which employs 7000. The Lazarus Department Store employs 5000. And the aforementioned Nationwide Insurance Company employs 3000. Timken Roller Bearing Company employs 2600. Lazarus Department Store, by the way, which was founded in 1851, offers behind-the-scenes tours. Also you can tour the Omar Baking Company, the city's oldest and largest bakery; it has a monster oven that can bake 7000 loaves of bread an hour. All told, the Columbus area has over 800 manufacturers of diversified products—and for a state capital, that's real good. Columbus is a lot more than a tax write-off.

Other than the more obvious schools of higher education in the Columbus area, the city itself has four business schools, a half dozen beauty schools, two barber colleges where you can learn to talk batting averages, two places that give instruction in automation, a charm school, and a place you can learn to give massages. And, with a little luck, you can learn a lot of non-academic stuff by strolling the Ohio State campus after dark.

Columbus as a city is a reasonably flatland community filled to brimming with sophisticates, coeds, hayseeds, smart cookies, people with civil service minds, and politicians testing to see which way the wind is blowing. Columbus is also wide and airy streets which, if they were not lined with middle-class buildings, would have the beauty of boulevards. Columbus is also many new buildings, theatrical structures in the downtown section attesting to the vitality that Columbus seethes with. Around the central city, though, neighborhoods deteriorate—fast. Grim and lonely and tumble-down. No one could call that stretch between the capitol building and the university a street of anything but bad dreams. Columbus is not alone in this affliction. All cities suffer the same. But lest you quickly decide that Columbus is a falling-down rural-legislative-education conglomerate only, we suggest you quickly lest again because much in Columbus is charming and welcome as the roses in May, whatever that means. Label Columbus, for all its midwestern twangs and airs, reasonably cosmopolitan. Culturally, insofar as the legitimate theater goes, there's the Hartman Theater which, upon occasion, is blessed with Broadway productions. Community and summer theaters abound. Musically, the culture bug has the Columbus Symphony

293

Orchestra and its powerful and compelling concerts in Veteran's Memorial Hall. Or, for something quieter, try the public library, which has over 800,000 books, fifteen branches, five bookmobiles, and two county stations. The Columbus Gallery of Fine Arts is the area's chief art center. And admission is free. The Ohioana Library (the Martha Kinney Cooper Ohioana Library Association) is in the Department of State building, eleven floors up. This library collects books by and about Ohioans as well as collecting musical compositions of the same sentiment, clippings, photographs, and just about everything that says Ohio and isn't nailed down. The library lacks only the Dick Winfield paperbacks which have Ohio settings but which are sold only in bus stations to people whose lips move when they read. One of the major factotums of the Ohioana Library is Bernice Foley, former television performer, member of the Kappa Kappa Gamma sorority, and a most charming lady. The historic German village is in a league by itself, being a restored area a half mile south of downtown. Here once the Germans lived. Now the district has been refurbished historically by private citizens after the fashion of Philadelphia's Society Hill section. Here you will find many interesting private homes from yesterday, looking cheerful as new, and here also you will find shops, selling stuff. To give Columbus a quick-once-over, your best bet is the LeVeque Lincoln Tower, the city's tallest skyscraper which rises 555.5 feet above the gum wrappers in the street, and from whose observation tower on a clear day you can see everyone taking umbrage with Woody Hayes, another Columbus institution.

And in Columbus you can be sure Woody Hayes *is* an institution. He is the high priest of the Ohio State University football team. At times he is rated only slightly below the President of the United States and other times, when the scores are lean, he is considered less favorably and with more violence. Mr. Hayes, though, weathers each storm and football without him wouldn't seem like football which, even with him, sometimes it does, but sometimes it doesn't. Columbus also has a baseball team: the Columbus Jets play in the International League. Its hockey team, the Checkers, is in the National Hockey League. In other words, there's always something to see in Columbus.

Sightseers who collect state capitals will find much in Columbus to gape at. Care to drive by the governor's house? Drive to 358 North Parkview Avenue in Bexley and honk. Downtown, of course, is the capitol building, a Greek Doric heap of beauty underneath which is a 1200-car three-layer American Doric garage. That gloomy antique clink called Ohio State Penitentiary is on West Spring Street; getting in is easier than getting out. If your sympathies were with the South during the Civil War, go out Sullivant Avenue to Powell Avenue. That's where you'll find 2260 Confederate soldiers buried in a Confederate Cemetery.

View from the top. Columbus.

Ohio honors people as well as things. Starting in 1949 the Governor's Award has been given each year to some outstanding Ohioan, so the award reads, who has enhanced the state's prestige throughout the world. Other than people like Louis Bromfield and Dr. Albert Sabin and Charles F. Kettering, the enchancers have proved a mixed lot: Earl Wilson, Joe E. Brown, Hopalong Cassidy, Norman Vincent Peale, and Teresa Brewer—just to give you a sampling. And Ohio has— of all things!—a Teen-age Hall of Fame located in the south corridor of the capitol. There you will find such teen-agers as the Mills Brothers, Roy Rogers, Lillian Gish, and Milt Caniff. Or, at least, the inspiration for teen-agers. Also in the building is the mural *Dawn of a New Life* by Ohioan Howard Chandler Christy, commemorating the life of Thomas A. Edison. Incidentally, tours are available through the state capitol. Contact the state house capitol guide—or call the governor and tell him we sent you.

Columbus, as we have been saying right along, is also Ohio State University, established in 1873 as the Ohio Agricultural and Mechanical College. It is now the largest institution of higher learning that Ohio has. Other than being pre-occupied with learning stuff, the campus—and everyone else in Columbus—is preoccupied with Woody Hayes, the football team, and the marching band which is a fast-stepping gem. The campus is a collection of every kind of architecture you'd ever expect to see, plus a few kinds you didn't. Is the university academically sound? Of course. And it is sound socially, too. It has many myths. For instance, along one of the many paths that crisscross the campus is a statue which shall, for sake of propriety, be nameless because the myth is, each time a virgin passes, the statue blinks, and you know how statues are. More educational stuff: Capital University is in Bexley, where the governor lives.

And over there is the ferris wheel, giant slide, and the Ohio State Fair. As suggested at the beginning of this book, the fair traveled a lot before settling down, for keeps, in 1886, in Columbus. It started in Columbus with a 115-acre tract. It has since expanded to cover 370 acres. Each year at the fair thousands of exhibitors, pom-pom girls with bare legs, and animals assemble. You see—free! free! free!—such stars as George Kirby, Roger Miller, Johnny Carson, Jack Samuelson, the Smothers Brothers, Al Hirt, and Bob Hope. By staying ever alert as you stroll the crowded midway you will also be rewarded with the pleasant sight of the hog-, buttermilk-, or peanut-butter-queen, trim in her brief swim suit that glitters with sequins. As in any such assemblage, the midway contains the usual pitchmen and the gypsy peddlers of trivia: funny hats, canes, food cutters, and cotton candy. Also, every other booth seems to be selling soft drinks or hot dogs—or both. Bands from Ohio's many high schools give free concerts on the mall to an audience of pooped old-timers whose feet hurt and wide-

Visitors not—quite—welcome. Columbus.

Dorm. Ohio State University.

Giant slide. State Fair.

Midway. State Fair.

eyed young swains who, as they gape in wonder at the pom-pom girls, find their ids are hurting, too. In the various permanent buildings everything wonderful seems to be happening simultaneously: here a horse show, there a circus, over there a band concert. All free. Pay at the gate and, if you can avoid the carnival crowd, you can get away without spending a dime. In the stadium, big-name performers perform—free. But the ferris wheel ride costs. You must allow for that. And scattered about the grounds, in separate little trailers, radio disc jockeys spin records and watch the pretty girls go by. A most wonderful carnival.

But the fair, spectacle that it is, is more than spectacle. It is also that pair of Belgian horses that Early Grubbs brought from Eaton. The horses—powerful brutes that each weighed 4200 pounds—pulled a 10,000-pound concrete block sled twenty-seven feet to win the horse-pulling contest. The fair is also the Ohio State Junior State Fair, an event that brings both joy and heartbreak to Ohio's nicest kids. Here, in the Lausche Building, bubbling with youth, you see the largest agricultural shop exhibit ever to be set up. So big was the exhibit, the hall could not contain it, and exhibits spilled over to the outside area, too. One project: a steel spiral staircase by Mike Penn of Morrow County. Another project: a farm tractor which New Concord's Ronnie Spiker created from bits and pieces of this and that. The junior division live stock entries totaled over 5000 animals, chickens, and creepy crawly things. Beauty is everywhere. Leslie Shroyer—a trim blue-eyed blonde from New Carlisle—competed with 137 equally as charming and beautiful to win the title 1968 FFA Queen. Her folks, Merle Shroyer and his wife, were proud of her—and so were the rest of us. But what chance does a beauty queen have when a lad has steers on his mind? While she was winning her title, a 950-pound Angus steer belonging to Dennie Howsman of London was winning itself the championship in its four-legged category. Judy Jagger, the nineteen-year-old daughter of Mr. and Mrs. Richard Jagger of Mount Gilead, brought a pen of three lambs to the fair to see what they could do, and what they could do was win top honors. Proud girl. Nancy Campbell of Washington Courthouse brought only one pig to the swine show but she brought the winner, beating out 300 other snorting beady-eyed entries. Horses? Well, more than 300 4-H youth competed in the horseshow—being the cream of 10,000 other 4-H members who ride the nags, too. Probably the most shattering event among the youth events was when Bill Longbrake of the Marysville FFA gave a fire prevention demonstration. He unnerved the audience by setting a fire in the demonstration area and then proving his skill at putting the blaze out to win himself a gold medal. The purpose of the demonstration, they say, was to develop an FFA member's poise and ability to speak before a group. To which they should have added,

Youth, youth, youth!

his demonstration also developed the audience's poise and ability to sit while the place seemed to blaze about them.

If you prefer nature uncaged, then the Ohio State parks are for you. So while you're in Columbus see the man who runs the woodland spreads. He's Melvin J. Rebholtz, one of the key men in the Department of Natural Resources Divisions of Parks and Recreation—and one of the nicest people in Ohio you could ever hope to meet. The state park system offers camping in thirty-three state parks which means there's one near you. In these parks, the camp sites fall into three categories. Class A digs are reasonably luxurious items that have approved water under pressure, drinking fountains, waste water drains, flush toilets, laundry facilities, shower houses, numbered lots, and your own picnic table. Class B sites are a little less civilized; they contain usually a well or hydrant somewhere, pit-type latrines, waste water drains, either marked or unmarked lots, picnic tables, and that's about it. Both A and B sites have fire rings or grills handy. But in the last category you're on your own. Called Primitive Areas you can find a pit-type latrine, waste containers, and Mel Rebholtz getting away from it all. Logically the Class A areas cost more, the top being about two dollars per camp unit per night. The Primitive Areas are free. And several of the state parks have lodges that are so posh they put some hotels to shame. Ohio is also 250,000,000 acres of Lake Erie fishing, 100,000 acres of inland lake fishing, plus the 36 acres in Sandusky Bay, plus 7000 miles of stream—all, says Mel Rebholtz, just filled with fish waiting to be caught, but if you don't land one, don't blame him. Also, hunters are welcome on 500,000,000 acres of free hunting areas. Besides that over 10,000,000 acres of farm land can be hunted upon, if you are decent enough to make your peace first with the farmer. Rather than list here where *all* these places are and where you might best catch a muskellunge, whatever that is, we suggest only you query the Department of Natural Resources, Division of Wildlife, in Columbus. They'll send you maps telling you where all the wild life is, except the kind we had been looking for.

As you can probably tell, we have just about reached the point of desperation. Franklin County—and *all* of Ohio—is too much and too diverse to be compressed between the covers of any book, especially this one. Ohio, simply put, is everything but the kitchen sink. It is America's first billionaire: Cleveland's John D. Rockefeller. It is where, in New Washington in 1897, the first commercial chick hatchery turned on. Menthol cigarettes were invented here in the early 1900s by Lloyd (Spud) Hughes of Mingo Junction where George Washington slept but no one knows exactly where. Ohio is Daniel Decater Emmett from Mount Vernon; in 1842 he organized the world's first minstrel show. Ohio is the nation's first shopping center: the Town and Country in Columbus. Ohio is the first

303

Exhibitor. State Fair.

We'll toast Ohio at Marzetti's . . .

interurban trolley line; on December 28, 1888 it connected Newark with Granville. Ohio is the two national monuments that each year attract over 100,000 visitors: Mound City Earthworks near Chillicothe and the Perry Victory and International Peace Memorial in Put-in Bay. Ohio is the trio of ladies who went on to become Miss America: Mary Campbell of Columbus in both 1922 and 1923, Marilyn Meskeke of Marion in 1938, and Jacquelyn Mayer of Sandusky in 1963. Also, Ohio is farming—lots of it. Farming is Ohio's number one industry, yet it employs only 4 per cent of Ohio's manpower. How many farms? 114,000! Ohio is 3053 public elementary schools and 706 non-public ones; 1082 public secondary schools and 178 non-public ones. Ohio is, as we said, everything but the kitchen sink. And Ohio is that, too. We have no statistics on kitchen sinks, though.

Thus, having visited the four corners of the state and everything in between, here we stand in Columbus at our starting point: the intersection of Broad and High. Some of the communities we visited will be pleased. Others, we are certain, will not be. It saddens us, but that is the way things are. May we again suggest—amiably—that all the opinions in this book are subjective, personal, and ours? This is the way Bruce Goldflies saw Ohio with pictures. This is the way I saw it with words. Two others would have seen a different Ohio. Ten others would have seen an Ohio that would probably please or sadden us. Books about places, if the books are to have meaning, will ever be thus. Should anyone mutter, "But who are you to make judgments on Ohio?" we would only smile in a friendly way, and say, "Who do we have to be?" Point is, we enjoyed wandering about and discovering Ohio because, as we said at the beginning, we happen to be fond of this state and we would like to think that you feel the same.

But the journey is over. Bruce and I will leave Broad and High. We'll sit in Marzetti's and drink a toast to this state. Join us, won't you? First, we toast the fact that Ohio leads the nation in the manufacture of balloons, then to Ohio's number one position as a maker of coffins. Then, because here is where most of the canned Chinese food is made, we'll toast to that—and toast racing sulkies, pretzels, and police whistles because Ohio leads in the manufacture in these things, too.

The list is long. We may not last the night.

Geographical Index

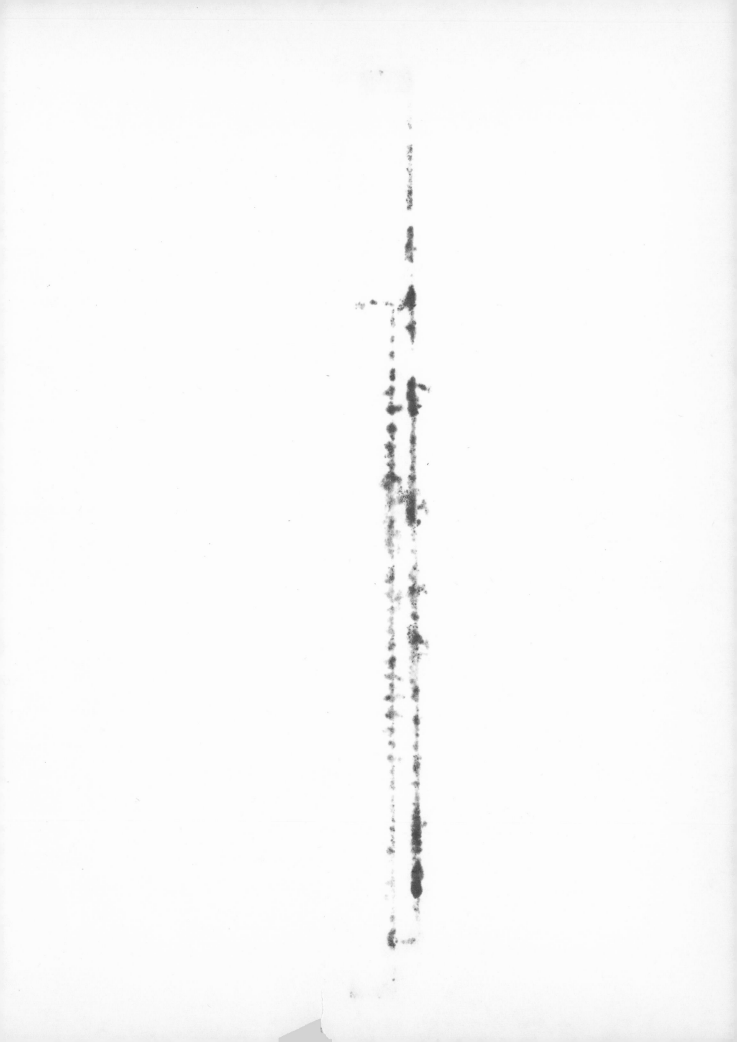